D0031456

"A must-read for anyone who wants to get real about frontline transformation." —JOEL KLEIN, executive vice president, News Corporation; former chancellor, New York City Public Schools

"Innovation is no longer the providence of those at the top or in R&D departments—it starts at the front line." —VIJAY GOVINDARAJAN, Earl 1924 Professor at Tuck School at Dartmouth; bestselling author of *Reverse Innovation*

"A must read for leaders seeking practical and pragmatic ways to leverage the capabilities, experiences, and judgments of frontline employees to create a competitive advantage for any company."

—MIRIAN GRADDICK-WEIR, executive vice president, Human Resources, Merck

"This is not another book written by academics. Tichy and DeRose share their lifelong journey of actually working at the front line in numerous organizations, which makes the content of this book so compelling."

—ROBERT KNOWLING, chairman, Eagles Landing Partners; author of *You Can Get There from Here*

"DeRose and Tichy have written the most compelling and well-crafted book ever written about how to harness the wisdom of people on the front lines. It is the most useful management book I've read in years."

—ROBERT SUTTON, Stanford Professor; author of *Good Boss, Bad Boss*

"The front line–focused organization is the organization of the future, and leaders on their journey to a new kind of relevance will welcome *Judgment on the Front Line*." —FRANCES HESSELBEIN, president & CEO, The Frances Hesselbein Leadership Institute; recipient of the Presidential Medal of Freedom

"The DeRose and Tichy framework for activating the potential energy and insights of the front liners is compelling." —EDWARD A. SNYDER, dean, Yale School of Management

"DeRose and Tichy make it easy to see how leadership, frontline employees, and the bottom line all grow as boundaries are broken."

—BRIAN A. GALLAGHER,
president and CEO, United Way Worldwide

"This is both a down-to-earth and an uplifting book. Well done!"

—ROBERT A. BURGELMAN,
Edmund W. Littlefield Professor of Management, executive director
of the Stanford Executive Program, Stanford Business School

"*Judgment on the Front Line* turns years of research and experience into innovative, pragmatic ideas readers can use in their companies today."

—CAMILLE MIRSHOKRAI,
global director of leadership development, Accenture

"Tichy and DeRose have created a powerful blueprint for those seeking to radically improve the value they deliver to their customers."

—TOM TORKELSON,
founder and CEO, IDEA Public Schools

Judgment on the
FRONT LINE

Also by Noel Tichy
Judgment
The Cycle of Leadership
The Leadership Egine
Control Your Destiny or Someone Else Will

Judgment on the
FRONT LINE

HOW SMART
COMPANIES
WIN
BY TRUSTING THEIR PEOPLE

CHRIS DEROSE AND NOEL M. TICHY

Portfolio / Penguin

PORTFOLIO / PENGUIN
Published by the Penguin Group
Penguin Group (USA) Inc., 375 Hudson Street,
New York, New York 10014, U.S.A.
Penguin Group (Canada), 90 Eglinton Avenue East, Suite 700,
Toronto, Ontario, Canada M4P 2Y3
(a division of Pearson Penguin Canada Inc.)
Penguin Books Ltd, 80 Strand, London WC2R 0RL, England
Penguin Ireland, 25 St. Stephen's Green, Dublin 2, Ireland
(a division of Penguin Books Ltd)
Penguin Books Australia Ltd, 250 Camberwell Road, Camberwell,
Victoria 3124, Australia
(a division of Pearson Australia Group Pty Ltd)
Penguin Books India Pvt Ltd, 11 Community Centre, Panchsheel Park,
New Delhi – 110 017, India
Penguin Group (NZ), 67 Apollo Drive, Rosedale, Auckland 0632,
New Zealand (a division of Pearson New Zealand Ltd)
Penguin Books (South Africa) (Pty) Ltd, 24 Sturdee Avenue,
Rosebank, Johannesburg 2196, South Africa

Penguin Books Ltd, Registered Offices:
80 Strand, London WC2R 0RL, England

First published in 2012 by Portfolio / Penguin,
a member of Penguin Group (USA) Inc.

10   9   8   7   6   5   4   3   2   1

Copyright © Chris DeRose and Noel Tichy, 2012
All rights reserved

Illustration credits
Page 80: Steelcase
Page 143: Intuit

LIBRARY OF CONGRESS CATALOGING IN PUBLICATION DATA

DeRose, Chris.
   Judgment on the front line : how smart companies win by trusting their people / Chris DeRose and Noel
M. Tichy.
      p. cm.
   Includes bibliographical references and index.
   ISBN 978-1-59184-388-7
 1. Customer relations.   2. Management—Employee participation.   3. Organizational behavior.
4. Corporate culture. I. Tichy, Noel M.   II. Title.
   HF5415.5.D467 2012
   658.3'14—dc23

                                                                                    2012018023

Printed in the United States of America
Set in Minion Pro
Designed by Elyse Strongin

No part of this book may be reproduced, scanned, or distributed in any printed or electronic form without
permission. Please do not participate in or encourage piracy of copyrighted materials in violation of the
author's rights. Purchase only authorized editions.

In memory of Eleanor Josaitis (December 17, 1931–August 9, 2011), cofounder of Focus: HOPE, whose work changed the lives of thousands of people, including ours, through her commitment to "intelligent and practical action to overcome racism, poverty and injustice."

Contents

Preface

This book is the unexpected by-product of the more than forty years that Noel has spent as an academic and consultant and the nearly twenty years that we have worked together, with our colleague Patricia Stacey, consulting to CEOs of organizations large and small. In our consulting practice we partner with CEOs on their organizational transformation agendas, which often entail developing the next generation of leadership as CEOs reconsider what is required to achieve long-term success. In nearly every case, we are required to work with leaders from top to bottom in an organization to ensure enterprise-wide execution of the strategic agenda and to help thousands of employees align with the organization's vision.

We have had the great fortune, as a result of our clinical practice, to find ourselves in some unusual circumstances. Over the years we have collectively stood alongside frontline associates working on deep-sea oil rigs and retail sales floors and ridden with them on installation trucks. We have been in manufacturing factories of all sorts, pulled all-nighters with software teams, in call centers listening to customer complaints, and in warehouses unpacking boxes. We have even found ourselves in customers' homes or in retail stores trying our best to assist with sales. In the process, we have witnessed firsthand how frontline workers deal with unpleasant customers, broken work processes, burdensome bureaucracy, and overbearing bosses.

In spite of these obstacles, we have walked away from these encounters amazed and inspired by the sincere desire most frontline workers possess to help their organizations, serve their customers, support their teams, and grow personally. As Noel has taken to saying as a result of these many interactions, nobody we have encountered woke up in the morning and decided to come to work so they could produce a piece of junk or aggravate a customer. On the contrary, nearly everyone we have met wanted to learn and contribute more. They had a sincere passion to make a difference through their work and the underlying hope that their involvement would lead to greater opportunities for them and their families in the future.

After more than a dozen years of making these observations across a wide variety of industries, and in both the private and social sectors, the importance of investing in an organization's front line snapped into focus for us in one galvanizing moment during a meeting at a big-box retailer on a cold winter morning in Chicago. The team discussion was led by a store manager who had just spent forty-five minutes training his retail associates, many of whom were paid less than ten dollars per hour, reviewing the store's profit-and-loss statement, teaching the group how to understand the store's return on invested capital, and discussing options for improving the business. The twentysomething manager, who did not have an MBA, had done a remarkable job of making complex financial topics accessible to the group. At the end of the discussion he asked if anyone wanted to comment before the group broke up and prepared to open the store.

After a pause, just as it appeared that the meeting would end, a young woman stepped forward. "I just want to say thank you to everyone," she started, a jittery nervousness in her voice, "for helping me realize that I'm smarter than I thought." In the few moments that followed, she shared her personal tale of being advised by teachers at a young age that she was not good at math, struggling in school, getting pregnant at age seventeen, dropping out of high school, and living with the self-image that she was, as she said matter-of-factly, stupid. The company's investment in helping her learn business math had demonstrated to her that she not only understood the concepts but actually enjoyed doing the calculations. In fact, she continued, she was most excited about an experiment she was running with several coworkers to try to improve the product margins in their department. Taking a deep breath and visibly trying to fight back the tears that had started down her cheek, she committed to the group to get her high-school diploma equivalent by taking the GED test within a year. As she finished, she said simply that the support of her colleagues and her company had changed not just her life but her daughter's as well.

That moment led us to reflect more deeply upon the millions of men and women of all ages and backgrounds who are often paid minimum wage to labor on the front lines and serve as the face of their organization to customers and their communities. Many have stories as moving as this young woman's and have an equal desire to both get from and give more to their daily work.

In the United States, at least one-fifth of the entire workforce might be classified as frontline employees. In fact, retail and service workers alone total more than fifteen million people.[1] These associates are experienced in the ways of customers, square off against the competition each day, and have insights into where the machinery of their organization consistently breaks down. Yet most organizations do little to learn from these wise workers or expand their ability to deal with the complexities they face. The prevalent corporate tagline stating that "people are our most important asset" notwithstanding, we don't see many company leaders who tap into more than a tiny fraction of the knowledge, creativity, and judgment of their largest group of employees.

This book sprang from our desire not just to help organizations improve the day-to-day working experience of these millions of people but also to help CEOs and senior corporate leaders recognize the tremendous missed opportunity that results from not more productively engaging frontline workers to solve customer problems, fix broken work processes, and innovate new products or services. We have attempted to formalize what we have learned from our clinical experience and supplement it with research into more than twenty organizations that we view as excellent at engaging their frontline associates. Once more, our research took us into call centers, quick-service restaurants, banks, and retail stores, as well as onto the front lines at hospitals, schools, police departments, and even on a midnight foray for a training exercise with the U.S. Navy SEALs.

This book is organized around a five-step process that simplifies the process of transforming an existing organization into one that is front line focused. As we discuss in later chapters, we understand and sympathize with much of the academic literature calling for wholesale change of how organizations are managed. Nonetheless, we don't view it as practical for most companies that have large workforces, entrenched cultures, and established organizational routines. Instead, we suggest a stepwise and systematic approach for more fully engaging frontline associates in everything from improved service to wide-scale experimentation.

The first chapter offers a case for engaging frontline workers more fully, while the second chapter provides an overview of the five-step process. The subsequent chapters explore each step in more detail, offering both more explanation and additional case studies along the way. Chapter 8 provides a case study of a company that engaged in many (albeit not all) aspects of the five-step approach we advocate, as well as a cautionary tale of how challenging it can be to maintain success. We close the book with a discussion of how the front line can engage in corporate citizenship efforts, which we view as turbocharging the transformation process as workers become more involved with the community members they serve and organizations more broadly define the "front line" to include people who are not directly on their payroll. Finally, at the end of the book we have included a handbook with exercises to help readers apply the five-step process and actively consider how to make changes to their organizations.

While we are confident in the book's findings and prescriptions, we do not suggest that building a front line–focused organization is the only requirement for success. Ultimately, organizations succeed or fail based on their ability to offer something unique and valuable to the customers they serve. Decisions about a company's strategy, where it invests resources, and which customers it chooses to target ultimately rest in the hands of senior leaders. Nonetheless, once those decisions are made, most companies have hundreds, thousands, or tens of thousands of people whom they can better involve in defining exactly how to win in the market. Our sincere hope is that as a result of this book more leaders and more organizations will recognize the opportunity to both ask more of and give more to those who work on their front line.

1

THE FRONTLINE INNOVATION FACTORY

In my experience, innovation can only come from the bottom. Those closest to the problem are in the best position to solve it. I believe any organization that depends on innovation must embrace chaos. Loyalty and obedience are not your tools; you must use measurement and objective debate to separate the good from the bad.

—**Greg Linden,**
former developer and software engineer, Amazon.com

- ■ **THE FRONT LINE IS THE RICHEST UNTAPPED SOURCE OF IDEAS AND INNOVATION**

  - ▪ Those closest to the customers understand their needs best.

  - ▪ Frontline leaders have the know-how to solve operational problems.

- ■ **WINNING ORGANIZATIONS EMBRACE THE PARADOX OF CREATIVITY AND CONTROL**

  - ▪ Leaders control by setting context and boundaries.

  - ▪ Leaders creatively unleash their front line by teaching them to make judgments.

Today, shopping-cart recommendations are regarded as a critical differentiator in Amazon's remarkable online retail success story, and one of many unique and innovative products and services that have enabled Amazon to prevail in its competition against much larger and formidable competitors, including Wal-Mart and Barnes & Noble. But when Greg Linden joined Amazon straight out of graduate school in 1997—at a point in its evolution when the company occupied a few floors of a run-down brick office building across the street from Seattle's famed Pike Place Market that Linden later recalled "enjoyed a view of the local methadone clinic and a bizarre wig shop"—the burgeoning Web site was a much simpler affair, with few of the bells and whistles that in the years since have kept Amazon a steady pace ahead.[1]

As a new hire brought into a fast-growing start-up, Linden wasn't surprised to find personal space at a premium. Still, he was taken aback to be shown to a desk parked in a cramped corner of the company kitchen, with an elderly PC perched on top. Linden was new to Amazon, but early on he displayed initiative by putting a bowl of candy out on one corner of his desk. This prompted other "geeks," as they fondly referred to themselves, to occasionally stop by for free candy, while Linden tried his best to suck knowledge out of anyone who passed by too closely.[2]

It was actually Linden's fondness for candy that led to his first major innovation at Amazon, as he recalled that in supermarkets, customers often find candy, potato chips, and other "impulse buys" on the racks directly adjacent to the checkout lines. Why not personalize recommendations for similar impulse buys, Linden wondered, based on the items in a customer's virtual shopping cart as it approaches checkout, just as a Wal-Mart or Shop-Rite would? Linden later wrote in his blog:

> The idea of recommending items at checkout is nothing new. Grocery stores put candy and other impulse buys in the checkout lanes. Hardware stores put small tools and gadgets near the register.
>
> But here we had an opportunity to personalize impulse buys. It is as if the rack near the checkout lane peered into your grocery cart and magically rearranged the candy based on what you are buying.

So like any enterprising young recruit at a dynamic, entrepreneurial company, Linden hacked up a prototype of the Amazon.com shopping-cart page to recommend additional items customers might enjoy adding to their carts. When he started running it by colleagues for review, he garnered mainly positive reactions, with the important exception of a senior vice president of marketing, who "was dead set against it." As Linden later recalled, "his main objection was that it might distract people from checking out." While Linden was forced to concede that it was "more common to see customers abandon their cart at the register in online retail," this sole objection failed to convince him that the concept was not worth pursuing.

But even at a start-up like Amazon, hierarchies and command-and-control thinking reign to some degree. Linden was expressly prohibited by a direct superior from proceeding with the project. "I was told I was forbidden to work on this any further. I was told Amazon was not ready to launch this feature."[3] In the vast majority of other, larger, older organizations, the idea would have been killed right then and there. But Amazon was (and is) different. Customer centricity has been deeply ingrained in Amazon's culture from the company's outset. When attending meetings, Amazon CEO Jeff Bezos "periodically leaves one seat open at a conference table and informs all attendees that they should consider that seat occupied by their customer, 'the most important person in the room.'"[4] Fortunately for Greg Linden, the company's overriding respect for the customer and for any experiment that might yield an insight into customer behavior trumped internal corporate hierarchy.

While Linden continued to prepare the feature for an online test to measure its sales impact, he heard through the grapevine that "the SVP was angry when he discovered I was pushing out a test." However, Linden notes that at Amazon, "even for top executives, it was hard to block a test. Measurement was good. The only good argument against testing would be that the negative impact might be so severe that Amazon couldn't afford it, a difficult claim to make. The test rolled out."

The results of the test were clear and irrefutable. Not only did the online test succeed, but the feature was so profitable that not having it live was costing Amazon a noticeable chunk of change. With new urgency, shopping-cart recommendations launched. For Linden (and for us) the lessons to be drawn from this story are as clear as the results of his test.[5]

In my experience, innovation can only come from the bottom. Those closest to the problem are in the best position to solve it. I believe any organization that depends on innovation must embrace chaos. Loyalty and obedience are not your tools; you must use measurement and objective debate to separate the good from the bad.

Of course, Greg Linden's virtual shopping cart experiment could have only succeeded and been widely implemented under the aegis of a CEO who created a culture where experimentation and adoption was the norm as opposed to the exception.

The Turtle Tank

During the course of our clinical work many years ago, a manager of a retail branch in San Diego known for innovation and employee engagement shared an instructive lesson.[6] He told us that if you buy a young turtle and put it in a small aquarium, it will only grow to a size that fits the tank. We looked into this. Not only is it true, but it is also a practice that infuriates animal-rights advocates. Unfortunately for the turtles, the practice stunts their growth, leading to health issues and an uncomfortable living environment.

So what do turtles have to do with frontline workers? As this manager shared with us, most organizations where he had worked earlier in his career had boxed in their employees with rules, bureaucracy, and hierarchy that stunted their personal growth and organizational contribution. Those at the top of the organization not only failed to ask for ideas but were often dismissive when frontline employees generated suggestions. When middle managers and senior leaders claim that frontline leaders lack the necessary strategic context or see criticism of their organizational processes as resistance, this behavior has the same effect as the turtle tank.

The HiPPO Corollary

The fact that many organizations commonly suffer from turtle-tank syndrome can be readily explained by the HiPPO corollary. HiPPO is a term originally coined at, appropriately enough, Amazon, that stands for "highest-paid person's opinion."[7] In most organizations, people reflexively bow to the HiPPO or forsake their own opinion because they do not have the ability to override the HiPPO. This is a direct outcome of the hierarchical organizational construct that assumes intelligence and capability are related to a person's job title. Fortunately for Greg Linden, as we saw in the previous story, Amazon is a company that values data and customer insight over intuition. As a result, his shopping-cart experiment prevailed despite the marketing vice president's (i.e., HiPPO's) opinion that it was not worth pursuing.

People: The Most Ignored Asset

The mantra "people are our most important asset" is commonplace today in business circles. You can find it in so many annual reports and press releases that it has lost all of its original meaning. Yet few companies have absorbed the primary lesson we seek to impart in this book: You can learn from the workers who are closest to problems and interact with customers on the front line every day. While many organizations frequently invoke the mantra of "customer-centricity," most don't pay enough attention to those who are closest to the consumer.

In most organizations, we find a number of initiatives overlaid on a command-and-control structure designed over a century ago for mass production instead of a comprehensive process or framework designed to tap into the well of information and knowledge available on the front line. In many cases, these approaches have been built on a foundation of earlier initiatives such as open-book management, lean manufacturing, service-profit-chain excellence, and prototyping. Most companies lack a blueprint for how to truly arm frontline leaders to better serve their customers and generate ideas that can reap potential windfalls when applied across the enterprise. In the worst cases, these initiatives are implemented poorly and actually contribute to greater cynicism among frontline employees, who hear rhetoric but do not see real change.

As opposed to treating frontline employees as their most valuable asset, most organizations fail to engage them at all. One recent study of the *Fortune* 500 estimated that companies get less than 50 percent of the potential contribution from their people.[8] Put that in the context of the average payroll and HR budgets of large companies (in the tens of millions), and you have to ask how any self-respecting businessperson can live with that level of inefficiency. Imagine the value that would be destroyed and the waste created if every manufacturing organization simply accepted 50 percent productivity. There is an idea-generating engine and innovation factory that remains untapped in most organizations simply because leaders do not know how to connect the experiences and insights of their front line to solving customer problems.

Consider the amount of downtime in most jobs: the wasted minutes that quickly add up when people are waiting for customers, having their requests processed, or simply taking a short break. We refer to these spare moments as *fractional time*.[9] They are the small, unused minutes that usually lead to idle employee conversations about fantasy sports leagues, midday naps, or the dawdler who works hard to make himself appear to be busy while accomplishing very little.

We're not suggesting that employee interaction or the occasional break isn't necessary. However, if employees were challenged to make their organizations better and given evidence that their ideas mattered, they would choose to use these free moments to think productively. They would view their customer interactions through a new lens, ask how they could improve the transaction, or discover an unmet customer need. These small ideas can be quickly shared so that employees build on one another's thinking and observations. Tests can be formulated and executed at the local level so that a huge investment isn't required. Technology and social media make it possible to rapidly broadcast learning and scale success regardless of where people are located or which organizational seats they occupy. This is the massive productivity and creativity gain that most organizations leave untapped today. It is a hidden innovation factory filled with good ideas and potential experiments worth billions of dollars.

The unfortunate reality is that most organizations continue to operate a twentieth-century management structure that dates back nearly one hundred years to Alfred Sloan, the genius who designed the siloed structure that caused General Motors to thrive in its early years but resulted in the fourth-largest bankruptcy in U.S. history in 2009. Most organizations are built around the notion that strong hierarchy, with formal reporting relationships and clear role prescriptions, can reduce complexity and thereby leverage economies of scale. The CEO and management team build the strategy, middle managers interpret it in operational plans, and frontline employees execute it. The amount of thinking required is correlated to your hierarchical level, with the expectation that frontline workers are doers, not thinkers.

While such a model was well suited to past business conditions, it simply does not hold up in a world where customers expect more personalized service, the Internet makes everyone's pricing transparent, and customers or employees can share a company's deficiencies online or via Twitter. The single service mistake a frontline leader makes doesn't just impact one customer anymore; it can instantly be broadcast to millions, as we shall see.

The Organizational Paradox: Control Versus Creativity

A perception of excessive risk attached to operating differently causes organizations—particularly those with thousands of employees—to employ policies and procedures expressly designed to limit individual autonomy. After all, what is less predictable than human behavior? Rogue traders have brought down entire firms on Wall Street, so it seems only sensible to keep tight control systems in place. Jack Welch, the famous former CEO of General Electric, used to liken his company of three hundred thousand people to a small city. Cities, Welch would observe, have jails and police forces because on any given day there is someone who is breaking the law.

It is the paradox of all organizations that they require control yet succeed most spectacularly when they unleash the imagination and energy of their employees. Companies cannot afford to completely give up either one, but their perceived inability to manage the operational risk of putting more power in the hands of rank-and-file employees tends to tilt the balance strongly in favor of control. Yet as you will see in the case studies we present in this book, the even more painful paradox is that companies that feel compelled to impose obsolete command-and-control protocols in an attempt to tightly govern the actions of frontline employees are actually running an even greater risk: Frontline workers will fail to provide these organizations with the information, wisdom, and judgment required to solve problems and meet their customers' ever-changing expectations.

Before we look at how to build a front line–focused organization, we would like to highlight the costs of failing to tap into the judgment and experience of the lower ranks. We will explore three examples—Meijer, Bank of America, and BP—to highlight the price paid by employees, customers, and shareholders when the front line is neglected.

1. "Out-of-Control" Control: Meijer

On November 17, 2008, the *Wall Street Journal* reported that Meijer, a large regional grocer in the Midwest akin to a Super Walmart, had installed automated clocks that timed every cashier's transactions.[10] The system was geared for "labor waste elimination." According to the article,

> a clock starts ticking the instant he scans a customer's first item, and it doesn't shut off until his register spits out a receipt. To assess his efficiency, the store's computer takes into account everything from the kinds of merchandise he's bagging to how his customers are paying. Each week, he gets scored. If he falls below 95% of the baseline score too many times, the 185-store megastore chain, based in Walker, Mich., is likely to bounce him to a lower-paying job, or fire him.

Subsequent interviews with Meijer cashiers indicated that the new system did spur many of them to speed up the checkout process, just as intended.[11] The quota system, with its looming threat of termination or demotion, pushed employees to go faster. This would have been great if

Meijer's only concern was output per hour. But Meijer's twenty-first-century customers were looking for more. Many elderly consumers complained of being rushed at the checkout lane, while frequent shoppers missed the personal exchanges with employees they had come to know. Employees were also unhappy and said they felt stressed. Some employees said they actively avoided eye contact with customers so they would hurry along. Others even figured out how to beat the system by using special buttons that would temporarily stop the clock.

In our view, Meijer applied old-school Taylorism in the worst possible way. What may have started as an attempt to make the customer process more efficient instead reduced the last point of customer contact to a "just get 'er done" moment. The shopping experience lacked connection and employees were stressed to the point that they started to cheat. Meijer applied a mass-production mind-set to the customer experience. The implicit logic underlying the initiative suggests that Meijer believed customers value quick transactions above all else. This may be true for some customer segments but is surely not universal. While it may seem that efficiency initiatives rarely garner a lot of employee enthusiasm, Toyota, Steelcase, and many other companies have demonstrated that employees are quick to identify and support efficiency initiatives that make their jobs more productive. Not only did Meijer fail to build employee support for the new process, but the company tried to reduce the tasks of cashiers to a computer algorithm. Unfortunately, computer programs can't supply the value of an employee's smile, the time it takes to answer a customer question that may lead to future business, or the appreciation of a customer who gets extra help loading his groceries.

2. Setting Up the Front Line for Failure: Bank of America

Shortly after the onset of the U.S. recession in 2008, an economic period when many Americans lost their jobs, watched their home values evaporate, and were contending with a restricted credit environment, Bank of America offered what it touted as an innovative program to convert customers' credit card debts into a fixed-fee loan. This was promoted as an escape hatch for customers burdened with double-digit-interest credit card loans. Unfortunately, the requirements for customers to qualify, based on monthly earnings, liquidity, and a host of other net-worth variables, meant that those most likely to qualify were least likely to actually need the program.

As Jackie Ramos, a fired employee, shared in a YouTube video later picked up by media outlets including the *Huffington Post* and CNN, the bank derived millions in profits from charging late fees or mandating increased annual interest rates when consumers missed payments. Although employees were admonished to "do the right thing for the customer" and "think of yourself as the customer," Ms. Ramos acidly observed that too many frontline customer advocates felt the prevailing rule was "do what is right for the company." Frontline employees were frequently left to explain to disappointed, angry customers why the purported benefits of the loan-modification programs weren't available to them.

In her video, Ms. Ramos pointedly recalled having to deny a loan modification to a twenty-four-year-old single mother recently diagnosed with cancer, who had lost her mother and husband in the past year but was seeking a way to pay off her six-thousand-dollar debt. As Ms. Ramos shared with the world,

> she sobbed on the phone telling me she couldn't afford the 30 percent interest . . . that we had her account on. She couldn't afford the $39 late fee, the $39 over-limit fee. She told me that we were her first credit card when she turned 18, we were her only credit card, and that she was a loyal customer. And given the time to be on this earth a little while longer she would have always remained a loyal customer. According to Bank of America, she doesn't have enough income to be put on a program, but she can however keep paying the high interest rates on the account, and fees, because at the end of the day, it is her account, she did rack up the debt, she was late, and she did deserve the 29.99 percent interest rate.[12]

In Bank of America's defense, it claimed it had modified over one million customer accounts in 2009. It's not that this wasn't a beneficial program. The problem, in our view, was that it was mass marketed, potentially raising customers' hopes even among the many who would not qualify. In fact, it most likely smacked of hypocrisy to many customers who were denied and the employees who were left with the emotional toll of denying them. Bank of America's debt-modification program failed to take into account the daily realities of the people at the front line—those who would execute it—or how the program would be perceived by customers and community members who didn't qualify.

Perhaps the greatest failing of the bank's program was that it obliged frontline employees to emotionally distance themselves from customers, when in reality they could have served as the customers' most concerned advocates, lending credibility to the repeated claims of the bank's senior leaders that it was evolving a "customer-centric" culture. Absent the ability to help distressed customers and often the targets of customer outrage, employees likely had to build some indifference to individual customers—precisely the opposite of customer-centricity. In fact, Ms. Ramos was fired from her customer-advocate role precisely because, unable to distance herself sufficiently from her customers' desperate needs, she by her own admission encouraged customers to lie on their loan applications in the hope that they would improve their chances of being approved.[13] It should be noted that in this case, just as at Meijer, a poorly designed frontline program led to dishonest employee behavior.

3. Crisis at the Front Line: BP

> I saw the mud shooting up, then it just quit. I took a deep breath thinking, "Oh, they got it under control." Then all of a sudden the degasser mud started coming out of the degasser. It's in a gooseneck, and it points down to the deck. And it come out of it so strong and so loud that it just filled up the whole back deck with gassy smoke. It was loud enough so that it was like taking an air hose and sticking it up to your ear. Then something exploded. I'm not sure what exploded but just looking at it, where the degasser is sitting, there's a big tank and it goes into a pipe. I'm thinking that the tank exploded.[14]

This anonymous eyewitness account of the moment before escaping hydrocarbons from the Macondo well caused the explosion of the Deepwater Horizon, an oil-drilling platform anchored forty-eight miles offshore in the Gulf of Mexico, is a chilling reminder of how underinvestment in or neglect of an organization's front line can lead to calamity. The quote above is just one among many independent observations relied on by investigators to assemble a complete picture of a tragic disaster that left eleven people dead, seventeen injured, nearly five million barrels of oil spilled, and the reputation of BP, the international oil company that leased the offshore rig, in tatters for years to come. As an internal investigation commissioned by BP soberly concluded,

> no single action or inaction caused the accident. Rather, a complex and interlinked series of mechanical failures, human judgments, engineering design, operational implementation and team interfaces came together to allow the initiation and escalation of the accident.

A U.S. federal investigation seemed to concur with BP's assessment when it later found thirty-five contributing causes leading up to the explosion, of which it found BP solely responsible for twenty-one and partially responsible for eight more.[15] While some of the critical contributors to the worst offshore oil spill in U.S. history, such as a questionable well design, occurred far from the oil rig, there seems to be little doubt that those who worked on the rig, and those who were responsible for safeguarding those workers, ignored warning signs that might have averted the disaster. The time line of the days and hours leading up to the event reveals that an operations drilling engineer noted in an e-mail to a colleague that BP had not taken the usual precautions to ensure a pipe had been properly cemented in place. "Who cares," he wrote just four days before the catastrophe, "it's done, end of story, will probably be fine."[16]

BP's 234-page internal report, while dismissed by many lawmakers and BP's partners, Transocean and Halliburton, as "self-serving," does recognize lapses in oversight of the rig's operations.[17] Mark Bly, the company's head of safety and the leader of the internal investigation, noted that "where there were errors made they were based on poor decision-making process or using wrong information."[18] A reading of the numerous reports on the incident suggests that poor judgment was at play as BP's drilling engineers failed to detect anomalies during crucial tests and the crew failed to detect the initial influx of oil and gas that ultimately led to the explosion. In fact, a technician who stepped away for a ten-minute cigarette break missed a warning that would have alerted the crew to disaster and likely saved lives. While he was smoking, the monitors he was assigned to watch revealed pressure data indicating the well was filling with a mixture of explosive gas and oil, but by the time he returned the gauges had reverted to normal. The technician, who escaped the tragedy, told an investigatory commission that he realized something had gone wrong only when the air conditioner in the ceiling began to melt.[19]

Sadly, we will never be certain of how events unfolded leading up to the explosion, as those who were on the front line that day—those who were closest to the action and who knew what really happened—were lost in the accident. BP maintains that cost pressures to finish the well, which was "running significantly behind schedule," never led to decisions that directly compromised safety.[20] Nonetheless, there is widespread recognition that the daily costs of running a rig—more than one million dollars—played a part in the company's decision making. As the chairman of a U.S. congressional committee scathingly summarized, "BP appears to have made multiple decisions for economic reasons that increased the danger of a catastrophic well failure."[21] At the heart of this tragedy seems to lie a "culture of recklessness"[22] that failed to take the necessary precautions to safeguard workers' lives and failed to arm those on the operational front line that day with the right mind-set and work environment to detect crisis before the worst had happened.

Surprisingly, in the notoriously cozy petroleum industry, one of the more searing yet credible critics of BP's business practices was Peter Voser, CEO of BP's archrival, Royal Dutch Shell. "Shell clearly would have drilled this well in a different way and would have had more options to prevent the accident," Voser flatly insisted, referring to Shell's own protocols.[23]

What stands out most about this comment, apart from the fact that Voser was willing to make it at all, is that it was deeply rooted in what Marvin Odum, chief of Shell's U.S. operations, described to the U.S. government commission charged with investigating the disaster as a "culture of safety" carefully cultivated by the company over decades. Gary Steele, a longtime Shell executive who later joined the Swiss construction giant ABB, advised us in an interview.

> Health and safety is one of those areas where you never add up the cost of killing someone. I've often said to my guys, "Let's charge the business a billion dollars if somebody dies in the business." Of course, we never actually do it, but the beauty of that number is that nobody can challenge it because nobody else has ever added up the number. Suppose it's half a billion; I'm wrong by one hundred percent. It's still a big number.[24]

Steele recalled a concrete manifestation of the culture of safety based on decades of experience at Shell.

> I was visiting one of our major voltage factories in the north of England. In many factories they have yellow lines that you have to stay inside if you're not one of the people trained to work in that space. I inadvertently had stepped outside this yellow line, and one of the operators physically picked me up and moved me back in. Now, that guy had understood that I would be okay with that because he was making sure I was safe. He was taking corrective action.

Would such an incident have occurred at BP? Maybe yes, maybe no. But as Steele contends, the critical process of instilling a truly transformative cultural change in any organization must start at the top yet quickly cascade down the ranks deep into the front line. "Safety," he points out, "is an area where you quickly learn that you can't dictate or define from the top every point of risk across an organization. You've got to carefully delegate and cascade the whole responsibility right down to the factory floor."

The comprehensive system of responsibility that Steele describes as deeply embedded at organizations like Shell and ABB is one we call "judgment on the front line." This leadership model is predicated on the discovery that knowledge, judgment, leadership, experience, and wisdom naturally reside among the frontline members of every organization and that it is an important responsibility of every organization's top team to design reliable methods of accessing and incorporating this knowledge into its broader strategy.

What if, for example, BP had created and implemented a comprehensive, enterprise-wide internal tool kit that asked the members of the rig crew, the tool pushers and drillers and outside contractors who actually lived on the rig day to day, to collaborate in devising a safety and compliance system that would have ensured their own safety and, indirectly, safeguarded the exposure of BP shareholders and stakeholders to virtually limitless reputational risk and legal liability?[25] What if that tool kit had contained actionable methods for accessing frontline workers' knowledge and judgment not just of safety protocols but also of exploration, production, and other critical components of the company's strategic goals?

Gary Steele provided us with one pertinent example of such an approach, adopted under his guidance at Shell. As part of an executive development program we helped devise over a decade ago, a team of high-potential Shell executives were assigned to identify operational cost savings. The team reviewed many ideas but felt that most of the major savings available to Shell without compromising safety standards had already been realized. Nonetheless, the team traveled to Brazil in search of ideas to cut maintenance costs in its retail gasoline operations. The executives' first stop was a gasoline station, where they were ushered around the facility by the outside contractors in charge of maintenance. After a customarily cursory question-and-answer period, the team was on the verge of pushing on to its next destination when one of the executives asked a maintenance technician if he had any cost-saving ideas.

Whipping out a wrench from the pocket of his overalls, the technician promptly pried open one of the gas pumps to reveal a rubber fuel line that connected the pump to the station's underground reservoir. He proceeded to point out that Shell's maintenance schedule dictated that these rubber hoses be replaced once a year, while they came with a manufacturer's warranty that guaranteed them for five years. "Don't know why you do this," the mechanic bluntly pointed out, "because it amounts to trading in a five-year warranty every year." The technician, who serviced the pumps every day and personally faced danger if a pump were to fail, was confident there was no safety risk in replacing the hoses every five years.

The upshot of this exchange was that the visiting executives returned to headquarters with a seemingly trivial idea that, extrapolated across Shell's entire global operations, saved the company many millions over many years in many countries. Only after these not-insignificant cost savings had been duly noted did one of the original team of high-level executives return to the scene of the breakthrough to ask the technician one simple question. "You've been working in pump maintenance for a long time," the executive began, to which the mechanic readily agreed. "Why didn't you tell us any of this before?"

"Because," the technician cheerfully volunteered, "no one ever asked me."

The moral of this story, Steele later reflected, "is that regardless of what a person wears to work, or what tools they use, they've got a reservoir of information and knowledge that historically, few organizations have any reliable way to tap." The identity of one of the team's high-potential executives who over ten years ago thought to ask these questions is not incidental to this story. He was Peter Voser, future CEO of Royal Dutch Shell, the same man who in 2010 broke his industry's unwritten code of silence by daring to publicly criticize BP's operations for not, in effect, being more like Shell's. Take the twenty-billion-dollar escrow fund that BP was obliged to set aside for damages incurred as a result of its spill and add to it the potential liability incurred when the U.S. Justice Department sued the company for an additional twenty billion dollars, and BP's failure to access the reservoir of judgment and skill available to it at the front line—at negligible cost—snaps into focus as potentially critical not just to a firm's bottom line but to its very survival.

Summary: The Frontline Leadership Paradigm

Changes in consumer behavior, a generational swing in employee attitudes, and the growth of social media have all contributed to an erosion of command-and-control organizations. In their place, organizations that emphasize decentralization and collaboration are rising in order to more nimbly respond to consumer needs. Those who embrace these changes and learn from their front lines are able to create a virtual factory of new ideas and innovation.

Some of these organizations, like Zappos, IDEO, and Google, began in the past decade or two as small start-ups. More established organizations like Pepsi, Steelcase, and the Providence Police Department have fundamentally altered their organizational structures and employee relationships. In the course of our research, we have learned from all of these, while also examining organizations that have a history of relying on frontline leadership, including the Navy SEALs, the Mayo Clinic, and Ritz-Carlton.

While our benchmark organizations differ in many respects, they share certain features that we have defined as essential to driving frontline judgment and innovation. The first is that they display strong leadership from

ABRIDGED RESEARCH LIST

- ABB
- Amazon
- Charoen Pokphand Group
- Disney
- Facebook
- Google
- Grupo Salinas
- Hewlett-Packard
- IBM
- IDEO
- Intuit
- Mayo Clinic in Arizona

- PepsiCo/Pepsi Bottling Group
- Providence Police Department
- Ritz-Carlton
- Steelcase
- 3M
- U.S. Navy SEALs
- Wal-Mart
- Yum!
- Zappos
- Zara

the top. If leaders don't want employees who act as dumb terminals only capable of carrying out tasks they have been explicitly assigned, then they must have faith that giving employees power carries more reward than risk. This faith is one way in which the organizations we researched set themselves apart from the norm. Rather than spout the usual platitudes about empowerment or engagement, the leaders in these organizations really believed it. Rather than deploy an initiative or pursue a management fad, they fundamentally altered how their hierarchies operated.

Leaders in these organizations usually began with a cultural revolution in mind. They weren't after suggestion boxes or the occasional good idea; they wanted profound change in how their organizations looked at the expected contribution of leaders at all levels. All of this was in pursuit of providing better products, services, or experiences to the customer, patient, or community member.

While it is easy to get lost in the power-to-the-people positive vibe in many of these organizations, these leaders demanded accountability for results and often measured progress relentlessly. As they did so, many struggled with the difficult task of creating a performance-based environment that simultaneously fostered individual initiative and risk taking. What they have accomplished, individually and collectively, has been the result of deliberate investments in technology, tools, and training. In the next chapter we explore the process of creating a front line–focused organization in more detail and highlight Ritz-Carlton as an example of a company that has embraced this paradigm since its inception, discovering along the way that fostering leadership, judgment, and innovation at the front line cultivates customer relationships, employee engagement, and the creation of long-term value.

2

BUILDING THE FRONT LINE–FOCUSED ORGANIZATION

My name is Herve Humler and I am the president of Ritz-Carlton . . . and I am a very important person. But you are more important than I am. You are the heart and soul of this building.

—**Herve Humler, addressing hotel staff shortly before the grand opening of Ritz-Carlton's Hong Kong property**

■ **STRONG LEADERSHIP IS REQUIRED TO UNLEASH THE FRONT LINE**

- Senior leaders use their authority to create the architecture and support systems.

- The organization's top team must stay directly connected to those in the field.

- Information from the front line should be used to define and refine the strategy.

■ **BUILDING A FRONT LINE–FOCUSED ORGANIZATION IS A PROCESS**

- An integrative framework is needed to replace a collage of initiatives.

- The process helps whether starting from scratch or rebuilding a decades-old institution.

The popularity of CBS's hit reality TV show *Undercover Boss* is rooted in a simple if not always convenient truth: Many CEOs have little actual knowledge of how work gets done in their organizations. They lack an appreciation for the conduct and skills required of frontline workers, who all too frequently perform repetitive and strenuous tasks day in and day out, at an infinitesimal fraction of a CEO's compensation. In one typical episode, Joe DePinto, a former army officer, a West Point graduate, and the CEO of the U.S. 7-Eleven chain of convenience stores, openly vows to go "on an undercover mission to find out what's really happening inside my company. By working on the front line, I'll learn about the good and the bad, which will ultimately change the way I manage the company."[1]

"I want to find out how the communication from our headquarters in Dallas flows out to the stores and back," he announces to his assembled senior leadership team before bravely venturing into the field, where—as he puts it—"the rubber meets the road." Disguised as an out-of-work real estate salesman seeking an entry-level job, he spends a day at a convenience store that sells more coffee per day than any other in his vast empire of 7,600 stores, another day on a bakery assembly line that produces a fair proportion of the sixty million pastries the chain sells annually, and an overnight shift with a delivery driver distributing products and stocking store shelves.

At every semicomic turn, the CEO learns that he lacks the skills and experience required to complete his assigned tasks. His inability to keep pace with a line of thirsty customers dying for their morning joe and his awkwardness trying to mesh with an assembly line teach him that his co-workers are good-hearted, kind, and competent. Although they are frequently exasperated by his work, they continue trying to train him. More than anything, DePinto also sees that his frontline workers, though paid little, are talented, intelligent, and wise in the ways of keeping customers happy. After spending a week on the front line, he freely concedes, "I thought I knew our stores and our people, but the fact is, I was wrong."

While much of the comic undertone of this Emmy-nominated reality show is derived from a senior manager's incompetence at performing routine tasks, nearly every episode of *Undercover Boss* ends the same way. The CEO solemnly and sincerely vows to change his perception of the frontline workers, to institute policies and procedures designed to improve their lot, and to manage his company differently based on the lessons he has learned. It appears that there is nothing uniquely American about this disconnect from the C-suite to the front line; there are versions of the show, which originated in the United Kingdom, in production or scheduled to launch in ten other countries across Europe and the Middle East.

Leadership in a Front Line–Focused Organization

As a communications expert lamented in a blog commentary on *Undercover Boss*,[2] surely there must be a better way to keep an organization's CEO in touch with frontline employees than having the boss spy on them incognito. The importance of ensuring that CEOs and senior managers maintain a communication pipeline with frontline workers is greater than ever. Not only can they validate whether a strategy is working in practice, but they are also able to pick up subtle cues about changes in customer behaviors that should influence the refinement and evolution of any given strategy.

Yet what gives this "reality" show bite is that there are so many challenges to providing a CEO with real, unfiltered feedback from the front line, not least of which is the fact that when the head honcho comes to town, many people suddenly feel inspired to do their best work. Layer on top of this the combination of awe and fear that the person sitting atop the organizational pyramid typically inspires in those near the bottom, and the multiple barriers to facilitating an open two-way conversation between senior management and the front line become readily apparent. However, the perceived gulf between the organizational apex and its front line is often more a matter of structure, process, and leadership than simply a CEO's personality, title, or individual style.

If CEOs and senior leaders don't create routines for understanding customer needs through the eyes of frontline workers, they run the risk of creating strategies that can't be put into operational practice. Building a business model that is aligned with customer needs is only a fraction of senior leaders' responsibility. Once customer needs are identified, CEOs and senior leaders must work backward from the moment of truth when customers and frontline employees find themselves face to face. They must imagine what the ideal customer interaction will look like and ask where breakdowns may occur throughout the process, from generating customer awareness to building postsale relationships. Some may argue that this is more operational grit than a CEO needs to absorb. Unlike *Undercover Boss*, however, we don't advocate that CEOs try to *do* the jobs of their frontline workers (though there may be some educational and symbolic leadership value in choosing to climb down into the trenches with the foot soldiers). Before settling on a strategy, senior leaders need to design an organization that is prepared to execute, or at least be aware of the limitations of the organization as necessary changes are being implemented.

In a front line–focused organization, senior leaders have five primary responsibilities:[3]

♦ **Define a Customer-Based Vision:** First, they must set the vision and define a customer-based strategy for the organization. The accountability for where to compete, against whom to compete, and how to differentiate an organization in the marketplace ultimately rests with the CEO. As we will discuss below, however, these judgments aren't just passed down from the mountaintop but must reflect observations, feedback, and learning from the field. Senior leaders must mobilize organizational expertise to craft a customer-value proposition that matches the product and service capabilities to what the organization can deliver.

♦ **Develop a Front Line–Focused Culture:** Second, the leaders must create a culture of front line focus. This starts with the leaders' personal attitudes and behaviors: They must deeply care about the opportunities their organization affords frontline employees and they must sincerely respect the importance of their insight. In our experience working with CEOs and other senior leaders who fit this profile, they often have had life lessons that taught them to value everyone's perspective. Some have worked their way up from entry-level jobs as dishwashers or salespeople. Others have felt the sting of being socially different—whether as the fat kid who couldn't climb the rope in gym class, as the only male in a household of women, or as the kid who moved so often he went to nineteen schools before graduating from high school—and have had their opinions discounted by others.

Senior leaders who respect the potential insight that can come from any individual can infect their organizations with their deep-seated respect for people. They are hierarchically positioned to embed values and model leadership behaviors that ensure their organizations actively consider the needs of those on the front line and learn from their experiences. They also have the power to define the organizational structure, job designs, customer policies, and work environment to enable those on the front line.

♦ **Obsess over Talent:** While they deeply respect views that come from anywhere in the organization, these leaders also know that they will win only by having the best talent and the right kind of leadership at the customer interface. They are hard-nosed about the recruitment and hiring process, not content to leave this to human resources or middle management to work out. Not only do they protect the front doors of their organizations with a watchdog mentality, but they also ensure that training and support systems are in place to teach newcomers how to be successful with customers.

◆ **Define the Judgment Playing Field:** Armed with a customer-based strategy, front line–focused culture, and the right players, these leaders actively define the judgment playing field for their teams. They define the boundaries for employee decision making, clarifying when frontline leaders can act autonomously and which issues are outside of their authority. When employees are empowered to act, senior leaders ensure that they are equipped with the right resources to make good judgments on behalf of the business and in the interest of the customer.

◆ **Live on the Line:** Leaders—especially the top leadership—need to go where the action is. They must interact with workers at the customer interface to understand whether the front line feels capable of executing the strategy. Front line–focused leaders do far more listening than talking when they are in the field. Field visits are neither an old-school, white-glove audit nor just a rally-the-troops moment, although a senior leader may subtly try to do both of these when mixing it up with lower-level employees. More important, this is a reality check in which leaders try to understand at a deep level:

1. Are individual employees committed to our organization, our mission, and our customers?
2. Are we incorporating all of our knowledge about customers to meet or exceed their expectations?
3. Are we providing our employees the right tools, resources, and work environment to create value for customers without unnecessary bureaucracy or delay?

Giving Frontline Workers What They Want

The concern that senior leaders exhibit for employees in front line–focused organizations translates into strong cultures and improved work environments. According to our research and that of other observers, implementing components of the methodology that will be described in coming chapters has led to statistically significant improvements in employee engagement scores, customer satisfaction, and financial results.[4]

Perhaps the best case to date has been made by the authors of *The Service Profit Chain,* which quantitatively linked employee satisfaction to customer loyalty and ultimately to profitability. As the authors observe, providing employees with the skills, latitude, and resources to do their jobs directly translates into a more positive customer experience and improved financial performance.[5] In their words:

> Their satisfaction stems, at least among the best frontline employees, from their desire to deliver results to customers. In order to deliver results to customers, they must have the ability to relate to customers, the latitude (within well-specified limits) to use their judgment in doing so, the training and technological support needed to do so, and recognition and rewards for doing so.

Involving employees in decision-making processes, enabling them to innovate, and providing the autonomy and resources to solve customer problems without escalation collectively offer frontline workers the essential elements that have been shown to drive employee satisfaction and engagement. Although academic research has provided many labels for the drivers of employee commitment, we summarize them as the "four C's":[6]

- **Context:** Frontline employees want to connect their daily interactions with the customer to the achievement of larger long-term goals. This requires an understanding of strategy and customer and business objectives.
- **Control:** Frontline workers, like most people, want to feel empowered to make autonomous decisions and take action when necessary. There must be established boundary conditions in which employees feel free to make decisions, and they must be given the training and tools to make effective judgments.
- **Care:** Ultimately, if employees do not feel connected to their organizations and have a sense that coworkers and managers are unconcerned with their well-being, they will not care about the organization or their job.
- **Creativity:** Work is a personal endeavor that occupies the majority of waking time for most people, so frontline employees need the opportunity to exercise their individual thought and creativity and invest their own personality in their work.

Building a Front Line–Focused Organization

When leaders provide the building blocks and employees are encouraged to actively share their intelligence and creativity, we find organizations that are better places to work, provide a better customer experience, and generally perform better financially. Although we still run into command-and-control managers who question the sensibility of entrusting employees to make real decisions, we more typically encounter leaders who appreciate the benefits of front line–focused companies but don't know where to begin in building their own. They recognize the basic tools and techniques but, like architects gazing at the pyramids, they aren't quite sure how to build such a formidable structure. Throughout the book we will highlight the many benefits of building a front line–focused organization—and the potentially devastating costs of failing to do so—but we focus our attention mostly on the process of *how* to build such an organization.

It isn't startling news that organizations benefit from empowering employees, solving customer problems, and engaging more experienced minds in the process of innovation. What we see lacking in our clinical practice and research—just as we saw on *Undercover Boss*—is an integrative framework for assessing how much an organization is focused on the front line and a process for closing the gaps. The remainder of this book is organized around a five-step process for leaders to build or, more likely, rebuild their companies from the front line so that the ingenuity, innovation, and emotion of thousands of employees can be harnessed.

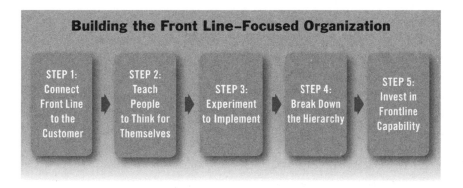

Building the Front Line–Focused Organization

STEP 1: Connect Front Line to the Customer

STEP 2: Teach People to Think for Themselves

STEP 3: Experiment to Implement

STEP 4: Break Down the Hierarchy

STEP 5: Invest in Frontline Capability

While we depict this process in a step-by-step fashion, the building of a front line–focused organization may not occur in such a neat, linear manner. Nevertheless, we have found that all of the elements are necessary whether building an organization from scratch or transforming a decades-old institution.

We will introduce the process below and then use the example of the famed Ritz-Carlton global luxury hotel chain to illustrate how each step is put in motion. Subsequent chapters will explore each step in more detail.

Step 1: Connect the Front Line to the Customer

After so much emphasis on the leadership, judgment, and customer knowledge of frontline employees, it may seem paradoxical that our process starts with the CEO setting a clear vision of the customer.[7] The CEO and top team must be clear on the type of customer experience they expect the front line to provide so they can help to engineer the supporting organizational infrastructure to make that happen, day in and day out. In sum, the CEO and senior team have three fundamental responsibilities in step 1:

1. Understand changing customer needs based on feedback from customers and employees.
2. Ensure that the organization's capabilities match the customer promise.
3. Connect the front line to delivery and improvement of the customer value proposition.

The matrix below illustrates the relationship between the degree of frontline judgment required and the level of customer complexity. In general, if customer needs are predictable and fairly homogenous across different customer groups, frontline employees may focus on delivering consistency. In cases where we find relatively little deviation from one transaction to the next, businesses are able to make do with employees who follow rules and rote processes. In the most extreme cases, employees aren't needed at all and technology can take their place.

At the other end of the spectrum are highly individualized, unique transactions that require employees to anticipate solutions to complex customer needs that customers may not even be aware they have, much less be able to precisely articulate. Employees act more as caseworkers, acting flexibly and adaptively to grasp the nuance of the customer's needs so they can assemble a customized solution. In such cases technology may be used to connect employees to foster collaborative innovation or the rapid spread of best practices.

A simple example of a highly routine customer transaction occurs at bank branches when tellers deposit money or cash a check. These straightforward exchanges are usually governed by strict standard operating procedures and in most cases can be replicated through an automated teller machine. By contrast, a financial planner would want to understand the customer on a much deeper personal level—the customer's financial goals, risk profile, and other characteristics that would influence the appropriate type and time horizon of investment choices. In practice, we find that the

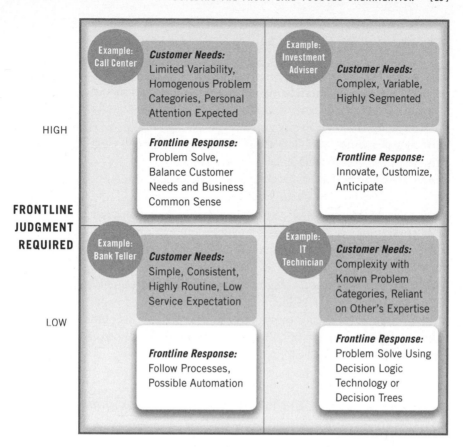

TRANSACTION COMPLEXITY

dichotomy between highly routine jobs and highly variable jobs isn't so clear-cut. In fact, the bank teller who accepts a deposit should be able to intelligently refer a customer to an investment specialist or suggest alternative banking products directly.

Rather than consign frontline staff to routine work and standard operating processes, leaders must consider how employees can add value by engaging actively with customers. Identifying the increased service and innovation capabilities of the front line should be part of the strategy, not an afterthought.

Once the business model and ideal customer experience have been identified, the senior team must articulate how these are made operational throughout their organization. As we have written elsewhere, leaders do this most effectively by developing a Teachable Point of View (TPOV)[8] for their business that clearly articulates what is required to win in the market. This starts with identification of the role that leaders at all levels must play to execute the strategy, and the allocation of resources to build the necessary support systems.

The need to define and teach the business strategy may seem like common sense, but as Harvard professors Robert Kaplan and David Norton revealed in their influential work on the balanced scorecard, only 5 percent of frontline employees truly understand their company's strategy.[9] Unless the frontline leaders know the target customer and recognize their role in creating value, employees will be far less motivated and capable of solving customer problems when breakdowns occur.

Once senior leaders have defined how the organization will win with customers, they must more fully outline the values that will lead to the successful execution of that strategy. These serve as operational guidelines that define employee behavior and customer interactions and articulate the unique culture of the organization. The degree of autonomy and creativity expected of employees should be explicitly expressed so that workers understand the strategic and cultural boundaries for serving customers. If a company demands little differentiation in the customer experience, employees won't be expected to innovate, so operational discipline might be valued, while in organizations requiring more tailored customer experiences, creativity and innovation may be prized.

Ideas and Values at the Ritz-Carlton Hotel Company

We have selected the Ritz-Carlton hotel chain to explore each step of the process in practical application because the company has a long history of being both customer and front line focused. Steeped in history dating back to the 1800s, when famed Swiss hotelier César Ritz catered to European royals and celebrities at his pleasure palaces at the Savoy in London and the Ritz in Paris, the Ritz-Carlton brand has always been synonymous with luxury and service. Many decades before customer-centricity became a buzzword, César Ritz was widely admired for his oft-stated point of view that the customer was "never wrong."

The current incarnation of the Ritz tradition dates back only to 1983, when a group of five investors purchased the Ritz-Carlton Boston and, over the succeeding nearly three decades, expanded the portfolio to include more than seventy properties worldwide where customers have come to expect consistently outstanding service in beautiful facilities and premier locations. Just three years after its founding as a modern entity, with only five hotels to its credit, Ritz-Carlton was voted the best hotel company in the global industry. While the superlative physical surroundings are impressive, these are merely table stakes. As Herve Humler, president and chief operating officer, is fond of saying, "Luxury is wanted, not needed. . . . With luxury you always have to look at personalized service. Luxury is rich in detail."[10]

Service has been embedded deeply in the DNA of Ritz-Carlton and is a hallmark of its brand mystique. The company's approach to service is spelled out clearly as part of the "Gold Standards" that define the company's purpose and relationships with both customers and employees. The "Three Steps of Service" are quite simple:[11]

1. A warm and sincere greeting. Use the guest's name.
2. Anticipation and fulfillment of each guest's needs.
3. Fond farewell. Give a warm good-bye and use the guest's name.

The Ritz staff of several hundred valets, front-desk employees, house-keepers, and the like at each property make up the front line responsible for providing that special, personalized service, as captured in the company motto: "We are Ladies and Gentlemen serving Ladies and Gentlemen." Horst Schulze, one of the founding five investors and the company's charismatic leader until 2001, noted of the motto:

> "Ladies and Gentlemen" has two values to us. Of course, the first is the expression of our expectations of our employees, from the president to the vice president to the last housekeeper or dishwasher. It expresses to them an expectation of how to behave, look and so on. At the same time it expresses a promise to the same group that they are all important to this organization. Their jobs may be different, but they're equal. They are in service but aren't servants.[12]

The Ladies and Gentlemen are charged with "making memories" for guests during their visits. These special moments and experiences that the Ritz hopes will stay with guests for a lifetime account for as much as 90 percent of the company's value proposition. Such memories not only encourage customers to spend more—actively engaged customers tend to drop 23 percent more on food and services[13]—but also to visit more often, making the lifetime value of the best Ritz-Carlton customers more than one million dollars.[14]

Keeping customers for a lifetime has required frequent and precise calibration by top leadership of how the company delivers its famed luxury to guests. In order to stay relevant in a crowded, competitive market, Ritz-Carlton's leaders have had to stay abreast of generational changes that influence guests' desires for property design, amenities, and how the company delivers its "bespoke" service. As Simon Cooper, president from 2001 to

2010, once remarked on the chain's changing clientele, "If you had cast your eye across the lobby of The Ritz-Carlton Boston in 1982, it's likely that most guests would have been mature, formally dressed, and male. Today's guests are much more diverse—younger, more casually elegant, and less formal. There are many more women guests, as well as more families."[15]

Over the years, Ritz-Carlton has steadily decreased its reliance on standard operating procedures, encouraging more local innovation and nurturing employees' exercise of in-the-moment judgment. This began in 1989 when Ritz-Carlton pursued the Malcolm Baldrige National Quality Award, ultimately winning the honor twice, and recognized the critical role of individual employees in driving continuous improvement. Ed Staros, one of the founding team members and currently managing director of the company's Naples property, explained to us, "Back in the early days we said we've got to put the decision making on the front lines. And then we coach and mentor the people who make decisions to either help them create a better decision cycle the next time around or reward them for a great decision that was made on the spot."[16]

Ritz-Carlton's leadership has maintained a steady presence in the field, traveling extensively to listen to customers and meet with employees to refine both strategy and operations over the years. As Herve Humler says, "You have to listen to your customer. You still need to solicit the opinion of your ladies and gentlemen around the globe; it's so important that you get as many opinions as you can before making a decision."[17]

One critical decision was updating the hotel chain's physical image. Based on customer and employee feedback, it became clear by the mid-2000s that the Ritz-Carlton's traditional standards had created an experience that felt too cookie-cutter and slavishly formal to a new generation of guests. Adherence to global procedures had led to uniformity in design details, such as a decorative harp, that didn't fit the aesthetic of locations such as Miami's South Beach or Hawaii. "We had no sense of place," recalls Humler. "Even Kapalua had the portrait of someone's grandmother on the wall."[18]

In response, Ritz-Carlton hired the famed Palo Alto design firm IDEO to make the decor and guest treatment more unique and personalized to the specific ambience of a property's location. Ritz-Carlton executives had decided that instead of a universal playbook with prescriptive service standards that would be identical in all locations, they needed localized "scenes" that would capture the essence of customer-service exchanges tailored to each property's diverse clientele. IDEO orchestrated a process in which creative staffers from each hotel brainstormed local touches that would ever so subtly play on their particular property's strengths. Whether these meant a handwritten note from the chef or an invitation to a wine tasting,

Ritz-Carlton added flexibility and localization as hallmarks of its service strategy.[19]

By the mid-2000s, Ritz-Carlton's leadership had also refreshed the company's service platform to keep its staff connected with a younger, less formal clientele. While the Ladies and Gentlemen had always been given suggestions for appropriate guest interaction, phrases such as "at your service" and "my pleasure" had become too stilted for the type of communication that guests expected. Such phrases were never intended to become habitual but, according to Ed Staros, people had started using them "as if they were scripts, often not varying their choice of the phrase 'my pleasure.'"[20]

To prompt more personal and flexible service, Ritz adopted twelve "Service Values" to describe expectations for behavior and leadership action at all levels. Each value begins with *I* to help employees identify specific behaviors that will create memorable experiences for their guests. Rather than embodying a set of blunt and inflexible dictums, the values provide employees with a sense of responsibility and personal investment in the service they deliver. With the simple title "I Am Proud to Be Ritz-Carlton," the value statement openly acknowledges that people—and most notably frontline, customer-facing employees—are the essence of the company's value proposition and brand.

As values should, they provide guideposts for making judgments as employees confront the daily challenges of meeting ever-shifting and often unpredictable customer demands. Frontline employees are encouraged to adapt service based on cues taken from customers, whether speeding up the dining process for a business traveler or offering a less formal greeting to a casual guest. The only steadfast expectation is that all employees carry a laminated card with them at all times that contains the twelve Service Values so that they have a quick reminder if they are ever in doubt about how to handle a customer issue.[21]

Overall, Ritz-Carlton has provided the type of leadership that is essential to creating and sustaining a front line–focused organization. Leaders have clearly articulated that the company's long-term prosperity is reliant on lifetime relationships with customers, and these happen only if the Ladies and Gentlemen generate special memories for guests. Ensuring that they are equipped to do so has led to investments in updating the hotel properties, including adoption of local design ideas taken from staff, so customers' needs are met and employees' efforts aren't focused on making up for disappointments with the physical product. More important, by adopting the new Service Values, Ritz-Carlton leaders have entrusted their front line with the latitude and flexibility to make service personal and contemporary.

SERVICE VALUES: I AM PROUD TO BE RITZ-CARLTON[22]

1. I build strong relationships and create Ritz-Carlton guests for life.
2. I am always responsive to the expressed and unexpressed wishes and needs of our guests.
3. I am empowered to create unique, memorable and personal experiences for our guests.
4. I understand my role in achieving the Key Success Factors, embracing Community Footprints and creating The Ritz-Carlton Mystique.
5. I continuously seek opportunities to innovate and improve The Ritz-Carlton experience.
6. I own and immediately resolve guest problems.
7. I create a work environment of teamwork and lateral service so that the needs of our guests and each other are met.
8. I have the opportunity to continuously learn and grow.
9. I am involved in the planning of the work that affects me.
10. I am proud of my professional appearance, language and behavior.
11. I protect the privacy and security of our guests, my fellow employees and the company's confidential information and assets.
12. I am responsible for uncompromising levels of cleanliness and creating a safe and accident-free environment.

Step 2: Teach People to Think for Themselves

Once employees have a basic understanding of the organizational strategy, customer requirements, and their role in fulfilling the value proposition, they must be taught how to make the right customer-friendly judgments while protecting the business's long-term health. This requires continuous teaching and discussion of how judgment is applied in actual situations. In short, step 2 requires

1. Teaching everyone deeply about customer needs and basic business math;
2. Coupling organizational values with a problem-solving framework that can be used by frontline employees and coached by their leaders.

Many organizations are tempted to dumb down customer-segmentation and strategy discussions for fear that frontline employees won't understand such ostensibly sophisticated subjects. This line of thinking is rooted in the all-too-commonly held assumption that less educated workers—many of whom may not possess an undergraduate college degree, let alone an MBA—aren't capable of absorbing financial concepts such as return on invested capital or the nuances of different segmentation schemes. In fact, we have sat in rooms with frontline hourly employees who had a far better grasp of both the concept and the application of return on invested capital than *Fortune* 500 senior executives earning hundreds of thousands of dollars.

Senior leaders all too frequently confuse complexity with intelligence. In fact, the responsibility of senior leaders is to undo the MBA-speak and meaningless technical details rife in corporate PowerPoint presentations. The CEO and top team must find clear, simple (not simplistic) ways of talking about customers and financial concepts that every employee can embrace and apply to his or her work.

These ideas need to be taught continuously so that when employees are confronted with a customer problem or a service opportunity, they can align their solutions with the strategy. If employees do not have a deep understanding of customer needs, they are likely to miss opportunities or offer the wrong solution to customer problems. Similarly, if employees do not understand the importance of operating the business profitably, they may be tempted to give away too much or be too stingy in their responses. Equipped with this knowledge, it will become a habit for workers to ask, "Am I doing what is necessary to please our customers? Am I earning a respectable profit for our business?" And in situations where these seem incompatible, "Am I making the right choices for the long-term health of the business?"

Those at the customer interface also need to be prepared for the inevitable customer problem or breakdown in service delivery. Frontline staff are in a position to see all of the broken plays in an organization. They are there when processes don't work as expected or the infrastructure supporting customer service breaks down. In many cases, they have the ability to fix the problem in the short run and recommend, if not actually change, the process for the long run.

Frontline employees need problem-solving frameworks for addressing customer complaints as they arise and contributing their ideas to improve products, services, and business processes. The path to a customer's heart in any business rarely lies in an escalation protocol or in transferring the customer to a supervisor.

As many of our benchmark companies have learned, it is dangerous to assume that employees have a framework for problem solving. Values can serve as a guidepost, but employees also need to understand how to weigh customer input, business calculations, and other data in order to make good choices. Each person comes to an organization with different thought processes, and people ascribe varied levels of importance to the factors involved with everyday work. For example, what if a customer wants to return a product one day after the return policy has expired? Left to his or her own devices, an employee may assess the value of the customer relationship as greater than the cost of accepting the product that can no longer be returned to the vendor that sold it to the company. What if the customer is returning the product late on behalf of his sick mother? What if his sick mother is one of the company's best customers?

The answers to such questions are rarely black and white. In fact, problem solving at the front line is similar to case law in the U.S. legal system; leaders look at individual cases and begin to set boundaries based on precedent. In order to create a common language and shared framework for examining such cases, they must teach employees a problem-solving methodology that is shared throughout the organization.

When employees are provided with a methodology to identify problems as they occur and diagnose root causes, they are often better equipped than supervisors two or three levels above them to identify the right solution. In our research we discovered that which methodology organizations selected for problem solving—whether TQM, Lean Sigma, or one of a host of other possibilities—was less important than that the entire organization shared a common language and thought process. While it may seem heretical to the proponents of specific methodologies, we found that the true value in unleashing people's problem-solving initiative came from coupling a consistent methodology with shared values, so that any customer problem could be discussed and debated among employees at all levels. A common problem-solving framework engendered trust and enabled those at the middle and senior organizational levels to act as coaches instead of dictating answers.

The Ritz-Carlton Approach: Lineup, Wow Stories, and MR. BIV

Each Ritz-Carlton employee receives hundreds of hours of training. The organization's "Key Success Factors" are taught so that everyone understands Ritz-Carlton's profitability model and customer needs. This includes customer analysis showing that guest engagement is directly tied to drivers under frontline staff control: (1) providing a sense of enhanced well-being, (2) anticipating needs through personalized relationships, and (3) ensuring that service basics such as room condition and check-in are in good order.[23] Employees understand how each is tied to maximizing revenue and profit and their role in helping to do so.

One of the company's most effective teaching methods starts daily at 9:00 A.M. sharp at every property around the world when all employees, from housekeepers to floor managers, gather for fifteen minutes to review guest experiences, resolve issues, and identify ways to improve service. This concept, called Line-Up, borrowed from the French restaurant tradition in which a chef convenes the entire staff shortly before opening every evening to review new menu items and alert staff to VIP guests and other issues of the day. The Line-Up concept was expanded to cover every staff member, to be run at each property separately, and to be repeated three times per day, once at each shift change.[24] Line-Up reached a new level of success following a benchmarking trip Ed Staros took to FedEx.[25] Staros observed that the delivery company used its satellite network to hold daily meetings in order to align business goals and resolve operational issues. Ritz-Carlton couldn't afford to invest in its own satellite network but, at Staros's suggestion, Line-Up was expanded to incorporate broader business issues and began tightly integrating the company's values.

These are far from dry staff meetings; employees are typically smiling and high-fiving with team members throughout the session. In order to align the company globally, topics for each day, including one of the twelve Service Values, are sent to each property from corporate. Local leaders of each hotel area use Line-Up to address basic operational issues, review the prior day's financial performance, and reinforce the Service Values. Typically the selected value is highlighted each month and employees start their day by reading that value aloud and discussing its application. Three days per week, on Mondays, Wednesdays, and Fridays, the Line-Up ends with a "wow" story that is shared across every hotel in the more than twenty countries where Ritz-Carlton operates.

Wow stories single out staff members who go so far above and beyond the call of duty that they epitomize the best of Ritz-Carlton's culture. The wow stories demonstrate the Service Values applied to everyday situations that include helping distressed customers or showing how staff can go the extra mile.

In one story, the bartender at the Los Angeles property discovered that a young couple was in LA so the husband could receive chemotherapy treatment for a particularly difficult form of Hodgkin's lymphoma with which he had just recently been diagnosed. The couple had booked a stay at the Ritz's Kapalua, Hawaii, resort but feared they might not make it in time. In response, the LA staff created a Hawaiian atmosphere for the young couple without their knowledge, upgrading them to a honeymoon suite that had been redecorated with Hawaiian-themed posters, Hawaiian decorations, and even a cooler of sand that they dubbed the couple's "private beach."[26]

The wow stories not only provide global recognition for an employee's commitment, reinforcing a Service Value in the process, but also serve as an example of how staff should resolve problems and treat guests. In fact, the

Line-Up represents a tremendous investment in teaching about the business, customers, and Ritz-Carlton service culture. Just do the math: Fifteen-minute lineups, which happen thrice daily, multiplied by over seventy properties, three hundred sixty-five days per year, with over thirty thousand staff daily. The cost of the staff's time preparing for and attending such sessions is unquestionably in the millions of dollars. This is an investment for Ritz-Carlton; each full-time employee receives more than seventy hours of development annually.

While staff members may not create a wow story daily, they are expected to resolve guests' issues at all times. As Service Value six states, "I own and resolve all guest problems." This philosophy was perhaps most clearly articulated by Horst Schulze when he said, "When something went wrong at your home as a young child and you told your mother about it, she would say, 'I'm here for you,' and she fixed the problem. Mom didn't say she'd check with someone else to see if they would take care of it, and she wouldn't start arguing with you or blaming you for the problem."[27]

One analysis by Ritz-Carlton determined that there are 970 potential instances where a problem might occur in dealing with an overnight guest.[28] Multiplying the number of potential problems by three hundred or more guests, it is evident that, as Ed Staros has commented, "it takes everyone on staff having the skills, training, confidence, and above all else, the faith of their leadership to fully and consistently step into creative-problem-solving mode when things go awry."[29]

To assist employees in identifying problems, preferably before they damage a guest experience, Ritz-Carlton introduces its employees to "MR. BIV." This playful acronym helps employees recognize telltale signs of a problem and determine where things have gone awry in service delivery:

Mistakes
Rework
Breakdowns
Inefficiencies
Variations in work processes

The open approach to problem identification and correction encourages employees to speak up and take responsibility for initiating immediate corrective action.[30]

Equally important, leadership uses problem-solving frameworks such as MR. BIV to engage staff in solving problems, never blaming them for defects and continuously looking for ways to bolster support systems as they do their jobs. As Schulze has said, "The problem is never with the people. The problem is always with systems."[31] For example, when Ritz-Carlton recognized that some housekeepers were upsetting guests by entering rooms before giving customers the opportunity to answer the door, sometimes catching them in states of undress, the company didn't respond by firing employees or issuing knocking procedures. Instead, it listened carefully to housekeepers and realized that it was difficult for employees to hear guests behind closed doors. The company was able to respond with a technological solution enabling guests to indicate whether the room was occupied, sparing their housekeepers and customers unnecessary embarrassment.[32]

Step 3: Experiment to Implement

Once frontline employees understand their customers, business model, and problem-solving framework, they can be encouraged to innovate entirely new solutions. Beyond simply improving existing processes or products, frontline workers have the ability to dream up new ways of delighting customers and opening their wallets, whether through a business-process improvement, a new product, or enhanced service. We have seen companies unlock millions of dollars of value simply by offering frontline employees the autonomy and resources to put their ideas into practice. However, innovation is a difficult endeavor in any business, so encouraging hundreds or thousands of people to innovate can be dangerous if not handled properly.

Innovation isn't a free-for-all. The boundaries around when and where employees are free to exercise their judgment need to be drawn clearly. Paradoxically, companies need to begin with strong operating methods well documented and understood among their employees or they risk unnecessarily sacrificing a consistent customer experience and coherent brand.

The act of innovation also requires strong process discipline. Whom frontline employees work with, whether individually or in teams, as they generate ideas needs to be clearly explained. Likewise, the methodology for testing an idea scientifically, evaluating results, and determining whether to continue or kill an innovation must be taught at all levels of the organization. In short, there are three requirements for step 3:

1. Define the innovation areas (products, services, or business processes) where frontline innovation is desired.
2. Explain how employees work with others in the organization to generate, review, and select innovation ideas for implementation.
3. Provide a methodology for experimentation and measurement in the marketplace.

Innovation at Ritz-Carlton

Innovation at Ritz-Carlton is quite literally every person's job. Service Value number five states: "I continuously seek opportunities to innovate and improve The Ritz-Carlton experience." Like most hotel companies, Ritz-Carlton maintains a customer relationship management database that is shared across its properties. In large measure the information that goes into the database results from the observations made by frontline employees. Standard issue as part of every employee uniform is a "preference pad" on which employees slyly jot down observations of customers. If a guest prefers a specific wine with dinner or is late leaving her room in the morning, Ritz staff will notice. The guest will likely be offered his or her preferred wine the next night or get a midday visit from housekeeping as a result.

The ability to actively but unobtrusively observe guests, a trained skill that is referred to as "Radar On, Antennae Up," is at the heart of meeting customers' unexpressed wishes. Scaling this program globally resulted in a 3 percent to 5 percent customer-satisfaction improvement at most properties, on top of their already impressive achievement levels.[33] It empowers associates to act before a customer even asks for help. For example, if a guest leaves a suit button on the desk and a jacket sans button nearby, he's likely to return to his room to find the button has been sewn on without his ever needing to ask.

The freedom given to individual employees turns daily service into an art and creates innovation opportunities with each customer interaction. Ritz-Carlton not only encourages innovation in service delivery but also seeks employees' engagement with new product ideas.

Line-Up is one useful vehicle for harnessing employee brainstorming. During one daily meeting where innovation was the focus value, the session leader shared ideas that had been generated by staff for driving incremental food and service revenue. After highlighting an idea for a prepaid children's debit card for use at resort areas such as the pool and snack bar, and another proposal to invest in hardware that would enable guests to customize their television programming, the leader invited staff members to blurt out ideas on the spot or use the day to think creatively and bring their thoughts back to Line-Up the following day.[34]

While daily meetings provide a helpful venue for idea sharing, the company introduced a more rigorous four-step innovation model in 2007 and 2008.[35] The model provides a structured approach to engaging employees at multiple levels to generate out-of-the-box solutions. The innovation process deliberately takes employee innovators through the process of creating a customer-based vision, assembling a team, conducting customer research, benchmarking, stimulating new ideas, and testing innovations commercially.[36] Whether creating a fine-art event in Boston or finding ways to charge a premium for club-level guest rooms in Naples, the new process provides a conduit for harnessing frontline knowledge.

The pièce de résistance in Ritz-Carlton's innovation and guest-satisfaction armory, however, might be considered the ability of every employee in the company, regardless of rank or position, to spend up to two thousand dollars of the company's money to improve a guest's experience, handle a complaint, or fix a problem. While employees are expected to take responsibility for their actions, no advance written authorization or verbal permission is required. Frontline employees are trusted by Ritz leaders to use their judgment no matter how unconventional their approach may be.

Step 4: Break Down the Hierarchy

Engaging the front line in problem solving, innovation, and experimentation can have profound bottom-line benefits, but these may never materialize in a traditional hierarchy. Most organizations have embedded assumptions about power roles and cultural norms governing decision making that limit the autonomy of frontline associates. Leaders must recognize the structural and behavioral challenges that will result if their organization has a history of formalization in rules and regulations coupled with strong centralization of decision-making authority.

Senior leaders need to invigorate the change process by resetting the organizational context, deliberately changing how people talk about the importance of the front line while reinforcing respect for those who do the work that delivers value directly to customers. They must actively diminish the detrimental aspects of hierarchy—disrespect, intimidation, and oppressing opinions—through the careful use of language, symbolism, and open discussion of role expectations.

Becoming a front line–focused organization also requires eliminating unnecessary work that bogs down workers with time-wasting bureaucracy or menial work. If the front line hasn't been asked to identify inefficient policies and processes and lacks the authority to make changes independently, it is likely that their time will be squandered on unproductive activities such as assembling customer data from multiple systems or performing tasks better suited to automation.

Technology can be deployed to eliminate wasteful guesswork by frontline employees, providing them with real-time intelligence or decision-support systems. It can also be used to flatten an organization, providing fluid communication among leaders at different hierarchical levels. When technology is used in this way, it enables intelligence to flow from the front line to the rest of the organization and permits frontline workers to share solutions with their peers.

Finally, senior leaders have the positional power to create new structures, work groups, or other organizational constructs that encourage collaboration across hierarchical levels. Creating such organic collaborative networks in traditional organizations with thousands of diverse, multigenerational employees is no easy task. It has been demonstrated that executives play a critical role in organizing both formal and informal networks by bringing together groups, defining job responsibilities, and creating an atmosphere for open dialogue.[37] Internal collaboration fosters conversations that bring different perspectives to bear so that frontline experience can be supported by the resources and leadership of senior executives.

In sum, leaders cultivate respect for frontline contributions and ensure that associates maximize their value creation by

1. Setting the organizational context through language, symbolism, and role modeling that highlights the importance of frontline associates;
2. Eliminating unnecessary work and bureaucracy for frontline workers;
3. Deploying technology to increase frontline intelligence and encourage fluid communication flow;
4. Creating new structures to promote collaboration among frontline workers and leaders at all levels.

Demonstrating Respect and Building Trust at the Ritz

As discussed above, Ritz-Carlton has supported frontline activities through technology, such as a shared customer database that enables staff to review guest preferences before arrival and guest-room technology to alert housekeepers when a room is occupied. To flatten the organization and nurture open communication among employees and customers, Ritz-Carlton has also embraced social media. Former company president Simon Cooper joined Twitter, leading the way for employees to use it as a means to congratulate colleagues, comment on local trends, and communicate with regular customers.

Line-Up also propagates collaboration among employees at all levels. Line-Ups surface service challenges and enable employees to have open communication up the chain of command on a daily basis. Problems are less likely to fester, and leaders can quickly organize employee teams from different hotel departments to address any concerns. The leader of a Line-Up facilitates the conversation, but the solutions can come from anyone.

The most important achievement by far, however, has been to preserve the legacy of respect accorded to the Ladies and Gentlemen that is part of the company's heritage. While the Ritz was founded with this belief, senior leaders have worked hard to sustain it and build on this foundation through efforts such as the Radar On, Antennae Up program.

Respect for the front line permeates all levels, with hotel and senior managers routinely helping associates with activities such as checking in guests, carrying luggage, or valet parking. Such acts not only demonstrate concern for staff and bolster teamwork but also make it clear that a person's title isn't a reflection of the value he or she contributes. Current president Herve Humler captured this leadership attitude good-humoredly when he addressed hotel staff at the grand opening of the Hong Kong property:

> My name is Herve Humler and I am the president of Ritz-Carlton, the president of Ritz-Carlton Residences, and the president of Bulgari Hotels & Resorts, and I am a very important person. But you are more important than I am. You are the heart and soul of this building.[38]

Step 5: Invest in Frontline Capability

The final step in building a front line–focused organization is essential to its long-term health. The organization can only be successful if the right type of employee is hired and brought into an environment that enables frontline associates to reveal their distinctive personality and creativity in their work each day.

The employees who are selected to join an organization should be screened against the values defined in step 1. These values reflect the behaviors that are necessary to create the desired customer experience and to act autonomously when making judgments. For frontline positions, particularly for frontline leadership roles, values and attitude must trump experience. Skills can be taught, but mind-set and beliefs are hard to change. When hiring, leaders cannot compromise on values or they are likely to open their doors to someone who can degrade their culture and erode trust. Instead, selecting someone should feel like a celebration, an invitation to join the family. This may seem herculean in industries with high turnover and in organizations needing to hire thousands of people each year. Front line–focused organizations relish the challenge, watchfully guarding entry to their organizations and holding frontline hires to scrupulous standards that would be reserved for senior managers in many places.

Once someone has been selected, induction becomes a vital process. The cost in time and dollars required to develop a productive employee who is capable of exercising individual judgment can be significant. Training cannot be simply relegated to the HR department or local managers. Instead it must help to indoctrinate and integrate the new team member, ensuring that the new hire has not only the technical skills but also an understanding of how to make decisions effectively on the fly.

This massive investment in recruiting, hiring, and training can be wasted, however, if employees live in local environments that don't afford the desired respect and freedom to frontline associates. If the managers to whom frontline associates report do not reflect the desired culture and are not taught to be effective leaders themselves, the commitment and judgment capability of frontline workers will fade away with time.

In short, step 5 is concentrated on preserving the talent, culture, and local leadership to sustain a front line–focused organization by

1. Selecting candidates rigorously and in alignment with the values and customer expectations;
2. Developing frontline judgment capability through an immediate and sustained investment;
3. Teaching leaders of frontline associates how to be effective in their critical roles.

Investing in Frontline Talent at the Ritz: Selection to Day 365

Ritz-Carlton is committed to finding the top 1 percent of hospitality professionals[39] and insists that it "selects" rather than hires them. The difference, Ritz-Carlton managers maintain, is that hiring is about filling a job, while selection is a meticulous process of getting to know someone, which could take weeks, and making a commitment to have them join you.

The Ritz-Carlton selection process is indeed lengthy and laborious. If you make it through the telephone screening process, over the course of a dozen or more interviews you may be asked to share a time in your life when you cared for someone else. For a brand that places so much emphasis on service, it is no surprise that the hotel searches for employees who can share "extraordinary" examples of helping others. Likewise, interviewers are likely to assess your level of empathy and whether you are able to imagine guests' emotional response to a situation.

The select few who are then invited to Ritz-Carlton training will receive two intense days of cultural and practical immersion covering not only functional job responsibilities but also every element of the Ritz-Carlton Gold Standards. These include the Ritz-Carlton credo, motto, Three Steps of Service, twelve Service Values, Sixth Diamond characteristics, and Employee Promise. New associates are taught to understand the drivers of guest engagement, their role in creating this, and the important difference between the job functions they perform and their higher purpose of creating memorable moments for guests.

Unlike many organizations, which might send a new recruit home with a binder and a pat on the head, Ritz-Carlton follows up its initial training with what has become known as "Day 21." Approximately three weeks after initial orientation, employees must pass a certification exam to demonstrate their knowledge of the Gold Standards. But development of new associates doesn't end here. On top of training from their direct supervisor and participation in the daily Line-Up, frontline employees also are brought back on "Day 365" for an annual recertification.

Employees know that they can't stop developing and, as Service Value eight says, they have both the opportunity and the responsibility to continuously learn and grow. In fact, upward mobility is an important part of career development at Ritz-Carlton, where homegrown talent is preferred.

As Staros shared with us, senior leaders are deeply committed to the ongoing development of their staff. This is more than routine coaching and mentoring and is built on making a personal connection with individual employees. "You don't just give direction but share stories about the mistakes you made or when you could have done a better job," says Staros. "I give them what I can from my toolbox and share my experiences—the good, bad and ugly." Leaders at Ritz-Carlton, like Staros, open the kimono and share these stories to help develop employees' judgment and reasoning capabilities. The goal, Staros enthusiastically explains, "is to give everything you've learned to help make the next generation better than you are."[40]

Summary: Architects Needed

The summary of the Ritz-Carlton should make it evident that the frontline engagement and innovation occurring are neither an accident nor the product of any single initiative. They come from a system that is engineered to help frontline personnel detect and act upon guests' wishes. In the process, Ritz-Carlton employees have the opportunity to personalize service, fix problems without escalation, and contribute to ongoing innovation, all while understanding their role in the value-creation process.

As in all of our benchmark organizations, Ritz-Carlton senior leaders act as organizational architects who stay connected with what employees need through direct experience on the front line. They are able to constantly evolve and refine both their strategy and their operational approach based on customer feedback that comes directly and channels through frontline observations.

Those who wish to emulate their success—creating more engaging workplaces, happier customers, and better financial results—cannot simply copy their approach. Instead, leaders need a process for rebuilding their organizations to match their specific customers' needs with frontline action and the right organizational culture. The process that we have laid out in this chapter, and which we will explain in more detail in subsequent chapters, is predictable and repeatable but requires those with authority and resources in a company to help make it happen. Ideally this starts with the CEO, but we have seen leaders create this process in miniature within divisions, departments, and even teams. Those who make the commitment to rearchitect their organizations don't require fancy formulas or statistical correlations to measure the impact. They see the results in dollars tied directly to customer revenue from building customer relationships and creating new products.

3

STARTING AT THE TOP

We define for every person in this [headquarters] building what they do that impacts a restaurant manager. If you don't know, go out and sit in the lobby of a restaurant until you figure out what it is. And then figure out how you do it better because every single person in this building does something that eventually impacts the restaurant manager. If you're not doing it in the most efficient, effective way possible, you're not doing your job.

—**David Novak, chairman and CEO of Yum! Brands, parent company of KFC, Taco Bell, and Pizza Hut**

- **BUILDING A FRONT LINE–FOCUSED ORGANIZATION REQUIRES TOP-DOWN SUPPORT**

  - Senior leaders set expectations for how the front line connects with customers.

  - Top leaders must clearly define the scope of frontline judgment authority.

- **SHAKING UP LEADERSHIP AT THE TOP**

  - Senior leaders may be the slowest to embrace change to a front line–focused organization.

  - Adapting frontline solutions locally requires organizational support and resources.

Walk into a KFC in India and you feel a buzzing energy most people don't associate with fast food. The red and yellow graphics pop off the menu board welcoming you to the "Indian School of Lickonomics," a play on KFC's motto that its chicken is always "finger lickin' good." Informational posters on the brand's heritage show images of hip, youthful Indian consumers in various forms of gastronomic rapture, while another wall documents the restaurant's "drools"—instead of rules—which emphasize fresh food, healthy ingredients, and high-quality standards. The restaurant's clientele seem in step with the fun vibe, resembling many of the attractive faces gracing the heritage wall and drool board.

It's not just the restaurant's graphics and wordplay that have been engineered to target the more than 70 percent of India's population that is under the age of thirty-five. The restaurant layout is broken into "sip and snack" areas designed for groups of friends to hang out, while long tables toward the back are reserved for young families. Most important, the restaurant crew members, who sport "Lickonomics" T-shirts paired with funky, spiked hairstyles, remain connected with consumers and keep a watchful eye to make sure they are happy.

Frontline workers are chosen daily for roles that include a product champion who conducts random food samplings and kitchen inspections, and a "chef of the day" whose picture is displayed prominently by the cash registers. In addition to preparing meals, the chef of the day averages three kitchen visits per shift, in which customers are invited behind the counter to see the fresh-cooking process and the separation of vegetarian and non-vegetarian cooking areas ("because chicken and mutter don't get along," according to the menu boards).

They are joined by a "taste monitor" whose role is to make sure no customer leaves the store disappointed. Chosen for their ability to talk to people, resolve problems, and embody "Customer Mania," the taste monitors walk the restaurant floor quietly watching customer faces for any sign of displeasure. If a customer makes a funny face or turns their nose up at something they ordered, the taste monitor is quickly there to help. While exchanging food is the fastest and simplest remedy, the taste monitor—just like every other employee in the store—is empowered to spend the equivalent of ten dollars to ensure that the customer has a great experience.

KFC India's "branded service" program, involving frontline staff in outstanding service delivery and soliciting innovative ideas ranging from trendy store design to spicier chicken, is the fuel behind the company's rapid expansion in this hot market. By 2015, KFC India expects to grow from just over 150 stores now to 500.[1]

Starting at the Top

KFC's explosive growth in India is remarkable, but understanding the genesis of its success will lead you half a world away and more than a decade into the past, to Louisville, Kentucky, in 1997 when PepsiCo decided to spin off its iconic KFC, Pizza Hut, and Taco Bell restaurant brands. More than a dozen years and two stock splits later, the stand-alone company (now known as Yum!) has grown under Chairman and CEO David Novak's inspired, charismatic, and deliberately offbeat leadership into the world's largest fast-food (or to use the preferred industry term, "quick-service") restaurant company, with more than 37,000 outlets in 117 countries, over one million associates and 2011 revenues topping twelve billion dollars. An earnings powerhouse, Yum! stock has delivered over a 700 percent return since becoming an independent company.[2]

Yum!'s 1997 spin-off from PepsiCo created one of the biggest opportunities ever for a "corporate do-over," as Novak likes to refer to the raft of changes he's instituted over the years since he took the helm. He likens this corporate transformation to occasions when his daughter Ashley would play with friends, make a mistake, and say, "I get a do-over." Looking at the assets Novak inherited, it is clear that some mistakes had been made along the way under the stewardship of PepsiCo. Saddled with nearly five billion dollars of debt and annual returns that had lagged both the market and the industry, the newly formed company's restaurants operated as three independent competitors more than as corporate allies. Moreover, even as the restaurants' customer ratings steadily declined and their competitiveness slowly eroded, few investments were made in even routine modernizations. Simple operational infrastructure, such as the phone systems at Pizza Hut, which accounted for 70 percent of the orders, was sorely in need of updating.[3]

When Novak and his leadership team set out to remake the company, their first goal was to consistently treat those who served the customer—the restaurant managers and their teams—as the most important people in the organization. Novak also knew that since he was rebuilding his business for posterity, this couldn't just be the initiative du jour. He needed to fundamentally rethink virtually every aspect of how the company operated in order to ensure that all employees deeply felt the importance of their jobs and came to work prepared to put a "yum" on the face of each customer.

Step 1: Connect Frontline Execution to Customer Needs

In this chapter we will use Yum! to explore the details of how to connect frontline execution to customer needs, our first step in the process of building a front line–focused organization. We find Novak's story so compelling because he simultaneously faced the problems of a mature company and those of a youthful start-up. He had inherited the entrenched infrastructure, power structure, and embedded ways of doing business of a large, incumbent company. Yet at the same time, much as with a start-up, he had to create a fresh vision that would inspire employees and provide a road map for building a business that could stand the test of time.

Step 1 requires the CEO and senior leadership team to first understand changing customer needs based on feedback from both customers and frontline employees. Novak was no stranger to the quick-service restaurant (QSR) industry, having been president of KFC and Pizza Hut. His many days spent in the market touring restaurants and talking directly with restaurant teams, customers, and franchisees had taught him much about what customers wanted from their quick-service restaurants.

Above all, QSR customers typically look for cleanliness, speed, value, and great tasting food. Unlike with Amazon or Ritz-Carlton, there isn't much opportunity to create a personalized experience for customers on the spot. Instead, the best customer experiences tended to be defined by consistently good service, delicious menu choices, and well-designed restaurant layouts. To make all of that happen through a repeatable process, according to Novak, "you have to look at every customer touch point including assets, service, menus and delivery models to back-of-house cooking processes."[4]

Looking at those touch points, the industry's typical customer transaction (typically lasting at most a few minutes) doesn't seem to provide much opportunity to build an individual relationship. As the matrix below shows,[5] the average QSR consumer expects a fairly emotionless transaction and a restaurant worker who will deliver nothing more than the basics—most likely uninterestedly pushing food across the counter at the end of the exchange.

However, Novak recognized that there was an opportunity for much more. He saw that the best employees in his restaurants were able to infuse even those brief interactions with a smile and a positive personality that could turn a mundane moment into something delightful. His ultimate goal was to have employees intuitively and reflexively take care of the customer and resolve any possible complaints. As Novak has said, Yum! aspires "to not simply satisfy the customers, which is somewhat passive, but to actively try to make them feel welcomed and happy to be eating in one of our restaurants—to put a yum on their face."[6]

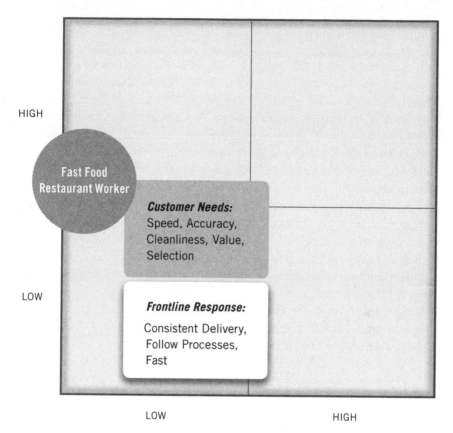

HIGH

Fast Food Restaurant Worker

Customer Needs:
Speed, Accuracy,
Cleanliness, Value,
Selection

LOW

Frontline Response:
Consistent Delivery,
Follow Processes,
Fast

LOW   HIGH

TRANSACTION COMPLEXITY

A Teachable Point of View for the Front Line

During step 1, leaders must connect the desired customer experience with the role of the frontline leaders. They must identify what their customer-facing staff (restaurant crew members, in Yum!'s case) can do and how they must behave to drive execution of the strategy. As we have written previously, leaders need to outline ideas for how the front line can create the right customer experience, the values and leadership behaviors required to drive execution of the strategy, and a method for emotionally energizing employees.

Beyond simply naming these, leaders must teach throughout their companies, helping people align their daily activities with organizational goals. For this reason, we say that leaders need more than a point of view; they need a Teachable Point of View.[7] Active teaching by top leaders is essential in the process of building a front line–focused organization in order to connect the customer strategy to employee roles, organizational processes, routine policies, reward systems, and the many other factors that lead to execution of the strategy.

Knowing the customer process and envisioning the ideal employee-customer experience that he wanted to create, Novak began to formulate a Teachable Point of View in his first days as CEO. At its core, Novak's Teachable Point of View was straightforward. The central idea guiding the rebuilding of Yum! was "People capability first . . . satisfied customers and profitability follow."[8] The laser focus and intensity of that people capability would be directed at creating "Customer Mania" with the singular employee passion of putting "a yum on customers' faces around the world." If this task were done correctly, the organization would achieve Novak's unwavering goal to "be the best in the world at building great brands and running great restaurants!"[9]

Novak's work with employees at all levels of the company produced a set of values and behavioral anchors called the "How We Win Together" (HWWT) principles.[10] These encompassed a belief in all people, customer passion, breakthrough thinking, continuous learning, recognition, and dogged commitment to execution that define Yum!'s Customer Mania culture. The principles begin with this simple statement:

"Believe in all people. We trust in positive intentions and believe everyone has the potential to make a difference. We actively seek diversity in others to expand our thinking and make the best decision. We coach and support every individual to grow to their full capability."[11] Another critical HWWT principle was an integral part of the foundation for creating the right brand of emotional energy in the company. "Recognize! Recognize! Recognize!" is a mantra at Yum! and an idea of such importance that saying it just once won't suffice. In an industry in which team member turnover typically exceeds 100 percent and an employee's tenure is more likely to be measured in weeks than in years, it can be difficult to overcome an underlying apathy that some employees have toward their work. Novak's experience taught him that instilling frontline workers with purpose and pride was the key ingredient in his Customer Mania recipe. Employees needed to care about their work and feel that the company and their team members cared about them in return.

The Frontline Judgment Playing Field at Yum!

The Teachable Point of View outlines what is required of the business and its people to win in the market with customers. Making it operational entails defining the judgment capability that is needed at the front line in order to deliver the expected customer experience.

When leaders look at the front line, they must determine the scope of decision-making autonomy they are prepared to give. Most organizations fail to articulate this clearly or elect not to grant frontline workers any meaningful independence. Front line–focused organizations, by contrast, tend to define plainly what is out of bounds and where staff is empowered to act.

Operating in an industry that necessitates strong brands and operational consistency, Yum! didn't afford its restaurant teams the freedom to play with store design, product offerings, or operating processes. While it sought improvement ideas from any quarter and has consistently benefited from countless suggestions shared by restaurant workers to stoke its epic growth, the primary focus of frontline employees' judgment has been ensuring a fantastic customer experience.

Once they understand the ideal customer frontline interaction, leaders must look at what is required to put it in play. Top leaders must establish what we call the Judgment Playing Field. We use this metaphor because those in charge of the organization have the power and resources to truly define how much space employees have to operate. They do so by delineating where the boundaries are, as Yum! did, but they also do so implicitly through the organizational culture and systems they cultivate. As the diagram below shows, senior leaders in an organization have the ability to architect the systems that make the Teachable Point of View come to life and enable frontline employees to act.

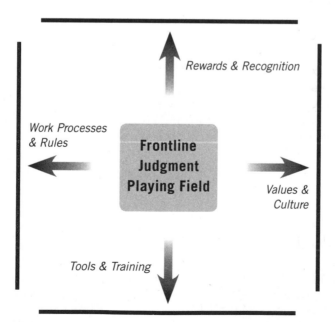

Each element of the diagram is essential for providing employees the latitude and support needed to execute the desired frontline actions and judgment. If the culture of the organization doesn't appropriately value frontline work or doesn't respect workers' immense contribution, individuals will not feel empowered to act, regardless of what the CEO may say. The room for employees to maneuver in this case will shrink. Similarly, if they aren't rewarded and recognized for making good judgments to create the envisioned customer experience, there will be little motivation to take risks or put forth extra effort. Even if they are motivated, frontline employees will not be capable without investments in support tools and training. Most difficult of all, organizations need to find the balance between operating discipline, embodied in the work processes and rules, and local flexibility to correct problems or innovate. In the sections below we will review how Yum! transformed in each of these areas to enable the appropriate scope of frontline judgment.

Values and Culture at Yum!

At Yum! the HWWT principles (the company's values) powerfully convey a culture of teamwork and respect that elevates the role of the front line. The importance of having great restaurant general managers (RGMs) "who build great teams" is articulated in the values statement because, as Novak told us during an interview, "If I show you a good leader, I'll show you a good business. I don't care if it's in India or your restaurant down the street."[12] Focusing on ensuring that the company has talented RGMs guarantees that Yum! restaurants have the right work environment and culture. It also gives RGMs a sense of importance and pride in their leadership role. Anne Byerlein, Yum!'s chief people officer, insists, "Telling our RGMs that they are the number one leader raises the level of esteem of that job in the organization."[13]

Reinforcing the premise that everyone who isn't working in a store is obliged to support those who are, Yum! also changed the titles of all senior managers above RGMs to "coaches" instead of referring to them as "bosses." As a result, Yum! explicitly revised the nature of the interactions that these leaders had when they set foot in a store. They were there to coach, not criticize.

To enable them to do so, the company carried out a detailed review of every operational position from store personnel through the regional managers to understand how people were spending their time. As Novak said, "it was eye-opening to realize that we had as many people working as many hours as they were, often inappropriately." Rather than simply change titles or send out new job descriptions, Yum! fundamentally restructured reporting relationships and spans of control to ensure that area coaches and regional coaches actually had time to work with people in the restaurants.

For those who didn't work in the field, Novak even changed the name of the corporate headquarters to "Restaurant Support Center" to remind everyone of the company's first priority: the restaurants and RGMs. This was much more than a titular change; Novak made a 180-degree shift in who served whom. The entire mind-set became to make it as easy as possible for the people in the stores. "I cannot call any restaurant from this building if the local time at the restaurant is between eleven thirty and one o'clock," Novak once told us. "I don't care what I need. We will not do anything to distract our people from taking care of customers and our business."[14] Yum! also adopted a clear etiquette for how the Restaurant Support Center actually supports the restaurants. Any call from a restaurant manager has to be returned, and either their problem should be fixed or a solution should be under way within twenty-four hours. No handoffs are allowed. The person receiving the call takes care of the problem, period. Novak continues,

> We define for every person in this building what they do that impacts a restaurant manager. If you don't know, go out and sit in the lobby of a restaurant until you figure out what it is. And then figure out how you do it better because every single person in this building does something that eventually impacts the restaurant manager. If you're not doing it in the most efficient, effective way possible, you're not doing your job. That's what RGM is #1 means.[15]

Yum! not only celebrates RGMs, however, but also holds them accountable for giving their team members the same respect and support that they receive. The HWWT principles have become the basis for the "Voice of Team," a 360-degree evaluation of leaders at all levels of the company. After reviewing the scores each year, Novak notes that the top-performing restaurant managers consistently have team members who trust them and want to learn from them.

Recognition at Yum!

An essential ingredient in Novak's recipe for a great culture was recognition. Spending weeks of his time each year in the field interacting with employees had taught him the power of recognition for reinforcing desired behaviors and achieving results. As Novak wrote in Yum!'s annual report:

> There's nothing that people want and enjoy more than recognition. Recognition says "I care about what you do. It matters." And I have to tell you . . . the greatest driver of the results we've achieved is the recognition culture we have created. . . . Our leaders have their own individualized recognition awards, from giant Taco Sauce packets to Camels in the Mideast, and believe me, we have fun giving them out to the people who deserve it most. This is creating a highly spirited work environment that is serving as a magnet to retain and recruit the very best talent. The fact is too many corporations are cold, impersonal, detached from the front line and frankly, boring.[16]

The individualized awards that Novak mentions started as his own practice while serving as president of KFC. In an interview with the *New York Times,* Novak recalled the origin of his much-touted "Floppy Chicken" award:

> When I became president of KFC, I wanted to break through the clutter on recognition, so I gave away these rubber chickens. They were called floppy chickens. I'd go into a restaurant and I would see a cook who'd been there for 25 years and the product was great, so I'd give him a floppy chicken. I'd write on it and tell him his "Original Recipe" was fantastic, and take a picture of him with me. And then I'd give him $100 because you couldn't eat a floppy chicken. I now give away these big sets of smiling teeth with legs on them for people walking the talk on behalf of our customer.[17]

Over more than two decades, Novak has amassed an enormous collection of photos of the people he has recognized, not just decorating his Louisville office from floor to ceiling but *covering* both walls and ceiling with pictures of himself personally presenting rubber chickens, mechanical chattering teeth mounted on spindly legs, foam cheese heads, and countless other fun awards. The photo displays don't end at Novak's office. The Restaurant Support Center has a brightly colored walkway between offices that displays hundreds of pictures of employees around the globe being recognized for their achievements. As Novak told us in a recent interview, "When people walk into this office, I want it to symbolize the idea that if you get the people capability right, you get the business right. Our formula for success is 'people capability first.' I want to really shock the system and show people an office like they've never seen before."

Part of the creativity that Novak looks for at the front line is how people engage with their team members. "What can you do to make your team members smile when they come into the restaurant? What can you do to make them feel appreciated and recognized?" Novak asks.

Tools and Training at Yum!

In addition to turning typical manager-employee relations into coaching events and building a culture of recognition, Novak set out to give the company's employees a sense of purpose. In company speeches and external talks he began to emphasize building employees' life skills. It was true that they might only be with the company for a matter of months, but in that time, Novak asserted, they could learn how to interact with others, how to work on a team, and how to care about customers—capabilities that would transfer to any job or industry they chose in the future. Novak liked to say, "We've elevated the importance of the jobs in our industry. I think people would rather come into a company that is committed to building life skills versus teaching you how to cook chicken for the rest of your life."[18]

To underscore this notion, Yum! made a significant investment in training *every* one of the 850,000 employees who were employed by the company, deploying corporate trainers and staff to visit stores every quarter. The training included content on how to listen to customers, how to be empathetic, how to exceed expectations within reason, and how to recover from a mistake.[19]

Employees have been able to do the latter, in part due to one of the training programs, initially called LAST. This is an acronym that provides an easy-to-follow formula for the resolution of customer disputes. *L* stands for "listen to the customer," *A* stands for "apologize," *S* stands for "satisfy" (even if that means replacing an entire order), and *T* stands for "thanks," a constant reminder to every frontline employee and manager that the old-fashioned mantra "The customer is always right" can provide a reliable guide to present-day conduct at the customer interface. Frontline workers and managers are encouraged and trained to empathize with their customers and to take independent initiative to resolve customer problems and dilemmas. Novak later recalled, "We had to change LAST to BLAST because we were finding that first the server had to *believe* what the customer was saying or everything else pretty much fell apart."[20]

Work Processes and Rules at Yum!

The focus and thoughtful design of work processes and rules is fundamental to determining the leeway given to employees to exercise judgment. On the one hand, the relaxing of rules or the design of flexible work processes enables frontline workers to adapt quickly to customers' immediate needs. On the other hand, compulsory processes can be a vital counterbalance to employee innovation, ensuring that a company maintains the operational discipline and brand integrity upon which customers in some industries rely. If leaders have carefully considered the domains in which they want frontline judgment, work processes can be designed to offer open space for unconstrained innovation in some areas, flexible rules that provide measured autonomy in others, and required adherence to nonnegotiable policies in still other situations.

For Yum! the choice was clear to have employees exercise their judgment to make service more personal and to help problem solve if customers were dissatisfied. It was equally clear that issues such as food safety and cooking processes could not be subject to employee improvisation or the restaurant might incur health-code violations and endanger customers. Similarly, because customers tend to frequent more than one restaurant in a brand, stopping by the KFC near their office for lunch while dropping into a different KFC close to home around dinnertime, Yum! couldn't permit employees to change menu selections, brand images, and other features that customers expected of every restaurant. As Sam Su, chairman and CEO of Yum! China and vice chairman of the Yum! board of directors, shared in an interview:

> Anything that has to do with food safety or food quality standards, there's no room for negotiation. You've got to do it and do it right. If you think our price is not as good as competitors, or you have a better idea, tell us and we'll listen. We'll evaluate and we may incorporate it, but once we incorporate an idea in these areas, it becomes the new standard again. So our standards are very, very sacred and cannot be touched.

> Then when it comes to the customer we encourage our employees to apply the Customer Mania principles and to really make it personal. Especially in Pizza Hut restaurants in China, which is a casual dining restaurant concept where we have different service standards than other countries. And there you can't be robotic. We teach our employees how to use visual clues, looking at a customer and seeing whether they need service or they actually need to not be disturbed.[21]

Clarifying the nonnegotiable elements is truly essential to the judgment-definition process and liberating for employees. It enables them to understand where their time can most productively be focused to exercise their judgment, knowing that support systems will be in place and senior leaders will be ready to listen and learn in these select areas.

The nonnegotiable operating processes needed on the front line to ensure consistent, high-quality food and service at Yum! were implemented with its CHAMPS program. CHAMPS, which stands for "Cleanliness, Hospitality, Accuracy, Maintenance, Product quality and Speed," was a standard way of assessing processes and desired outcomes in every restaurant, regardless of the brand and geographic location. CHAMPS looks at all the critical customer touch points to make sure that processes are in place with the right standards. "The basics never go away," Novak explained to us during an interview, "and you have to bring excitement and enthusiasm and new data and new perspectives to the basics. We just have to keep looking for ways and training people on ways to get better and better at it."[22]

As another executive noted, before CHAMPS, standards differed across the brands, so a manager at Taco Bell might argue that four pieces of trash in the parking lot was acceptable, while a KFC manager had set the limit at three.[23] With CHAMPS, restaurants and workers are graded against consistent standards on mystery shopper scores at least twice per month. Every receipt provided by a cash register at Yum! is branded with a toll-free number for customers to call in and rate their experience. Additionally, a Customer Excellence Review team of dedicated operations and recognition specialists visits each store approximately three times per year.

Novak and team set the bar high. One executive observed at the time, "In the past if someone got a 92 or above, that was considered good."[24] Under the new regimen, the expectation was simple: 100 percent in every restaurant. The goal was aspirational and developmental, but Novak held managers accountable.

It is important to remember how other changes aligned with Novak's Teachable Point of View came together to support CHAMPS. In many organizations, a goal of achieving a perfect score would be viewed as unreasonable and senior managers would quickly exhibit punitive behaviors when their expectations weren't achieved. By contrast, at Yum! converting managers above the restaurants to coaches and investing in their know-how helped build a supportive team environment in which senior leaders were seen as trying to make crew members more successful. Furthermore, the recognition culture led to many success stories shared across the company, so that managers could see and hear about actual examples of others who had achieved high standards.

Ongoing coaching and recognition are hardwired into CHAMPS reviews as well. If a score falls short, a Customer Excellence Review team member can produce a printed evaluation that summarizes opportunities and provides an action plan for remedies. If a restaurant achieves 100 percent, the recognition is immediate and on the spot, with high-energy hoopla and prizes.

Recognition isn't just confined to management. Anyone who observes positive performance can hand out a CHAMPS card to a coworker. The CHAMPS card includes a sticker with space for a handwritten comment from the person who presents it. Each week restaurant managers around the country draw from the pool of CHAMPS cards awarded in their restaurant and present the employee selected at random with a prize such as a pair of movie tickets. This simple practice encourages employees to provide peer support and reinforcement for achieving CHAMPS.[25]

The Ten-Dollar Judgment at Yum!

With the support systems in place and the focus of frontline judgment made clear, Novak demonstrated confidence in his frontline employees' ability to make good judgments when rectifying customer problems. Yum! gave every employee the power to spend up to ten dollars to resolve any complaint or service issue. This may not seem like much, particularly in comparison to the two thousand dollars given to a Ritz-Carlton employee, but if you consider that an average menu item at a Yum! restaurant costs less than two dollars and operating margins run around 15 percent, the amount is far from trivial. As some Pizza Hut leaders anxiously noted at the time, Novak had effectively empowered minimum-wage employees to turn any transaction into a money loser.

More than a few Yum! managers expressed concern that ten dollars multiplied by hundreds of thousands of restaurant workers created the risk of a seemingly innocuous policy inflicting a mountain of financial damage. In truth, as Novak later told us during an interview, employees exercise intelligent discretion and rarely use the ten-dollar allowance. Today, not only are Yum! restaurants run so efficiently that there are fewer disgruntled customers, but also the considerable investment in employee training has resulted in frontline workers who are able to listen and resolve problems amicably without frequently resorting to compensation.

Novak believes that the ten-dollar policy has imbued employees with the "self confidence to know they can do what's right for the customer. It's a sign of how much we trust them and our commitment to make Customer Mania real."[26]

Broadening the Frontline Contribution

While Yum! had targeted service aspects of the customer experience as the primary domain for frontline judgment, the company is constantly seeking input on how to improve organizational processes and execution plans. As a result, Yum! created local mechanisms for engaging frontline associates and RGMs to identify solutions to organization-wide issues. Roger Eaton, formerly KFC's CEO and now Yum!'s chief operating officer, recalls involving frontline RGMs to help with innovation while he was running Yum!'s South Pacific operations in 2003.[27] KFC's CHAMPS scores were falling short in Eaton's market, often rating below 50 percent, but it was initially hard to get people excited about improving operational efficiency.

As part of the effort to raise scores and create employee engagement around CHAMPS, one initiative that Eaton and the Australia team implemented locally was to invite restaurant managers to customer research sessions. As they sat behind mirrored windows, the managers would observe customers talking about their buying experience in KFC restaurants. The primary complaints were slow speed, poor communication in the drive-through, and lack of access to a manager to solve problems in the stores. The restaurant managers suggested improvements that were immediately implemented. Their recommendations included replacing the speaker system with an actual attendant who could take customers' orders and answer questions at the drive-through. As Eaton observed, "it's far more customer friendly."[28]

To address some customers' desire to speak to a manager, Eaton says that they acted on the frontline team's recommendations by taking "the best of our frontline workers, put[ting] them through additional training, [giving] them a different uniform and [giving] them both responsibility and greater authority for resolving customer complaints." This way, even if a manager was unavailable because he or she was out of the building or otherwise occupied by production or administration issues, there was always someone readily available to solve customer problems. As a consequence, according to Eaton, there was a dramatic decline in the number of customer complaints that made their way to company headquarters. It's important to note that although frontline leaders couldn't innovate on a daily basis, Yum! created mechanisms for involving them in defining innovation at the company and driving these new ideas to a variety of customer touch points.

Shaking It Up at the Top

One of the paradoxes of creating a truly front line–focused organization is that change must be driven from the top down, especially in established businesses. The Customer Mania program was initially questioned by some of the senior lieutenants of the company's brands. While some senior leaders did not want to lose autonomy as the three companies came together, others expected Customer Mania to be another short-lived initiative, and a few felt that Novak's methods were just hokey. As Eaton remembers, there was also widespread concern that the recognition and empowerment aspects were rooted in American culture: "The initial reaction in our management was a bit along the lines of, 'What's he on about! Australians won't buy into this, it's too American! What does it actually mean?'"[29]

Novak had performed his due diligence, however, and knew the proposed changes would have quick traction with frontline employees and the managers above them who dealt with customers on a daily basis. Eaton notes, "It was when we took the concept to the team leaders—the people dealing with customers in the stores—that the idea really took off. Their reaction was almost one of, 'about time!'"[30] Ironically, while some senior executives groused and camouflaged their personal agendas by saying that field leaders might resist Customer Mania, the momentum of the program with the front line put a squeeze on executives to get with the program. Eaton explains that the frontline reaction was "that senior management had finally got it together, and that, 'It's the customer, stupid!' Because the frontline workers were the quickest to get the concept and start running with it, it became a catalyst for change throughout the organization. The challenge then became how to support them."

Driving real transformation requires senior leaders to simultaneously deal with technical, political, and cultural obstacles to implementing changes aimed at the organizational front line. The technical challenges include the organizational structure, systems, processes, metrics, and compensation required to support execution. For Yum! everything from back-office information systems to job titles required refreshing. In most organizations the political forces at work tend to be most extreme at the top of the organization.

Leaders may also oppose change because they feel it challenges their power base or threatens the resources at their disposal. At Yum! those who were not willing to embrace the customer focus were dismissed. "That was the only way," Novak later recalled, "that we could have grown the business so fast and prepared it for the future."[31]

Finally, moving an organization to a frontline focus requires overcoming many of the traditional hierarchical norms to which senior managers have become accustomed. We've already discussed the initial skepticism among Pizza Hut leaders to instituting the ten-dollar policy on the grounds that employees couldn't be trusted not to abuse it. Likewise, establishing a set of shared values for Yum! was controversial. Some senior executives felt that each restaurant should have its own set of values instead. Taco Bell isn't the same as Pizza Hut, the argument went. Other leaders believed that national culture trumped corporate beliefs, so it would be impossible to generate a set of shared values that matched the company's diverse global employee base. Ultimately, Yum!'s statement of values, embodied in the How We Win Together principles, was formulated only because Novak at one point simply dug in and said, "Good values are universal. We need to have one culture for everyone in the company, no matter where they are."[32]

Novak didn't simply fire people or play the autocrat. He invested days of his time in helping the top leaders of the company, particularly those with high potential, understand and relate to the vision so that they could contribute to its execution. Novak personally led and taught a program of leadership workshops he called "Taking People with You," which was designed to teach the top five hundred leaders along with thousands of franchisees. During intensive three-day workshops, he did much more than impart the gospel of Customer Mania. Novak helped the leaders plan for their role in creating the company's distinctive culture and making the HWWT principles come alive in the stores and the Restaurant Support Center.

Yum! also created its own university aimed at helping managers and coaches of all levels obtain the important know-how to play their parts. Yum! managers teach the classes. At the end of each class, participants fill out an "I Will" card specifying how they will use what they learned from the session.

It's important to note that the process of building a company around frontline execution of a strategy can happen only if the leader is willing to use his or her power to make it so. As Novak realized early on, senior managers who aren't committed to the vision will undermine its execution, drive confusing signals down the chain of command, contradict the culture and values, and fail to commit the resources required to build an infrastructure that supports how the front line serves the customer. The technical, political, and cultural obstacles are numerous. It was Novak's dedication, with support from frontline associates and positive senior managers, which helped him stay the course and remake Yum!.

Making It Local

Novak's efforts to teach and align his top team were essential to put in place the necessary support systems—values and culture, tools and training, rewards and recognition, and work processes—that enabled the desired degree and focus of frontline judgment. Equally important, by cracking through resistance at the top, Novak enrolled his leaders to ensure that local organizations, whether in India or Illinois, engaged the front line to create the differentiated customer experience envisioned in "Customer Mania."

As we saw with the innovative approach to drive-through service in Australia and taste monitors in India, leaders who were committed to the Teachable Point of View adapted solutions to fit local needs and expanded the degree of frontline judgment appropriately. Perhaps the best example of localization is China, a critical market for Yum! that now accounts for more than 40 percent of its operating profit and has nearly five thousand stores.

Sam Su has been a steadfast advocate of Novak's transformative approach from the outset. Since joining the company in 1989, Su has led Yum!'s growth from its very beginning, building an operation that earned nine hundred million dollars in 2011 operating profits and plans to open nearly five hundred additional restaurants annually. From his early days in the market, Su and his team focused on the local Chinese consumer by taking "the best ideas from the US fast food model and adapting them to serve the needs of the Chinese consumer."[33]

Employing Customer Mania in China has meant adapting nearly every aspect of the Yum! restaurant experience, from product offerings to service. Whereas Americans view fast food as a quick in-and-out experience, Chinese consumers see Yum!'s restaurants as a place to enjoy food and company and linger awhile. Yum! China has created a KFC experience that is markedly different from the KFC experience in the United States and from the experience at many Chinese competitors, from the hostess who greets you at the front door to the highly professional staff members who take your order to the brightly lit, climate-controlled, clean interior. Stores go so far as to organize activities for children while parents eat. Pizza Hut, which opened in mainland China in 1990, is no different. Su has positioned the restaurant as a full-service experience, or what the company advertises as a "five-star dining experience at a three-star price."

While Su adapted to the local market, he held fast to Yum!'s core HWWT values, Customer Mania, CHAMPS discipline, and focus on building people capability. Su told us that Novak, who has been an ardent supporter, has "allowed us to link those visions with the reality and how we implement it in the restaurants in our market."[34] One twist that Su put on the company's approach to recruiting talent has propelled the division's extraordinary growth.

From the outset, Su viewed recruiting talented frontline workers who could deliver great service as essential to the long-term health of the company's brand and a vital ingredient in his growth plan. Although he came from a marketing background, Su told us, "People probably see and experience our brands more from their interactions at our restaurants than what they see on television or through advertising. That's the truth of brand building in this business, so to me the brand is the front line."[35]

Yum! China's breakneck growth made filling stores with new recruits who would act as brand ambassadors a considerable challenge. Every store had to become a training site and RGMs needed the skills to continually hire and teach new staff. Su's team has amassed an encyclopedic volume of best practices and introduced technology to help with the hiring process but, as Su concedes, "the most important decision that the frontline restaurant managers have to make is people decisions in terms of who we hire, how we train and develop them, and how we make sure that there are even better people behind them. At the end of the day it's the RGMs who are making the final call and hiring the right people, working with them to make sure we're the best in customer service."

Su also dreamed of possibilities for his young employees. Novak had emphasized building life skills, and Su repeated the mantra but adapted it. In many cases, Yum! China had to convince not only young recruits of the value of a part-time job but often their parents as well. In one-child China, a part-time job was usually a new experience for a young person. As Mark Chu, president and chief operating officer of Yum! China, has said, children in China "spend a lot of time on the computer, which is not the best preparation to enter society. A part-time job with Yum! is a way to begin to learn people relation skills, teamwork, how to enjoy team achievements and to celebrate with other people."[36]

The product breadth and service complexity in China meant that the inexperienced, sometimes socially awkward students who were the bulk of new recruits needed to be trained in virtually every aspect of basic operations. Yum! discovered that its newcomers often lacked the social skills and self-confidence to engage with customers. Whether offering to help a mother with a crying baby or recognizing that a customer needed assistance with a taxi, the part-timers often desired to help but were afraid to make a personal connection. Su told us that after hearing of this from the RGMs, his team immediately understood the importance of changing Yum!'s training approach to fit China's specific needs. "A lot of times in a big company we take for granted what people should know," Su said. "We came to the realization that we need to help these young kids make their first move. So we have developed training programs that encourage them to step out and greet the customer and encourage the crew members to work as a team."[37]

The program not only trains and encourages staff members to make the first move but also recognizes them after they do so. In all of Yum! China's restaurants, newbies are issued a different hat than the experienced workers. Once they have made their first move to help a customer solve a nonroutine issue, however, they are celebrated by the team for their courage. Their commendable customer service earns them a different hat. While the change in uniform is so subtle that customers would never recognize it, the difference is visible to other employees and becomes a source of pride. "When we go out and visit restaurants," Su says, "crew members walk up to us and tell us what they did to earn their new hat. They're very, very proud they made that first step and you can see the joy in their face."[38]

While adjusting a training program may not seem particularly noteworthy, it's important to understand Su's changes in the context of Yum!'s overall transformation. Had Su not believed in Customer Mania, not been committed to the idea of building people capability at the front line, not been earnest about building a recognition culture, and not seen the importance of supporting RGMs as they made their most important decisions, selecting the frontline workers who serve as Yum!'s daily brand representatives, it is inconceivable that the division would contribute more than a third of the parent company's overall profitability, as it does today.

Summary: Learning from Yum!

We find Yum!'s story so instructive because it defies many of the arguments we hear regarding the complexities of building a front line–focused organization. At the time of its spin-off, Yum! was already a massive company with more than its fair share of operational challenges and internal political conflict. Simultaneously, it was also a start-up that had massive debt and pressing strategic issues and lacked a cohesive culture and shared vision. Rather than let the company's deficiencies dictate its priorities, Novak and his leadership team focused their rebuilding efforts by working backward from the customer interface with the front line.

Novak's Teachable Point of View, developed through his many years of experience and hard work connecting with customers and employees in the field, envisaged Yum! as a fundamentally different organization: one that was built around the customer and focused foremost on building people capability. That perspective flouted conventional wisdom by imagining that frontline workers in a quick-service restaurant could make a difference and be entrusted to spend money to solve customer problems. Everything else in the organization, Novak insists, must take second place as a support function to the customer experience, which to a large extent rests in the hands of the front line.

Novak understood that the front line was not a panacea for all that was ailing Yum! and the company has invested heavily in the physical assets of its brands and in building its product-development capability over the years. However, Novak focused his frontline efforts on ensuring that employees felt appreciated, had the tools, training, and support systems to do their jobs, and were entrusted with the ten-dollar policy to demonstrate that "putting a Yum! on every customer's face" required active participation by every employee.

He made these changes over the cries of some senior managers. Aligning the Teachable Point of View and defining the judgment playing field for frontline employees are often the most difficult tasks in the process of building a front line–focused organization. They require breaking down and breaking through existing power structures. At Yum! as at other companies with which we have worked, middle and upper managers tended to disguise their own fears regarding the perceived erosion of their authority by claiming that the front line "won't get it." In truth, it was some of Yum!'s most senior leaders who "didn't get it," and their inability to align themselves with the company's new direction meant that some had to leave.

Novak's resolve and his leadership ability to bring others with him on the transformational journey created a shared global culture that has the ability to adapt and innovate at the customer interface, whether in Bangalore, Beijing, or Buffalo. Novak told us, "Our culture is that everyone counts, and if you drive that deep in an organization you'll get more people stepping up. We're not perfect . . . but I think we have more people in our company thinking that they count today than last year and the year before and the year before that."[39]

TEACHING PEOPLE TO THINK

It's really about thinking before doing. Somebody can always have a better price or come up with something that's more aesthetically pleasing, but by using these tools, we helped the customer make connections and solve problems they didn't even know that they had.

—Brian Shapland, salesperson, Steelcase Furniture

- **ACCESSING FRONTLINE INTELLIGENCE REQUIRES TEACHING PROBLEM-SOLVING SKILLS**

  - The front line needs a method and language for solving complex issues.

  - Decision making can't occur at the front line if people don't know how to think critically.

- **LEADERS MUST ARTICULATE, ALIGN, AND REFINE THE PROBLEM-SOLVING METHODS**

  - Common frameworks and language reduce hierarchy and enable frontline action.

  - Developing judgment skills requires experiential training, tools, and strong support.

United States Navy SEALs Lieutenant Commander Kevin Williams's eight-man team had just huffed eight kilometers across rugged terrain and concealed itself in a covert position deep in the mountains of Afghanistan when it received an unexpected radio call. The team had spent days preparing for a strike on the terrorist safe house that now stood tantalizingly close. Yet the radio call advised Williams that a new, more sensitive target—"a serious bad guy" in SEALs parlance—had just been located nearby. As a result, the optimal mission target had been changed at the last moment.

Since Williams was commanding the patrol on the ground, the radio call was posed more as a question than as a direct order: Could Williams's team hike to a new location, strike the target, extract the enemy, and get out before daylight? Complicating matters even further, the other half of Williams's platoon, which had inserted a few miles away to maintain cover, had lost radio contact with Williams as well as the mission controllers at headquarters. In that brief moment, Williams had to arrive at an independent judgment as to whether the seven men with him possessed the speed, capability, and firepower to pull off this revised mission. A miscalculation might mean that the enemy would get away or that some of Williams's men might not make it back.[1]

Living with Complexity

In this chapter we will look at step 2 of our process for building a front line–focused organization by examining the exercise of judgment on the front line in more complex, dynamic situations. Whereas a restaurant crew member at Yum! has to contend with relatively predictable customer needs, and the personalized care of a Ritz-Carlton staff member is directed toward solving sets of mostly homogenous service issues, frontline personnel in other industries must deal with more variables and higher degrees of unpredictability. We will use two very different examples, the U.S. Navy SEALs and the sales force at office furniture manufacturer Steelcase, to demonstrate how organizations teach their frontline workers to think about multifaceted problems.

In both cases, one military and one civilian, the organizational challenge is identical: to train people to make good judgments and reason for themselves often under extreme pressure—whether on the literal battlefield or when battling for a customer—and not simply to succumb to conventional wisdom or industry practice when such judgments may prove fatal to the outcome of the mission or cause. And in both cases, the SEALs and Steelcase, the solution lies in

1. anticipation of the types of problems frontline employees are likely to face;
2. repetitive training to develop judgment;
3. lower-risk opportunities for people to practice, again and again; and
4. contingency planning in case things don't go as expected.

All of these must occur before frontline employees find themselves facing do-or-die judgments.

The first stage of step 2 in our process of building a front line–focused organization is to consider the contextual variables that frontline leaders must understand in order to come to a good judgment. For most business organizations, these will include deeply understanding customer needs, knowing how the company makes money, anticipating competitor responses, and working with stakeholders who are involved in the process. The variegated nature of these more complex judgments—whether a furniture salesman proposing an enterprise-wide equipment overhaul, a technology consultant working with a hospital, or an investment planner restructuring a retiree's portfolio—often require frontline employees to weigh trade-offs as they work with multiple stakeholders, endure longer decision cycles, and face more intense competition.

The second requirement of step 2 is to teach frontline personnel how to think through complex problems, generate possible solutions, and select one from among them despite unknown data or ambiguous customer preferences. This entails moving beyond routine protocols and providing frontline employees with a thought process that relies upon contextual information to resolve knotty problems. The progressive shift to more complex problem solving can be thought of as a stair-step change, moving from recovery to resolution to reframing.

At Yum! BLAST was an acronym for the process of problem recovery. That is, fixing the situation for an already dissatisfied customer. In a Yum! restaurant, there are relatively few problems that customers are likely to raise, and the BLAST protocol provides a structured, step-by-step approach that results in a satisfied customer.

As we move to more complex problem resolution, however, the exact nature of a problem may not be immediately apparent to the customer, testing frontline workers' diagnostic capabilities. Complexity may also arise if resolving a problem requires employing broader technical or customer

PROBLEM REFRAMING
- Problem definitions may vary or needs are unexpressed
- May require new designs, dilemma resolution, or cocreation
- Likely to require support of multiple constituencies

PROBLEM RESOLUTION
- Fixing more complex, unstructured problems
- Multiple possible solutions; requires novel approach or rule bending
- Likely to require support of multiple constituencies

PROBLEM RECOVERY
- Addressing customer complaints or fixing service defects
- Typically defined problems with few solutions; use of protocols helpful
- Most often solved among individuals

knowledge or combining a company's offerings in a novel way that the customer hasn't anticipated. We saw an example of this type of problem-solving ability applied at the Ritz-Carlton and celebrated through the "wow" stories each week.

The most difficult skill is problem reframing, which we will explore in greater detail in this chapter. This requires having the customer or other involved parties look at and analyze a given problem differently as a result of frontline workers helping them to see unrecognized needs or broadening the context in which they view the problem. Problem reframing is a deliberate attempt to change a customer's perspective regarding his or her needs and potential solutions, which may result from new ideas proposed by frontline workers or from engaging in cocreation with customers.

Judgment on the Front Line for SEALs

In our opening story above, the nature of the decision faced by Lieutenant Commander Williams carried life-and-death consequences. Yet whether it's facing the wrath of an irate customer or facing an enemy sniper in Afghanistan, the fundamental principles of training, leadership, and judgment that empower and enable frontline people to make good decisions, often under pressure and at split-second intervals, remain the same across time and space. The recent demographics of new SEAL recruits make the analogy even more telling. In fact, approximately 70 percent of recruits come to SEAL training directly out of high school. With typical SEAL recruits ranging between nineteen and twenty-four years of age, with limited real-world experience, it's not difficult to imagine many of them working at your local Home Depot or Starbucks. Indeed, Williams's time after college graduation was spent as a vacuum salesman before joining the U.S. Navy.

SEAL teams, usually operating in small numbers, operate independently, far removed from the line of sight of their superior. Although their conduct is based on well-defined rules of engagement combined with precise mission orders, SEALs are trained to operate in the field semiautonomously, with limited direct communications and maximum latitude to make life-and-death, real-time judgment calls at the front line.

In fact, on-the-spot decisions made by SEALs have significant geopolitical ramifications. Although SEALs don't have customers in the business sense, they succeed by building local relationships with stakeholders as diverse as local tribes, politicians, and national governmental agencies that share information or provide other support. An individual SEAL's actions not only may endanger himself or his teammates but also may have much broader consequences for the entire military or even the U.S. government. In this context, the judgments that SEALs make in response to dynamic, complex problems, and in the face of direct opposition, typically require trade-offs when plans go awry on the battleground. For example, during the initial years of the war in Afghanistan, the military operated near the country's eastern border, but the U.S. government refused to sanction military action that strayed into Pakistan. Although the military would never publicly acknowledge making an unauthorized foray, SEALs have been called upon to make judgments between stopping the hot pursuit of a known terrorist and calling in an air strike that might cross a few hundred yards onto sovereign soil.

Captain Adam Curtis, a twenty-five-year SEAL veteran and former executive officer of the SEAL training school, shared with us the difficulty of training recruits to make rapid decisions on the battlefield. "If you're four hundred yards away and see a shadowy figure on the horizon looking in your direction, was your cover just blown? Is that a farmer with a gun to protect his land? Is that the enemy? Do you ignore, shoot, or detain him?"[2] SEALs often operate in very small teams in order to maintain their stealth advantage; how an individual SEAL operator answers Captain Curtis's questions may mean the difference between salvaging an operation and killing an innocent bystander.

How SEALs Develop Judgment

So how do the SEALs turn their young recruits into some of the most technically adept and versatile military specialists armed with weaponry but, most important, with discipline and good judgment? The short answer is intensive, Darwinian training that, even as it imparts new knowledge and skills, continually assesses and culls the numbers of new recruits. Even being accepted into this hardcore training is a long shot. Getting into the SEAL schoolhouse, known as BUD/S (or Basic Underwater Demolitions/ SEAL training), is comparable to getting into Harvard, which has an acceptance rate of 6.9 percent.[3] Aspiring SEALs must first pass a battery of physical and intelligence tests, in addition to personality profiling, which, while effective in predicting some qualifying factors, are quickly supplanted by the initial rigors of a grueling fifteen-week training program for which the historical graduation rate is approximately 25 percent of those who start.[4]

This rough training program culminates in an exhausting ordeal realistically known as Hell Week, during which candidates must function on a maximum of five hours of sleep—in a week, not a day. Physical demands aside, this trial by fire prepares recruits to make tough judgments at the front line by instilling a sense of confidence, courage, and commitment in each candidate. "Hell Week tells us what kind of man we're dealing with," says Lieutenant Commander Williams, formerly in charge of all SEAL basic training. "Hell Week is like one long mission," adds Captain Curtis. "We find out whether they're really willing to endure hardship to complete the mission."[5]

In other words, the herculean trials that SEAL candidates must survive are not simply macho tests aimed at measuring physical prowess. More than a few former Olympic athletes have failed the SEAL induction program. More important, the exercises demonstrate how a man performs and makes judgment calls under extreme duress, when sheer exhaustion and performance anxiety have stripped away reflexes and diminished reasoning capabilities. Those who succumb to stress are more likely to make bad judgments on the battlefield. While the diagram on the next page shows the essential technical skills taught during each phase of SEAL training, such as weaponry and mission planning, most would-be SEALs drop out due to their inability to cope with the psychological pressure rather than because of their aptitude for mastering the physical skills.

For example, what might seem like just another physical exercise, in which scuba-diving students are harassed by instructors while underwater, is also a psychological test of judgment. The BUD/S instructors perform a simulated attack on the student, simultaneously tangling his gear and causing disorientation; the test is exactingly designed to determine not just technical competence but also a student's capacity to maintain composure and make good decisions while under intense survival pressure. This challenging and potentially dangerous exercise is thoroughly planned by the instructors to ensure that panic attacks or erroneous responses do not

SIMULTANEOUS DEVELOPMENT OF SKILLS AND JUDGMENT

Training Phase	Weeks	Physical Capabilities / Technical Skills	Judgment / Leadership
SEAL Qualification Training	15	• Advanced tactics and equipment • Medicine, reconnaissance, insertion	• Leading the team under fire
Junior Officer Training	5	• Mission Planning • Team SOPs and Tactics	• Contingency Planning
3rd Phase: Land Warfare	10	• Land-based team tactics and shooting • Equipment: firearms, communications	• Situational Awareness
2nd Phase: Combat Diving	7	• Swim and dive competency • Use of scuba gear	• Judgment under pressure
1st Phase: Conditioning	7	• Intense running, swimming, and exercise • Withstand pain of Hell Week	• Commitment to the mission
Indoctrination	2	• Basic Fitness	• Being a team member

result in serious consequences, but failing this exercise will likely lead to one fewer future SEAL.

Each phase of SEAL training also hones judgment skills to develop sensitivity to the context in which SEALs must make decisions. When operating in a foreign country, every action has potential consequences for how the U.S. military is perceived by locals and whether the SEALs will be supported, shunned, or possibly attacked. SEALs are taught to consider situational ethical issues, such as what to do when taking hostile fire from what appears to be a fourteen-year-old girl armed with an assault rifle.

Other issues may arise far from the battlefield but have prolonged effects if handled poorly. For example, the SEAL teams function based on trust and the assurance that each man can rely on the others in life-threatening situations. One of the ethical issues SEALs might be required to ponder is what they would do if they saw the wife of one of their team members about to leave a bar with another man. To make matters more difficult, the trainees are told that the team member is someone with whom they have had conflict and don't particularly like. What follows is typically a vigorous debate among recruits and SEAL instructors about whether they have the obligation to act as a marriage counselor, what discovery of the infidelity might mean to the team member's psychological state on the battlefield, and whether surfacing the issue might cause distrust between the two men that could affect the entire SEAL team.

All of these scenarios and many more, some seemingly far-fetched, are derived from actual situations that one or more BUD/S instructors have faced. The purpose of such exercises is—as Captain Curtis put it to us—"to weed out the guys who think this is a movie or a video game, because

Rambo gets people killed in real life."[6] It's important to keep in mind that the desired outcome of this weeding-out process of selection is to field a recruit skilled not just with weapons but also with his own mind. The tight focus of this training is on providing a framework for thinking and developing problem-solving skills that may make the difference not just between life and death for the soldier but also for the mission itself.

Contingency Planning and Dress Rehearsals

In addition to debating moral issues, the SEALs also mentally prepare for judgment calls they may face tactically in the heat of battle. Achieving success in such inherently fluid situations requires that SEALs internalize standard operating procedures (SOPs), absorbing their mission routines more intently than an NFL quarterback reviewing a game-day playbook, while never permitting plans to inflexibly override unpredictable shifts in circumstance.

Despite reconnaissance and planning efforts, there is a high probability of an unplanned event occurring on the long march to a target, or of discovering an unanticipated variable after arriving on the scene. As a result, teams invest many hours doing their best to anticipate what might go wrong and planning how to regroup when faced with the unexpected. Contingency planning is the SEALs' antidote to the failure that can arise from blind adherence to prepared routines or, conversely, the chaos that can result from unstructured improvisation. They refine their judgment skills both in training and before complicated missions through live simulations, stress testing, and case studies derived from real-world experience.

In one training exercise we observed, for example, a SEAL team spent the day planning for a mock raid at a public location in order to extract a high-value target without engaging the enemy in open fire. In the process, they filled several whiteboards with plans, even using army men and Tonka trucks in the dirt to simulate the strike. The exercise ended in the dead of night, however, with utter failure and a training officer shouting expletives because the team had failed to foresee how much clearance would be required for a helicopter extraction if the mission went sideways—which, of course, it did.

Encouraging Failure

Developing judgment in any profession arguably requires experiencing failure and learning how to adapt in the face of the unexpected. This is particularly true for those whose jobs put them in the middle of dangerous, messy war zones. Contingency-planning exercises and live drills teach people to make judgments in circumstances where failure does not come at such a heavy price.

Prior to September 11, 2001, without the real-world influences that arise from sustained combat, some overly simplistic tenets had seeped into the training regime for Navy SEALs. However, as SEALs engaged regularly in ambiguous combat situations in Iraq and Afghanistan, the need for more tolerance of failure in training scenarios was highlighted, combined with a stronger ethos of learning from mistakes. Today, SEAL training for both new recruits and active teams is designed to confront simplistic decision routines, such as "always complete the mission," and challenge a young SEAL's judgment when forced into difficult and more complex trade-off positions.

"Before they leave training," Williams tells us privately, "we give them a mission that can't succeed. They realize their choices are between bad and worse." The challenge, according to Williams, is getting type A leaders to abort the mission. "They get through BUD/S and think there's nothing that can stop them. They're all about making the mission. But it can't be at any cost."[7] The ultimate cost-benefit analysis typically takes place in the field, at the front line, far from the officers at headquarters.

What factors should cause teams in the field to abort a mission? Answering this question correctly demands internal flexibility and tests trainees' ability to make appropriate adaptations in real-life situations. The only way to train or prepare for such scenarios, of course, is by running well-thought-through simulations. "A team leader may say he needs a minimum force of ten men or that he has to be in a certain location by a given time," says Williams. "We'll make sure one of those doesn't happen. In the heat of battle, do they go back to their planning or let the adrenaline take over?"[8]

Such risks become even harder to evaluate under hierarchical pressure in the military, but the SEALs' training directly confronts the paradox of respecting authority while trusting those on the front line to make informed decisions. At some point in a SEAL's training, he is likely to be given direct mission orders by a commanding officer that are doomed to failure. The point of the training exercise is to see not only whether the SEAL blindly adheres to mission orders but also whether he can effectively communicate with a commander to resolve the situation. The SEAL is forced to judge whether the mission will succeed if the parameters are changed and, if so, how to explain this to a superior officer brimming with confidence as he barks orders.

Williams's point is that in many situations a SEAL faces there is no right answer. His training regime emphasizes the ability to think under pressure, weigh options, evaluate consequences, and take action. Conceding that he has a bias to action himself, Williams adds thoughtfully, "You have to constantly ask yourself, 'What's the risk to the mission and what's the risk to our force?'"[9]

So how did the story of Kevin Williams's team in Afghanistan end? Williams determined that his men could in fact redirect to capture that "serious bad guy," a target who turned out to be a richer trove of information than even they had expected. This was the first domino to fall in a series of successful missions that led to the capture of a number of other key Taliban leaders. When serving as basic training officer in charge of BUD/S, Lieutenant Commander Williams shared his war stories with a precise purpose: developing and refining the judgment capacity of the young recruits who compose the next generation of elite warriors on the front line of the war on terrorism.

Teaching People to Think for Themselves

It may sound strange, or even condescending, to imply that adults need help learning how to think. After all, cognition is part of what defines us as human beings. However, individual thinking styles emerge as a function of experience, education, environment, and many other factors. Numerous studies have shown the difficulty of blending teams of people who have different approaches to problem solving.[10]

One of the greatest stumbling blocks we see causing individual managers and sometimes entire organizations to revert to command-and-control formulas is when employees solve problems differently from how their leaders would have. This is particularly true if the issue is of great consequence or the outcome has led to failure. In such situations, it's not uncommon to hear a manager berating the decision-making employee with lines such as "Why didn't you . . ." or "I would never . . ." In those moments, senior managers don't want to hear about empowerment philosophies or decentralization theories.

The point of hiring diverse and talented employees, however, is to tap into their unique insights and creativity. Most organizations lack a common language and shared culture for how to mentally tackle problems. As a result, individual leaders can brashly discount employee insight when they confuse cognitive style with cognitive ability. Just because someone approaches a problem differently from how their manager would, or is less articulate about their thought process, doesn't mean they are less intelligent or their proposed solution less feasible.

By contrast, organizations that offer shared frameworks, methodology, and models for problem solving take an important step toward promoting nonhierarchical dialogue that focuses on using the best available information—much of it from the front line. Such models ideally offer a structured approach for considering the relevant variables, generating alternative approaches, testing failure modes, and developing contingency plans. Used correctly, they promote debate and foster creativity by giving everyone equal footing in a conversation.

Organizations armed with such an approach realize two benefits. First, they are able to more quickly develop and integrate new employees. Whether new hires are frontline employees or vice presidents of strategy, they presumably have ideas to share. Offering them a methodology for testing the rigor of their thinking and a language for articulating how they came to their conclusions breeds self-confidence and facilitates communication, broadening their opportunities to contribute. Second, where employees may lack a structured thought process or be prone to jump to conclusions, managers have a common language and coaching methodology they can deploy to help develop the individual.

As we saw with the SEALs, once this shared context has been established and those on the front line have been given a tool kit for the types of judgments they are likely to face, it is critical that training affords the opportunity to practice making such decisions under stress and teaches frontline employees how to develop contingency plans.

In the remainder of this chapter, we will examine how office furniture manufacturer Steelcase implemented a shared approach to problem solving to address the extreme price competition, highly variable customer needs, and unpredictability of aesthetic design preferences that are endemic to the furniture industry. Steelcase's story is helpful because it demonstrates how a problem-solving approach can be adapted to the needs of a particular organization and hardwired into a company's culture. It is also instructive because it reveals the challenges of the process. The development of Critical Thinking, as Steelcase calls its approach, has taken more than a decade, as the organization's leaders have faced difficulties articulating, aligning, and then evolving the methodology.

Critical Thinking at Steelcase

As Brian Shapland hung up the phone, he knew he had his work cut out for him. After months of pursuing a large contract with a financial-services company, the field salesman's putative client had just informed him that it planned to put the deal out for a competitive bid. Shapland had been at Steelcase in Chicago long enough to know that open bids in the fiercely competitive furniture industry all too often lead to mutually destructive price wars. A deal this prominent would attract extra intense competitors' attention and very likely bury any hope of making a reasonable profit. As a salesman, this was the most frustrating kind of contract to win, because instead of focusing on customer needs, everyone's energy goes into wringing out pennies. But this was late 2009, the country was in the midst of the worst recession since the 1930s, and his industry's sales were down 35 percent. What was he to do?

Rather than play his competitors' lowball game, Shapland chose to pursue a different approach to winning the contract. He had just spent several days at company headquarters in Grand Rapids, Michigan, learning from a talented team there that called itself Workspace Futures. The members of this group had taught Brian, along with a number of his frontline sales colleagues, a different way of selling their products based on a different way of *thinking* about selling their products. The essence of the new way of thinking was that the sales team was required to create a compelling story based upon precisely defined customer needs, as opposed to price—the proverbial "commodity hell."

After phoning his colleagues in Grand Rapids, Brian assembled a small team, armed them with notebooks and cameras, and instructed them to fan out across the country, visiting some of the financial-services giant's hundreds of branches, snapping photos, and watching closely how people really worked in each location. They were aware that the client's business processes were changing dramatically, requiring more automation and a technology upgrade. They also knew that there were workstation ergonomic challenges and that the company needed to consolidate sites, compressing even more workers into some offices.

The story that Brian Shapland and his Workspace Futures colleagues ultimately presented to the client told a much richer and more compelling story than any of his cost-conscious competitors. Projecting pictures on a big screen, Shapland demonstrated how the client had much deeper ergonomic challenges as a result of the increasing weight of the average U.S. worker or, as he more delicately put it, "the sharply varying shapes and sizes" of employees in their offices. The pictures also graphically depicted how employees were routinely sitting with bad posture and trying to type sideways due to poorly designed work spaces. There were no spaces for spontaneous interaction, so people would stop in the hallway and lean against the wall to take notes. Worst of all, there were employee-made signs displayed in the customer areas that confused the company's brand image.

At the close of this candid conversation, Shapland's client knew that it had a far bigger design challenge on its hands than just furniture. As Shapland told us, the dialogue had shifted dramatically from "how much does your six-by-six workstation cost, or how much power can your cubicle panel generate, or what paint colors does that chair come in" to a multifaceted narrative "about the person sitting there all day, about how we can help that person with their job, about how we could save the customer money with a more effective work space."[11]

The moral of this story is not just that Brian Shapland won an enormous multiyear, multistate contract but that a local field salesperson located hundreds of miles away from Steelcase's corporate office had seized upon an opportunity to reframe the way his *Fortune* 100 customer was thinking about a multimillion-dollar deal by changing the way *he* thought about the deal. Shapland never had to ask for permission or hand the big deal off to more senior managers. He had been provided with the tools to think about the customer's needs and position his offering in the way that was best for the customer and helped Steelcase to build a broader, deeper, longer-term, and ultimately more profitable relationship with the client. He had been given the freedom to assemble a small, smart SWAT team to help him, and he had developed relationships with area experts in corporate headquarters that helped him to mobilize his team.

"It's really about thinking before doing," Shapland told us proudly. "Somebody can always have a better price or come up with something that's more aesthetically pleasing, but by using these tools, we helped the customer make connections and solve problems they didn't even know that they had."[12]

Finding Out What Customers Want

Shapland's ability to reframe his customer's problem more broadly, and in a manner that fit with Steelcase's unique abilities, was an outcome of a long journey that had started fifteen years earlier when James Hackett, a broad-shouldered former center for the University of Michigan football team, assumed the role of CEO at Steelcase in 1994. When he stepped into that role, he was disheartened by his employees' apparent willingness to accept declining growth rates in what was widely regarded as an industry in decline. "I was struck by the lack of people establishing future opportunities," Hackett told us. "This haze naturally settles over product categories, but why did we need to accept that there's no more growth and that the product has leveled off? For me, the solution to that question became, How could we find out what customers wanted that they haven't yet expressed?"[13]

Hackett had actually encountered this problem much earlier in his career, a frustration that led him on a deeper exploration of the innovative reaches of the design world. In 1987, after meeting David Kelley, the famously imaginative founder of the cutting-edge design firm IDEO—which helped Ritz-Carlton redesign its properties to emphasize localized scenes[14]—Hackett realized that he had discovered an ethos and methodology that might, if properly applied, help him ease Steelcase out of its long and deep slump into commoditization.

As Hackett later explained, here was a firm that could "take raw ideas from concept to market faster than any entity that I'd ever seen."[15] The firm had been credited with the design of an astonishingly wide variety of products ranging from Oral-B's Squish Grip children's toothbrushes, Dilbert's Ultimate Cubicle, the De Paul Hospital emergency room in St. Louis, and the interior of Amtrak's Acela high-speed train. But it wasn't IDEO's design skills that Hackett was really after. Much more interesting to Hackett, IDEO had developed a process combining anthropological and sociological techniques that engaged employees in the direct observation of customer behavior and designed solutions for what were often unexpressed needs.

Shortly after Hackett assumed the top job at Steelcase in December 1994, one of his first significant strategic moves was to take a substantial equity interest in IDEO. Transplanting the innovative DNA of IDEO into Steelcase's far more conservative culture would not be a cakewalk, Hackett knew. Yet he firmly believed that infusing IDEO's unique methodology into his own company would lead to strategies that could translate across different markets—from health care to education—and across different work styles—anticipating office environments, for example, that might stylishly serve an increasingly nomadic workforce.

IDEO's core methodology consists of a five-step process that Hackett and his senior team custom-tailored to meet Steelcase's specifications. Mark Greiner, who would go on to lead the internal group charged with adapting IDEO's methodology for Steelcase, later told us that "Jim saw the relationship with IDEO as an opportunity to work with a client to understand what was unique about their specific needs, and then to create high value. At IDEO, it was always about understanding the user at a deep level and then applying engineering skills in direct response to their needs. He wanted that spirit infused deep within Steelcase."[16]

IDEO'S INNOVATION PROCESS[17]

Step 1: Understand the market, the client, the technology and the perceived constraints on the problem

Step 2: Observe real people in real-life situations to find out what makes them tick

Step 3: Visualize new-to-world concepts and the customers who will use them

Step 4: Evaluate and refine the prototypes in a series of quick iterations

Step 5: Implement the new concept for commercialization

Initially at least, Hackett did not succeed in making much headway with his rank and file—his army of salespeople at the front line. "There was considerable and widespread skepticism as to the value of embracing the new mission," George Wolfe, the recently retired head of Steelcase University, told us. "Mostly, this was because people just didn't know what this new way of thinking meant for them."[18]

Frustrated yet determined to make the new strategy more concrete to his people, Hackett recognized he needed the company's top brass aligned in order to drive implementation. He assembled thirty senior executives at a time in classroom sessions, with a preclass homework assignment to write a paper outlining how the design-thinking principles adapted from IDEO would change the strategy of the area for which they were responsible. "Hackett blew these essays up to poster size and put them on a wall like an art gallery," George Wolfe later recalled, "all 30 of them. Everyone was invited to come to the class an hour before it officially started so they could read them."[19] Then he put grades on each paper in front of the entire class. "No one got higher than a C," Hackett would ruefully recall years later.[20]

During these sessions, Hackett did everything he could think of, short of standing on his head, to coach his executives on how to apply the new design-thinking principles. Yet try as he might, he simply could not get his message across. "It was exhausting," Hackett told us with a sigh. "By the time I was done, I still had gotten through only half the people. I made a little headway in the sense that people knew I was going to be super stubborn about this. But when they left, half of them were totally pissed off and we still didn't have a way to systematize it across the company."

Concluding that he was running up against a cognitive and emotional brick wall, he later conceded that he "was bloodied and battled, and in the end all we accomplished was to waste five years." Ultimately Hackett consulted with Wolfe, who was familiar with our work on leadership and its relation to learning. What Hackett desperately needed, Wolfe gently suggested, was to systematically revise the way people at Steelcase thought about facing the customer and going to market.

Taking the Time to Think

With Wolfe's prompting, Hackett stood back to figure out what he was really trying to teach. He realized that his entire approach was profoundly influenced by a failed product launch in 1994, when a new cubicle system the firm had designed from scratch ran into deep trouble right from the outset. Although the company ultimately rectified its problems with the product, Hackett told us, "misunderstandings arose over its design, the size of the capital investment needed to build it, and its impact on our dealer organizations. We even had a product recall involving its panel surfaces. The concepts were a breakthrough, but the development process was a breakdown."[21]

The root cause of this system failure was that his people had failed to consider, let alone plan for, the chance that something might go wrong. Although they had started out with what they regarded as a revolutionary approach to meeting customer needs, employees had jumped into action before having truly thought through the design concept and its implications for end users. The rush to execution had led people to confirm hypotheses without collecting facts from those at the front line, talking to customers, or considering alternate ideas. In short, Steelcase's people had failed to consider the context of their decisions and had created no contingency plans.

The central lesson that Hackett took away from this painful experience was that Steelcase's culture needed to shift from one based on "doing" to one based on "thinking before doing." That thinking needed to be directly aligned with tapping more deeply into not-yet-articulated customer needs, as he had learned from IDEO.

More determined than ever, Hackett assembled a leadership team of his top one hundred leaders, the debut of which was not without blemish. "Initially the sociology of users was going right over their heads,"[22] Hackett candidly recalled in retrospect. But he stuck with it and worked hard with George Wolfe to articulate what would in time become known as the Steelcase Critical Thinking Model (see box below).

Employing this relatively straightforward methodology permitted Steelcase leaders at any level to combine execution with deeper strategic thinking. The underlying idea was to help decision makers at all levels make good judgments and reach informed agreement with others based on a series of methods and tools that could be applied to virtually any project. No MBA required.

Phase one focuses on thinking deeply about the subject. Innovation emerges only from asking and answering the right questions, Hackett informed his leadership team, encouraging the group to read broadly, tap into their network of friends and acquaintances, have conversations about the topic, and above all, *observe the end user.* "The think phase works best if you approach it as a 'naive beginner,'" Hackett points out, using a term he picked up from IDEO. "You can't be an advocate for a given position or try to defend a preconceived notion."[23] Just as Brian Shapland had assembled his SWAT team to investigate how his customer's employees actually operated, leaders in the "think phase" have to invest the time to cast a wide research net, brainstorm, and try to discover patterns that otherwise might not have been apparent.

PRACTICES FOR
critical thinking

think	▶	point of view	▶	plan to implement	▶	implement

think	point of view	plan to implement	implement
ponder, question, and challenge	determine single owner	consider cross-functional impact	demonstrate conviction
listen to all perspectives	fact-based findings	anticipate obstacles/	align those being impacted
network internally and externally	drive rationale	create contingency plans	execute flawlessly
research the issue fully	visualize success (how it looks)	clarify and answer questions	determine process improvement
reflect on what was learned	develop point of view	reduce complexity/	scrutinize and evaluate results
confront emotional issues	only new evidence can change a point of view	determine measure	celebrate success
make your information visible		finalize implementation plan	
		communicate the plan and practice	

"How fast you get through all four phases is less important than ensuring you complete each phase before moving to the next one."
—JIM HACKETT

Steelcase

© 2005 Steelcase Development Corporation

Only then is an individual or team prepared to move on to the second phase—forming a distinct point of view. At this point, teams have discussions about the options for approaching the market or client that were generated during the think phase. Shapland and his SWAT team, for example, invested many hours in reviewing pictures and sifting through observational data to develop the conclusions they ultimately shared with their client. The goal at this phase isn't to reach consensus but rather to get to a clear articulation of the issue and a vision of success that is owned by the person who will ultimately be responsible for the project. Once established, the point of view can change only if there are new facts or overwhelming new evidence—a rule that Hackett adopted from the justice system.

At this point, a number of more customary business practices kick in. Leaders develop a plan to implement that includes a clear mission statement, business plan, and deliverables time line. What is different from most organizations is Hackett's insistence on practicing the rollout. By "practice" Hackett means everything from prototypes to simulations to training, depending on the nature of the project. Changing a manufacturing flow to meet more demanding customer specifications might mean a dress rehearsal with cardboard boxes that represent different machines or elements of the work flow. In the case of the failed cubicle system, Hackett laments, it would have been as simple as training line workers and the sales force so they could anticipate the coming changes.

"Taking the time to teach implementation is the epitome of respect in our organization," Hackett insists. "When implementation is poor, people are taken by surprise. By making practice integral to our plan-to-implement phase, we have created a unifying, aligning experience that builds trust, and trust speeds innovation and execution." The final phase of Steelcase's "thinking before doing" model of execution is implementation. Rather than skip from a poorly formulated idea into action mode, Hackett demands that employees slow down so that execution can be watertight.

The Critical Thinking Model (CTM) has been adopted across every part of Steelcase and became the focal point of the company's in-house training efforts through its Steelcase University. Hackett personally taught the one-hour courses for more than a year and then asked his executive leadership team to lend a hand. A typical class, such as one we observed, includes everyone from the front line to senior management and longtime veterans to new hires. Even the new vice president of strategy, a direct report to Hackett and a former McKinsey consultant, was required to attend the session.

Critical Thinking Takes Hold

The cumulative effect for Steelcase has been that "CTM gives everybody the opportunity to be a problem solver regardless of what level in the organization," George Wolfe insists.[24] Hamid Khorramian, Steelcase's VP of North American operations, was prepared to passionately embrace a philosophy designed to overcome the furniture industry's historical profit margins of less than 3 percent. What Khorramian saw in CTM was a direct analogue to Toyota's famed production system: a method of creating true frontline ownership of innovation that would empower and transform the culture in his manufacturing plants. He simply needed to tap into the reservoir of creativity that his employees already possessed.

In Khorramian's view, sharing ideas stems directly from this sense of ownership and accountability. Frontline employees need to be emotionally invested in their work. The production workers feel this when their team leaders—who typically come to management straight from the front lines—have a sense of ownership for their area. Khorramian's goal was to be present and supportive but let the zone leaders and frontline teams create ideas and let him know how they would be implemented. "If I take five engineers, they may do a better job of recommending improvements but the change won't last more than a month because the ownership isn't there."[25]

To kick-start the process, Khorramian defined a straightforward objective: get an average of three suggestions per employee per month. In order to focus the effort in the most meaningful areas, he defined the judgment playing field as ideas in the categories of quality, process, cost, and safety. The goal was to provide focal areas that weren't overly constraining but also provided employees with boundaries within which they could add maximum value. His commitment was that any ideas that were approved would go from concept to implementation within four weeks. In the case of safety, implementation would occur within forty-eight hours.

At last report, the manufacturing team had achieved an average of 1.9 ideas per employee. Nearly 80 percent of ideas are accepted and, in the cases where they aren't, the team leaders work directly with the people who generated the rejected idea to explain why or to help rework the suggestion.

While Steelcase was undoubtedly making progress toward Hackett's long-delayed ultimate goal of infusing his entire organization with an IDEO-like capacity to innovate from the point of view of the end user, he still experienced frustration that not enough people were engaged on the user side. The ownership and continuity of execution that Khorramian was driving in operations wasn't as seamless among different departments or between corporate headquarters and the field.

The Final Leap with Workspace Futures

Although people at every level of Steelcase were thinking more critically and focusing on the customer, the methodology and mind-set that Hackett had first observed at IDEO had not yet permeated the entire organization. "Jim wanted everyone—whether you're a foreman or a frontline salesperson—to be thinking about what I can do for the user and convert that thinking into an offer,"[26] Mark Greiner contends.

Clearly, scaling the ability to generate deep customer insights required providing frontline employees with new tools and capabilities beyond the CTM "think before acting" model. The goal wasn't to turn them into full-time market researchers but to enable them to look at the customer experience differently, document what they saw, and engage in a new type of conversation with customers.

That expertise resided in the Workspace Futures group, established in 2003 by Hackett when he tapped Greiner, a twenty-year Steelcase veteran, to lead the integration of the IDEO methodology. Greiner's team of researchers and marketers had modified IDEO's approach to put more emphasis on understanding and learning about the customer environment. "The difference between what IDEO did and what we do is that they are hired by a company. They don't need to understand the industry but rather what the company is trying to achieve. We have to understand the customer, our company, and the field. We have to study in depth—it might take up to nine months just to learn about a field like retail banking or health care. Nobody will pay IDEO for nine months to learn their industry, but our customers won't pay us unless we do."[27]

Greiner's group had been instrumental in landing a number of significant contracts for the company and had proven that their methodology worked whether it was applied with the Mayo Clinic, Bank of America, or Cisco. However, they were a limited resource and treated as the heavy artillery for the "deals we can't lose." Their ability to scale their impact would hinge on being able to engage more people in using the process.

"We couldn't ask our people to pretend to be researchers," says Greiner, "but we want them to be comfortable enough to do observational research."[28] When applying Hackett's CTM, frontline leaders would now have the tools to do that research. Greiner's team began inviting small groups of salespeople for workshops, including the one that Shapland attended, in which they were equipped with digital cameras and a problem statement and trained to deploy the Workspace Futures research methodology to solve the problem. Greiner's team dubbed the new methodology ARC Lite (Applied Research and Consulting).

For some of the salespeople, this was not an easy transition to make. "Some people want to sell features and benefits because that's what they've been doing their whole life," recalls Greiner. "They turn the chair over and talk about our wheel-base assembly compared to Herman Miller. If they were that type, we had to weed them out. That's driving us all down to commodity hell."[29] Fortunately, others viewed it as transformative, and they formed the core of Steelcase's revamped customer-centric sales force.

Critical Thinking at the Front Line

The process of embedding CTM and ARC Lite across the company has also impacted Steelcase's culture of collaboration. As Wolfe told us, "people can be on virtual project teams distributed around the world and everyone uses the same model. They state it up front and then they use it to track which phase of their thinking they're in or what tools they need to deploy. It doesn't matter where you come from or what your title is. It keeps everyone focused, aligned, and on board."[30]

It has also directly connected Steelcase's corporate headquarters to the front line. Today, salespeople like Brian Shapland exchange e-mails with their Workspace Futures colleagues on interesting articles or books. They sustain conversations as well as solve problems together. This also makes the corporate team understand that when salespeople call to ask for a pricing exception or special help with a project, it's more than just a Hail Mary pass. Corporate specialists know that salespeople have really thought deeply about the issue, identified options, and evaluated what's best for the customer and the company.

The training has not only built relationships but also broken down the hierarchy. Hackett likes to say that it flattened the organization as people became intellectually aligned. Shapland agrees: "Now I can mention to my boss that I'm going to reach out to whomever at corporate and my boss doesn't even care if I copy him on the e-mail."[31] Above all, the shared rigor and common language of CTM has encouraged corporate people to genuinely embrace opportunities to help field salespeople such as Shapland, whom they once regarded with suspicion. "They'll help you get that company jet or expedite the chair sample," Shapland adds. "Five years ago, when I called corporate I might have just said, 'I need this price to win.' I was dialing for discounts. Now I think much more broadly and really own the decision about what's best."[32]

While Hackett still isn't fully satisfied with the scope, speed, or scale of the transformation he has driven at the company over more than fifteen years since he first became CEO, there is no denying the tangible progress and forward momentum that Steelcase has achieved as a result of its conversion to the new way of thinking before acting. Hackett contrasts where the company is today with an anecdote he was e-mailed by a salesperson, Charlie Diez, when he first started teaching his Critical Thinking Model. Diez related the story of a multimillion-dollar deal he had pursued for two years and ultimately almost lost due to internal bickering and mistrust. "What we had," Charlie wrote to Hackett, "was your proverbial goat rodeo. Team members were making assumptions independently, not communicating and leaving the process without being briefed on what had transpired." Today, Hackett hears far fewer stories of swirling internal conflict and far more success stories like Brian Shapland's.

Summary: Thinking Is Everyone's Job

Thinking is a precursor to problem solving, experimentation, and implementation. Most employees at all hierarchical levels don't have a rigorous methodology to help them approach problem solving. In every organization, there's a balancing act between making customers happy, mobilizing and engaging employees, and achieving the desired results. While everybody thinks, many people lack a framework for how to think productively to solve their organization's problems, anticipate obstacles, and make tradeoffs between constituencies.

In traditional organizations, these are typically middle- or upper-management responsibilities. Frontline workers perform tasks, and when an issue obstructs routine execution, the issue is escalated up the hierarchy. Teaching the front line how to deal with these problems in real time reduces cycle time, leads to higher customer satisfaction, and may mean keeping a customer who otherwise might have defected to the competition.

As Steelcase discovered, teaching people to think for themselves and solve problems dynamically is no easy task. It's not simply overcoming the organizational tendency to look up the chain of command, or even the fear of failure, that can paralyze decision makers at any level. Teaching problem-solving skills to frontline leaders such as Brian Shapland requires first articulating an easy-to-grasp methodology for thinking about complex issues. The nature of problems that frontline personnel face and the constituencies they must address will vary by company and by industry.

Taking the methodology directly to the front line and bypassing those in the middle or at the top doesn't expedite the process, as Hackett taught us. Building a company with problem-solving capabilities at the front line requires aligning leaders at all levels, providing them with a common framework and language that accommodates different thinking styles and diverse perspectives. It also requires developing a tool kit and ensuring that resources, such as Steelcase's Workspace Futures team, support those who are deploying the methodology with customers.

In the end, whether at Steelcase or in the U.S. Navy SEALs, both stories converge on the need to train people repetitively and effectively to use good judgment under pressure—physical, psychological, or commercial. None of which happens without a considerable investment in experiential training that forces participants to use the tools, confront difficult judgments, and learn to develop contingency plans before failure happens in the field. This often means tackling the more difficult task of helping team members unlearn dangerous habits, whether failing to acknowledge when the mission will fail as a SEAL or drifting back into the comfort zone of pitching a prospective client on price at Steelcase. All of this must be taught and trained with close attention to situational nuance so that every employee is deeply schooled in using the frameworks as a reflexive thinking style.[33]

The notion of thinking before doing, or looking before you leap, is hardly novel. Yet if you reflect on what most organizations reward and recognize their employees for, it is almost always doing rather than thinking; organizations value output that requires action. It's not that Steelcase didn't value activity, but as George Wolfe told us, "the goal was to grow the importance of thinking, not shrink the importance of doing."[34]

EXPERIMENT TO INNOVATE ON THE FRONT LINE

If I had to pick one "how," it would be to install a culture of rapid experimentation because people develop judgment from making judgments—seeing the reaction, seeing what happens, then learning.

—**Scott Cook,**
founder of Intuit, speaking about how
companies develop the capability to innovate

- **FRONTLINE INNOVATION IDEAS ARE AN UNTAPPED RESERVOIR OF GROWTH POTENTIAL**

  - Frontline personnel see opportunities to create new products and services.

  - Most organizations lack a methodology for collecting and testing frontline ideas.

- **A CULTURE OF EXPERIMENTATION CREATES GROWTH AND COMMITMENT**

  - Frontline leaders grow as they put their ideas into action.

  - When employees experiment, they emotionally commit to their customers and coworkers.

"**O**ur inspiration came from *Iron Man 2*," explained Islam Sharabash before theatrically asking the crowd in the room, "Who saw that?" Responding to the raised hands and fast nods, he seamlessly segued to the next phase of a surprisingly polished pitch on the AirChalk application for Facebook that he and his brother Hani, both computer science majors at the University of Illinois, had dreamed up less than a day earlier. "So you saw the court scene where Iron Man whips out his phone and starts controlling stuff? We wanted to do that because it was awesome."[1]

Less than a day earlier, the Sharabash brothers had flown to Facebook headquarters to compete as finalists in one of the social networking juggernaut's legendary hackathons; a twenty-four- to forty-eight-hour Red Bull–infused programming fest featuring around-the-clock highly technical work aimed at taking nascent ideas and turning them into prototypes of new products in real time. It's a fast and furious product-development and innovation method Facebook founder Mark Zuckerberg reportedly adopted after talking to a couple of software engineers on a Saturday afternoon over lunch at Silicon Valley watering hole Gordon Biersch.[2] Since then it has become an integral part of Facebook's culture, occurring annually, and has even spread globally. But the hackathon in which the Sharabash brothers had been invited to participate was the first organized strictly for outsiders, with the gold medal being a sought-after internship at Facebook and an opportunity to test their ideas at the company.

Hackathons have been embraced by any number of technology firms as a way to optimize frontline employees' contributions or crowdsource ideas, but in our view Facebook's formula has turned these geek festivals into a particularly powerful component of the company's ongoing success. They are used to free up ideas, encourage employee engagement, and continuously reinforce the company's culture. As Zuckerberg has explained:

> We want to make sure that everyone can come and add their ideas. . . .
> Some of the best ideas throughout the company's evolution . . . have [come]
> from places all throughout the company, whether it's an engineer or
> someone on the customer support team or different areas around the
> company. So we've always had these hackathons, which are basically time
> that we allocate . . . the only rule [being] that you don't work on what you
> work on the rest of the time. It's an incubator for people to prototype
> different ideas, much in the spirit of how Facebook got founded originally.
> You can build anything good in a day.[3]

Such signature Facebook features as the iPhoto plug-in, which lets users tag and share pictures, Facebook Chat, and video messaging all had their start as hackathon projects. But for the first-ever university competition, the question remained how readily outsiders would adapt to what had formerly been a purely internal exercise. Facebook coordinator Paul Tarjan opened the session with a video in which he juggled, unicycled, and performed a multitude of other tricks before inviting the Sharabash brothers to face off against four other teams hailing from Berkeley, the University of Texas, the University of Wisconsin, and Georgia Tech.

After sitting patiently through presentations by the three other teams, Islam Sharabash promisingly kicked off his tag-team presentation by saying that what he and his brother had developed was "essentially a virtual whiteboard. You can go anywhere, use your phone, and interact with any screen." As Hani waved his phone in the air like Robert Downey Jr.'s character Iron Man, a line appeared on the screen behind Islam. Zigzagging across the screen, the line turned colors from black to blue to green. Handing the phone off to his brother, Hani quickly explained the technical specifications, with only a brief pause to try to recall all of the "trendy, cool" technologies they had integrated while creating their prototype in the wee hours of the morning. "We want to show you one more application that we think is cool," said Hani. "If you have it on a Web page, you can use the phone as a wand to draw on any screen. The idea is that you can use any display, even displays that are currently nontouchable. You walk into a movie theater and what do you see? You see this huge display. You can't touch that, you can't control that . . . but now you can. We want to make this so it tracks to your fingertip so you can start manipulating objects on any screen."

"The really mind-blowing thing," Islam exulted, "is that this can be collaborative. You're sharing a screen. You want to point out something in our presentation and you whip out your phone and manipulate it, draw something, or you switch a page. This will become the next interface for interaction. In the future you can start doing 3-D manipulations. . . . You walk into a movie theater and you can control the screen with interactive advertising, or maybe there's a car-racing game you play with other people before the movie trailers start."

"I especially like this application," Hani continued, "because it makes everything touchable. If you have this on a Facebook Web page, you just hold up your phone and start moving your finger and you can start swiping through your photos or touch a button for 'like' it. It's a new way to interact." Gearing up for the big photo finish, the brothers scrolled down the screen to reveal a tiny icon with the "like it" function from their own Facebook page.

Before they were even aware of the time flying by, the Sharabash brothers had finished their presentation and Paul Tarjan stopped the clock. After one more presentation, all activity in the room came to an abrupt halt and the Face-book leaders evaluating the teams' presentations briefly excused themselves. Shortly afterward, Mark Zuckerberg returned, accompanied by two other judges, Mike Schroepfer, Facebook's VP of engineering, and Kate Aronowitz, director of design, and launched into the feedback process. Even the feedback cycles are compressed in a hackathon. Zuckerberg and his colleagues spent three minutes or less with each team, quickly dissecting their respective strong points and Achilles' heels. He started by congratulating the team from the University of Texas at Austin, which had presented first, for trying to make a game out of real-life activities. Yet he made it clear from the outset that theirs was not the team taking home the prize. "You know, the bummer is that you didn't ship anything," Zuckerberg said, meaning that the team had not created a working product. "That's the only rule of hackathon. You have to ship some-thing. So I guess that's the feedback I'd give you for next time."

By the time the group came to the Sharabash brothers, there wasn't a clear front-runner. Zuckerberg commenced his critique of the University of Illinois presentation with some encouragingly positive feedback. "I thought that was awesome. It's clearly a pretty challenging technical problem. . . . I also like *Iron Man 2,* so I'm there with you. I thought it was really cool that you had a vision for how this could play out in the future."

Adding a moment of tension, Zuckerberg momentously lowered his voice. "But it wasn't clear to me how you were going to make that social until you broke out that two people could draw at the same time. Then I figured you were going to have something where you could invite your friends to it and be modifying something at the same time. But you didn't do that; you just did the like. But it's all good. It's only twenty-four hours. Overall, very impressive."

With no apparent sense of intended irony or humor, Zuckerberg con-cluded by announcing that it had taken ten minutes—an eternity by his measure—for the panel judges to come to a decision because they were so impressed by all of the teams' work. With no pomp or circumstance, Zuck-erberg announced that "we thought the best one was done by the brothers from UIUC. So congrats, guys." As he handed the Sharabash brothers a crystal plaque—with, as Zuckerberg described it, "some sort of hack thing" etched into it—everyone enthusiastically applauded the victors. Formally concluding the ceremony, Tarjan announced to the group, "Thank you very much. . . . You are now allowed to go and sleep."

Frontline Innovation Models

In this chapter we will explore step 3 of our process for building a front line–focused organization. In this step we move beyond problem solving, with its emphasis on improving the business's status quo processes or service experience, and move to how organizations can actively tap into frontline creativity to generate innovation. Innovation, typically defined as the process for finding, making, and generating something new,[4] is pursued by virtually every organization as a necessity for staying alive in today's ever-changing world. There are a multitude of well-documented challenges to building a robust innovation process. Companies must ensure that they are generating a steady supply of creative ideas, find ways to capture and screen those ideas, and then take them from concept to commercialization.

In many industries, innovation has been the sole province of centralized research-and-development organizations. Other organizations use dedicated cross-functional teams or venture boards to generate or screen innovations. Regardless of the mechanisms deployed, however, nearly every company feels that it does a poor job of successfully tapping into its organizational reservoir of creative ideas. In our clinical work we frequently hear the refrain "We devote X percent of our revenues to research" or "We have thousands of people," so why don't we generate more good ideas?

Our intent isn't to tackle innovation in its entirety—others have done that in greater depth and detail elsewhere—but rather to look more specifically at how innovation comes from the front line. We agree with the all-too-common executive lament that most organizations do a poor job of listening to their front line, encouraging them to innovate, and providing the infrastructure for them to do it well. As we observed in chapter 2, the front line may not conceive of entirely new strategies for the organization, but they are capable of generating breakthrough product improvements. And as we saw in chapter 1 with the Amazon shopping cart example, these incremental innovations frequently pave the way for emerging product categories and service offerings.

A Culture of Experimentation

The companies that we have examined and worked with that are best at frontline innovation embed it in their organizational culture by linking it explicitly to their core values. They make innovation a part of each person's job, often articulating this expectation in the organizational values defined during step 2 of our process. So that it doesn't become empty rhetoric, however, these companies also provide structure, resources, and opportunity for frontline employees to explore their ideas, test them in the market, and refine their innovations based on customer learning. This requires a balancing act between dedicating frontline energy to creating something new and executing today's business model.

At Facebook, hackathons are emblematic of the company's deeply experimental culture because they

1. Focus on Impact: The ultimate goal of a hackathon is to produce something that actually works. This is an opportunity for programmers and developers to scratch that creative itch that they don't have time to address during the normal workweek. But it's not just for fun. Unless the idea works in application, it can't be a winner.

2. Move Fast: Twenty-four hours seems like an impossibly tight time frame to accomplish much of anything useful. However, one of the designers who was responsible for creating Facebook video shared, "As we were watching our engineering culture take shape, we found that some of the best products that we've ever shipped arose from just a single night's effort." The time pressure of a hackathon develops focus and teaches people to avoid overthinking solutions.

3. Require Boldness: Hackathons invite employees to take risks and be creative. They require healthy doses of self-confidence and guts to commit to turning a great idea into a working application overnight. While there are no penalties for failure, the kudos go to those who dream big and execute crisply.

These characteristics make hackathons the most tangible proof of the company values Zuckerberg has extolled on numerous occasions, ones that he proudly proclaims are as integral to the organization's DNA as any other aspect of his legacy. They serve not only as a cultural reinforcement but also as a release valve for any latent creativity pent up in Facebook's exceptionally talented employees. This is truly the resident genius of hackathons.

Business as usual at the company tends to be focused on its core mission to help people share information, control information, and stay connected to the people they care about. The company deliberately and carefully keeps employees focused on executing ideas that tie to the company's plans for new features and products. Of course, Facebook employees are free to tinker on the side. Unlike Google and 3M, however, Facebook doesn't have a "20 percent policy" that allocates employee time to a research project of the employee's choice. Zuckerberg has said, "It's not like everybody has their own pet project that they're working on and we're going to have seventy-eight different products in beta, and we'll see what works."[5]

In this sense, hackathons become the means by which the new developer or longtime programmer can share a vision for a new product with the management team. Many Facebook employees are sold on the company because they have an entrepreneurial, creative drive and want to have an impact on the next Facebook features that will—or so the leadership hopes—help to keep the company from being overtaken in the innovation challenge by some as-yet-unknown nimble interloper. Ultimately and most important, hackathons serve as a powerful mechanism for Facebook to continue to attract the software industry's top talent. As Zuckerberg says, "the best people want to go to the place where they can have the biggest impact."[6] Stories of new frontline developers creating features now accessed daily by millions upon millions of users are deeply embedded in a corporate culture that reinforces at every turn the notion that everyone—from Zuckerberg to a frontline employee—can have a lasting impact on the firm's future.

Providing Structure for Innovation

As both academics and practitioners have documented extensively, unleashing creativity does not mean encouraging a free-for-all. On the contrary, as expectations for employees expand to include a broader pool and extend deeper into the hierarchy, it becomes imperative that innovation activities be conducted with focus and structure. Building a frontline innovation strategy requires, first and foremost, answering three fundamental questions:

1. **Innovation Area:** Should the front line focus on improving products, business processes, or both?

2. **Activity Locus:** Where will innovation activities actually occur? Will the front line put ideas into practice or simply pass their ideas on to others who will perform implementation?

3. **Experimentation Methodology:** What is the methodology for screening and testing good ideas?

We will discuss each of these in turn in more detail below.

Innovation Area: Should the Front Line Focus on Improving Products, Business Processes, or Both?

The first consideration for a frontline innovation strategy is whether the front line can contribute ideas related to *business processes, products, or both*. Since frontline employees are by definition those who not only interact with customers but also use front-end systems, policies, and procedures every day, they tend to be the most knowledgeable about what works in practice and what doesn't. They can identify ways to effectively reduce costs, speed processes, or develop alternative work methods.

Frontline customer interaction also provides incredible insight into customer segments that may be underserved by existing products and services, ways of better promoting products, or entirely new ideas for product features or categories. Two brief examples below from consumer electronics retailer Best Buy demonstrate the differences.[7]

Business-Process Innovation

Best Buy is one of the largest consumer electronics retailers in the world, with more than 3,400 stores and nearly 170,000 employees. Among its ongoing challenges—which include fending off lower-cost Internet retailers and declining consumer appetite for many of its higher-margin electronics products—is that in metropolitan locations, high rents typically dictate smaller stores, which in turn must carry a more limited inventory than a big-box store at a mall in the suburbs. While Best Buy has had great success with its smaller Manhattan stores, which are typically less than half the size of their suburban counterparts, a persistent lack of shelf and warehouse space has over the years led to consumer dissatisfaction with the frequency of out-of-stock products and limited product ranges.

Determined to do something tangible about the resulting customer frustration and subsequent lost sales, a district team identified an unused space that Best Buy owned in nearby Long Island. The empty facility had been used as a dumping ground and was piled high with discarded equipment, furniture, and building materials. By rallying hourly employees to lend a hand, the warehouse manager was able to clean and paint the converted warehouse and install shelving, desks, and a security system for less than five thousand dollars.

Creating an additional six thousand square feet of storage would have had a substantial financial impact. However, the Best Buy team did not stop there. Several stores had already been experimenting with same-day delivery service in Manhattan. Store personnel benchmarked the competition, met with delivery companies, and devised a pricing strategy. The customer-value proposition was simple: For less than forty dollars Best Buy would deliver any product to your home in less than four hours. In New York City, where many people don't own cars, this meant that customers would no longer have to bother a friend or struggle with their newly purchased television on the subway.

The benefits of same-day delivery actually extended further. Since the company has a transparent inventory system that lets employees see all product inventory in the warehouse and local stores, if a customer couldn't find a product in one store, they could have it delivered from another store or the warehouse without having to make the trip to a faraway location or wait several days for delivery from the Best Buy Web site.

This one team's innovation was able to pay for the warehouse conversion with the margin it made on delivery while also creating a new source of revenue and delighting the customers it had previously frustrated.

Product Innovation

The frontline judgment displayed by the New York warehouse manager and his colleagues is equally applicable to product or service offerings. For example, Scott Reams, a district manager for the company in Florida, had been working with his store managers and personnel looking for growth opportunities. A number of frontline associates had noticed that many high-end television and GPS purchases had come from customers who owned marine vehicles. Reams and his team had benefited from the company's commitment to teach all employees about both the business and customer segmentation. Using this knowledge, they began asking fundamental questions about the size of the population of recreational boat owners in U.S. coastal areas and how much they typically spent on gadgetry for their marine craft.

The team's business acumen led them to discover that over two billion dollars of marine accessories are sold every year in the United States and that more than half of that total expenditure is specifically devoted to consumer electronics purchases or service, of which Best Buy's share was less than 1 percent. This market was even more intriguing because many of these expenditures were made by relatively affluent owners of twenty-eight- to forty-foot boats that they were committed to maintaining in tip-top shape. This was a market historically served by small chains or, more frequently, mom-and-pop nautical-supply stores. A further appeal of this market was that it was highly concentrated on the country's coastline or in cities near inland lakes, which made it much more cost-effective to manage inventory. Putting the entire picture together, Reams's team was convinced that they had discovered an opportunity for the company that had a hundred-million-dollar potential.

Activity Locus: Where Will Innovation Activities Actually Occur?

The second key consideration is *where* the innovation action actually takes place. Most organizations don't fail at idea generation; the real challenge is putting ideas into practice.[8] Some companies prefer heavily decentralized models, where individuals work virtually autonomously. Google and 3M are two companies that have historically provided their engineers and researchers with up to 20 percent of their time to work on a project of their choice. Famous innovations such as 3M's Post-it notes or Google's orkut and AdSense[9] owe their genesis to individuals or small teams pursuing their private passions during their 20 percent free time at work.

Other organizations, such as Facebook, prefer tighter constraints and more directive focus for innovation activities. Some hackathons, for example, are aimed at improving specific features. Still other organizations utilize intermediaries who act as conduits between the front line and management to screen and test new ideas. In their simplest form these groups serve as internal venture boards that assess the feasibility and potential value of new ideas and then make decisions about whether or not to invest. In their more complex formulations, as at California-based software company Intuit, there may also be groups composed of full-time employees who not only collect ideas but actively test them.

Experimentation Methodology: What Is the Methodology for Screening and Testing Good Ideas?

The third and final consideration in building a frontline innovation strategy is the methodology for determining whether an idea is worth pursuing or not. As the locus of innovation is pushed closer to the customer interface, it becomes increasingly difficult to effectively screen ideas via conventional management controls. Individual leaders or review committees can be quickly overwhelmed by the volume of ideas generated in companies with large numbers of employees. The crux of the innovation problem in many companies is that when senior management approval is required for innovation, those managers' time is such a scarce commodity that they tend to focus on *bigger* ideas as opposed to *better* ones. Similarly, since they are further removed from the work being done at the front line, they tend to rely more on financial hurdle rates[10] and their business intuition rather than good analytics to make judgment calls.

By contrast, local employees can act quickly and nimbly to implement changes. The difficulty is that in most organizations the frontline employees have no reliable methodology for testing their ideas. Unless they have been taught the business, and unless they have ways to test the results of implementing their ideas, they are trapped in watercooler conversations about how they would change things if they were in charge.

Let's look at the Best Buy marine innovation as one example of what a frontline team can do with a robust innovation methodology. The process used at Best Buy for testing innovations was rooted in the scientific method[11] and asked the frontline leaders to answer the following questions:

1. *What* is the problem statement in one or two sentences that captures the unsatisfactory financial performance?

2. *How* are operational metrics affecting the overall financial perfor-mance?

3. *Why* are the operational metrics not where they need to be as a result of behaviors or processes?

For Scott Reams and the team working on the Best Buy marine initia-tive, the answers to these questions were as follows:

1. *What* is the problem? Answer: Significant missed revenue oppor-tunity in Miami store locations as a result of not effectively target-ing marine customers.

2. *How* are metrics affecting store performance? Answer: Average sales price and units per transaction with the marine customer segment are lower than they should be.

3. *Why* are the operational metrics not what they should be? Answer: We don't recognize this segment when they come in the stores, fail to probe their marine needs, and don't carry the right product mix to serve them.

Once these questions had been satisfactorily answered, the teams were prepared to construct an experiment. To do so, the teams were asked to identify a hypothesis, test it, and verify the results. These are the guidelines implemented at Best Buy:

- **Hypothesis:** Describe what you would do, over what time period, and the expected results.
- **Test:** Explain in detail who will do what by when in order to test the hypothesis.
- **Verify:** Detail the overall result expected at the end of the test, as well as the week-by-week milestones. Verification should be tied to the operational metrics highlighted in the *How*.

As noted above, the results of the Best Buy test were spectacular, with store personnel in selected Florida stores able to increase customer satisfac-tion and average sales to these marine customers. However, devising a methodology for experimentation is about more than simply hitting the numbers. An explicit framework for innovation and experimentation that everyone knows and that is shared throughout the organization can posi-tively transform a culture. It enables dialogue and helps employees form seemingly crazy ideas or partial thoughts into serious work. It is also a cul-tural antidote to the HiPPO problem cited in chapter 1.

The reason that the HiPPO dominates many organizations is that most companies lack sufficient data on which to make good judgments. It doesn't matter where you are in the hierarchy—at the CEO level or watching a Mc-Donald's franchisee deal with his staff. Typically, senior managers assume that generating the required data will take too much time or money, so the preferred method is to rely on the wise leader of the group. An experimentation methodology puts control back in the hands of employees, provided crafting the test isn't outrageously expensive or too onerous. For most experiments, an energized employee who is able to recruit a few coworkers to help is able to see whether an idea will work in practice. Since the format is consistent, once the test has been run, it is easy for an employee and manager to have a discussion about the results and intelligent next steps. The manager's intuitive judgment about whether an idea is stupid no longer carries much weight.

Such results-based experimentation, whether utilizing the scientific method, A/B testing as we saw at Amazon,[12] or hackathons as at Facebook, is always preferable to intuition. A difficulty in implementing this is that it requires employees to be trained in the methodology and leaders to be trained to change their behavior so they foster frontline innovation. Organizations that fail to make this investment may create pockets of innovation but never change their culture.

The process of using experimentation to break down hierarchy and give freedom to good ideas can be both exhilarating and exigent. Even famously innovative companies, such as oft-celebrated Intuit, frequently cited by the business media for its ingenuity, have only recently unleashed the power of experimentation by engaging broad numbers of employees. This is a recent phenomenon, due in part to new technology that has greatly eased the process of collecting, reviewing, and screening hundreds of individual ideas. However, we find that the most important variable in determining whether an organization pursues frontline innovation is the senior leadership team's willingness to embrace an experimentation philosophy and data-based judgment process. We will explore Intuit's experience and the lessons learned as it has built an experimentation culture in recent years.

Leadership by Experimentation at Intuit

In 1983, Scott Cook hit conceptual pay dirt after observing the intensity of his wife's aversion to the monthly routine of balancing the family checkbook. The California-based tax and financial software company he founded, Intuit, has a long history of customer focus and innovation. For the first few decades of its life, Cook's company thrived on the individual creativity that the founding team brought to the challenge of meeting consumer needs, based largely on learning Cook drew from his time at Harvard Business School mixed with his experience in the consulting industry and with consumer goods powerhouse Procter & Gamble. Innovation techniques included "follow me homes" in which Intuit personnel watched product users in their natural work environment—much as an anthropologist might do—scrupulously noting hassles and annoyances to remedy or new product features that would powerfully enhance the customer experience.

The company's entrepreneurial roots and nimble attentiveness to customer needs has enabled it to grow from a one-trick pony offering only its staple Quicken personal-finance software to a multiproduct, international corporation serving individuals, accounting professionals, and businesses through a suite of software and Web-based services. Its early foundation for growth was based on what Cook called "customer-driven invention." As he explains, customer-driven invention occurs after the company defines "an important customer problem that's still unsolved. We solve it so well and make changes so profound that customers can't imagine going back to the old way. If you do that, the financials tend to take care of themselves."[13]

Yet it was only after watching his ten-year-old son play at a Little League baseball practice did the realization dawn on him that after nearly three decades of growth, customer-driven invention was no longer sufficient for Intuit to continue conquering the growth curve. The company required something profound to occur that would fundamentally transform the creative relationship between employees and bosses at the company. Cook recently recalled,[14]

> I'm terrible at sports so I didn't coach, I just watched. But I observed that those kids were getting more frequent and closer coaching than we give our employees. The kid did something—threw a ball, caught a ball, ran for a fly—and then the coach would coach them on what they just tried to do. And I tried to figure out why was it that in Little League much better coaching goes on than in most businesses. In a single practice, every one of these kids would get multiple points of feedback on their own performance. Live! Right during and after the performance.

As Cook pondered this intriguing phenomenon from the sidelines, he came to the conclusion that Little League coaching was infinitely superior to the dynamic between bosses and employees at Intuit—and, indeed, in business in general—"because in Little League, the coaches can never take the field. The coach never bats, never pitches, never fields." In business, by contrast, the coaches, or bosses "take the field all the time. The boss will sweep in and make the decision."[15] It was in that moment that Cook resolved to "run [my] business closer to the way Little League is run—where your goal as a leader is to enable your people, and to set it up so they are fielding a lot of grounders, and so they are making the decisions that you can coach them on. And that's easiest to do with entry-level people."[16]

This was the genesis of a powerful frontline strategy that Cook also regarded as a means of attracting and retaining top talent in an industry that is heavily reliant on its people's brainpower to generate organic growth. The innovation-rich environment that Cook envisioned was based on the simple observation that people simultaneously feel best about their work and most committed to their organization when given the opportunity to act on their creativity. Enabling this, however, meant geometrically multiplying the number of experiments that Intuit undertook each year to drive growth. As Cook told us,

> Great people want to take their ideas and make them real. They want to learn from their ideas, not from their boss preaching at them. If you're in a division where you've got thirty people and you run two experiments a year, what are the odds that your idea will actually see the light of day? Somewhere between slim and none. But if you're in a group with thirty people and you run one hundred sixty-five experiments a year, now what are the odds? If you get a chance to iterate through real experiments, how do you feel? Which place would you want to work? If you're smart and entrepreneurial—the kind of people we want—you're not going to work in the first environment. You'll leave.[17]

Making Everyone a Genius at Intuit

Over nearly three decades, Intuit had adopted varied approaches to innovation, including enabling engineers and product managers to commit 10 percent of their work week to special projects they select—a model famously embraced by Google. The company has also maintained a work environment that remains fiercely committed to supporting individual initiative. The result of these efforts has been such employee-generated product ideas as the Medical Expense Manager, which an employee cooked up based on his personal distress coping with the complexity of dealing with the health-care charges following his son's heart surgery.

But only after observing his son at play on the ball field did Cook coalesce a vision of fostering the elusive gift of innovation by turning all of his people into "geniuses." When speaking more generally about nurturing innovation at technology firms, Cook frequently refers to five different models he has observed playing out over the years across the business landscape. The first is the lone genius ready and able to invent by himself—the rare

Steve Jobs of the world. The second model is "the boss as genius," in which the organization relies for its ideas on the collective brainpower of those at the top. The third option is to copy what competitors do; a fourth is to "cluster all of the geniuses in a lab" so they can conduct research and development for you. But the fifth choice—and the one that, not surprisingly, Cook prefers and has systematically built into his own business model—is to "make your people the geniuses." Only this last model, he believes, is sustainable over the long haul and, even more critical, effective in creating a culture of innovation across the firm.

"Our theory is that you should enable a lot of your employees—not just a small group—to invent business ideas or product features," Cook maintains, based on his own considerable experience. "If we build a great environment, a great place to work, and teach our people the skills of invention, only then do they create the kind of life-changing inventions that delight customers. And only in that way can we deliver the sustained profitable growth that delights our shareholders."[18]

Creating and sustaining such a free flow of ideas was part of the motivation behind a system implemented two years ago called Brainstorm, which enables anyone in the company to enter a business idea into the system in three to four minutes. Most of those ideas are entered by people at the working levels, not senior leaders, Cook proudly points out. Brainstorm has created an online innovation community that encompasses the entire

---

SCOTT COOK'S MODELS
FOR ORGANIZATIONAL INNOVATION

Option 1: Lone Genius
Find the single visionary who can guide your organization (think Steve Jobs)

Option 2: Boss as Genius
Rely on the top management to have all of the answers

Option 3: Copy Others' Genius
Figure out how to copy what others invent

Option 4: Cluster the Geniuses
Put your smartest people in the R&D center

Option 5: Make Everyone a Genius
Develop everybody's ability to initiate and test improvement ideas

company. As ideas are entered, other people comment on them, adding their own ideas or making edits. "The ideas morph, build, and grow all through the work of people at the working levels," Cook explains. "Then teams self-organize and self-assemble to start fleshing out and building these ideas—all with no management involved."[19]

In its first year, Brainstorm generated thirty-two ideas that were incorporated into products that shipped out to customers, ranging from product features to entirely new products. Cook informed us with visible satisfaction that in its second year, over five thousand ideas were entered into Brainstorm. The best part, he added, was that the system had been invented by two recent college graduates who had joined the company only four months earlier:

> They looked at how we processed ideas and managed it inside the company and they said, "That sucks, we can do better." And they were right; they built something much better. And we didn't have to force it into people's hands. It just spread through the company once the guys had built it.[20]

Part of the reason Cook is so quick to reel off Brainstorm statistics is the newfound love for experimentation and measurement that he has fostered throughout the company. In fact, by Cook's account, the single greatest accelerant of Intuit's innovation culture in recent years has been this focused approach to conducting business experiments that engage all employees at all levels. Cook told us, "If I had to pick one 'how,' it would be to install a culture of rapid experimentation, because people develop judgment from making judgments—seeing the reaction, seeing what happens—and then learning."[21]

Cook's approach is to engage everyone in the process of experimentation and then let the data do the talking. He straightforwardly refers to this as "leadership by experiment" or "decision making by hypothesis testing." Yet implementing this science-based approach required unlearning many habits that he and his senior colleagues had unwittingly accumulated over years of being the boss. As Cook explained to us, unlearning these habits unleashed a radical rethinking of what constitutes leadership.

> Most people think—and most bosses agree—that their role is to decide. Their role is to be like Caesar at the Colosseum—to give a thumbs-up or thumbs-down to every idea. My father, who's ninety-one now, learned leadership in the Second World War as a junior officer. For him, leaders are those who framed all the options, who made the choice and then told everybody what to do. Imagine Eisenhower, planning and then managing the D-Day invasion.[22]

In Cook's view, command and control was perfectly suited to managing the Normandy invasion or the conquest of Nazi-occupied Europe. But he challenges corporate leaders today to think of Thomas Edison as a better role model and encourages them to embrace the process of running experiments to find the answer instead of relying on the boss's ability to hierarchically impose an answer.

Cook is convinced that to drive a culture of experimentation, leaders at all levels throughout the company need to be thoroughly trained in applying the scientific method, in how to build rapid prototypes, and in how to learn from actual user data. Cook is ready and willing to concede that such experiments don't always have the highest level of rigor or the greatest sample size. However, he is equally quick to point out that any level of experimentation with reasonable methodology is a significant improvement over "zero experimentation, zero scientific method, no real learning. Compared to that desert of learning, a few drops of water are quite an improvement."[23]

As an example, Cook points to a team working on a new business idea. (He would only advise us cryptically that in this case, his people are "going after 'nonconsumption' in a novel way.") The previous process—before the advent of leadership by experimentation at Intuit—would have been for the market researchers to interview customers and then take up to a year to construct a prototype product. But since the advent of the experimental method at Intuit, "This team built one screen of the real offering they had planned. . . . And they didn't build it as they had planned; they built it as a Web-based concept rather than an app because it was faster and cheaper and they could do it in two to three weeks."[24] The team had three live users, all of whom continued using it and interfaced in ways that provided ideas for iterating a better product. "Now you'll never get statistical significance out of three users, but if zero of those users keep using it, that tells you something too."

Not just for product launches, experimentation reinforces launching entire businesses at Intuit. When the company wanted to launch a major product push in India—where the company historically had software-development and call-center employees but no customers—the business leader in charge of the region didn't go to market with a prepackaged strategy. Instead, as Cook recalled, the leader in India told his scant team to run experiments to figure out what business Intuit could build in the country. His managerial direction with a team composed of mostly entry-level programmers boiled down to "Let's run fast and cheap experiments."

In the first eighteen months in India, Intuit tested thirteen entirely different businesses that were identified by employees as having the greatest promise. In as little as four weeks, the teams mocked up, coded, and launched some of these ideas. Of the thirteen, ten failed. "I look at that and say that's good news and more good news," says Cook, "because we had three winners out of that, and we had ten things from which we could free up valuable people and time without wasting a year or two on something that would ultimately fail. We could redeploy them to other, better ideas."[25] As Intuit continues to develop its strategy in India, Cook notes, it will be iterated through the process of fast, cheap experiments.

Cook's affinity for experimentation is based in part on his mounting and increasingly confirmed conviction that running experiments develops employees who learn to make increasingly better judgments about customer needs, which product features are essential, and which businesses are most likely to succeed. "If you want somebody to make good business judgments in handling customers or in modifying a production process," he says, "if they have lots of practice running experiments and they've tried lots of things, they have a better sense for what works and what doesn't. Rapid experimentation can perfect and build their judgment through trial and learning."[26]

Cook contrasts this approach to leadership with his own managerial upbringing. Before adopting this method, Intuit relied on analysis and the boss's judgment rather than engaging employees in live testing. "We were in the mode that the boss made the decision based on a lot of analysis," Cook explains. "Yes, we always listened to customers well and we would expose things, but we weren't really running scientific experiments. We were still thinking we could analyze our way to success. I mean, I'm an ex-consultant. Old habits die hard."

In fact, while Cook says there was no single defining moment that caused him to change decades of managerial beliefs, he readily speaks about one experience on his proverbial road to Damascus.[27] Cook gleefully shares the story of how a young product manager, Catherine, worked around him to bring Intuit's QuickBooks software to the retail industry. Historically, QuickBooks had the lowest penetration in retail despite the fact that it was an enormous business opportunity, with many regional chains or mom-and-pop stores that needed it.

Catherine and another product manager followed Intuit's customer disciplines carefully, conducting "follow me home" visits to different types of retail stores. When they returned to Cook, they explained that the big problem to be solved for retailers was not a backroom accounting issue but rather an issue at the front of the store with their point-of-sale systems. Many retailers, Catherine noted, couldn't keep track of their inventory, out-of-stocks, and product orders. They had difficult point-of-sale systems that were purchased through resellers and temperamental to use, particularly for untrained employees in an industry that has one of the highest turnover rates in the world. "Why don't we make something so simple that the retailer can buy it in a box and install it themselves for a fraction of the price?" Catherine and her colleague asked. Cook loved the idea.

During the process of building it and test-driving it with potential sales outlets, however, the buyer at Staples objected. "That's not the right idea," he told them, noting that customers would need to not only buy Intuit's software but also assemble all of the hardware themselves: the cash drawer, the UPC scanner, the receipt printer, the credit-card reader. "Why do you want to force all that work on the poor small retailer? Why don't you put all that stuff in a box so the retailer can get a complete solution, just add a PC?" he asked.

When Catherine came back with the idea, "I did exactly the thing that I rail against today," Cook says. "I did exactly the thing that kills innovation, kills new ideas, and kills success."[28] In the meeting, Cook ticked off objections with a forcefulness that left no doubt about where he stood on the issue. "Hardware?!" he said. "We're a high-margin software company! Hardware is gritty and dirty; you've got obsolescence, repairs, warranty. Leave that to other companies!"

Instead, Catherine and her colleagues listened attentively to Cook's objections as he listed them one after another. "They figured out a way to work around every one of them. They figured out how to do the hardware on consignment so we never own it; repairs will be done by vendors; all we do is stick it in a box and sell it," Cook recalls. Seeing that the team had dissected his objections, Cook relented on the condition that they went to market with two options: one with the software only, and another hardware-and-software bundle that ultimately sold for twice the price. The sales results spoke for themselves: 60 percent of the units were in the hardware-and-software bundle, which translated into 80 percent of the revenue and 90 percent of the profits.

Cook recalls, "Putting this all in one SKU? I never would have done it. This business would have been a flop if they'd listened to me and, because they didn't, it's the number one selling point-of-sale system in the country."

Compare and contrast that story with Cook's description of the role of senior leaders at Intuit today:

> The boss's role is to champion some grand challenge, some ideal outcome, some change in the world you'd love to see—that's step one. Step two is to install systems so that your teams can rapidly run cheap experiments on how to get to that grand outcome, how to solve that global challenge, and then make it safe for those experiments to fail.

Coping with the frequency of failure has been one of the most difficult cultural challenges that Cook and his people have had to overcome at

Intuit. Cook openly tells people that most experiments are going to fail, and that is fine as long as employees are harvesting the learning from those failures. "Every failed experiment means there is something we didn't know when we started," he says. While successful experiments obviously prompt people to keep moving forward, failed experiments challenge people to figure out what didn't work, why, and how to iterate it into something that will win. "I think it is important to start by saying that you want such a velocity of experiments that you know most will fail," Cook says.

To reinforce his acceptance of failure as an outcome, Cook has gone so far as to give out "failure awards" as a form of positive recognition for failed experiments that prompted deep learning. Despite this, it has been hard to get people to embrace failure. "The tendency in organizations is to act like you already knew," says Cook. "Then there's no learning. You want to show the boss that you were on top of it. Let's not fib; let's treat a surprise as a surprise."

To combat such managerial bravado, Cook has one modus operandi in meetings and suggests the same for other leaders. "I teach teams and leaders to savor the surprise," he says. "I ask what was surprising or unexpected. Let's harvest what didn't fit our preexisting beliefs because that's where the learning is." By focusing on learning as a desirable outcome, Cook is able to remind people that there is success in failure. He goes so far as to counter the blasé, know-it-all manager by reminding him that if there is no surprise, there is no learning; the experiment has simply confirmed what was already known. "People start forgetting the fact that [the experiment] didn't work like they expected and start reveling in what they learned that was beyond their expectations."

The environment of learning and probing for unexpected answers that comes from experimentation also changes the nature of the day in, day out coaching discussions and boss-employee interactions. Rather than play the imperial boss, leaders at Intuit are expected to create systems that make it easy for employees to test their ideas. With team-based, collaborative experimentation, managers can't impose their views or do the work themselves. They have to truly coach and help their people develop the skills to build a good experiment, harvest the learning, or iterate their way to success.

Summary: Unleashing Innovation at the Front Line

Some of the greatest organizational payoffs for customers, employees, and shareholders occur when companies are able to engage their rank and file in innovation and experimentation. In its simplest form, enabling employees to contribute ideas demonstrates that they have a voice in making their organizations better. But we advocate moving far beyond the suggestion-box mentality that has permeated many businesses. Rather than simply ask for ideas, many of which will never be carefully considered, leaders need to provide targets in the form of real customer problems, whether products or business processes, so that employees know how they can have the most impact. To paraphrase Intuit's Cook, leaders need to provide that ambitious challenge and then offer the support to let employees creatively solve the problem.

Doing so requires an investment in building a shared approach for testing the quality of an idea and putting that into practice in a manner consistent with organizational values. There are numerous methodologies that can be deployed, as we have seen through the examples of Intuit, Best Buy, Amazon, and Facebook. As with problem-solving frameworks, we find that the specific methodology takes a backseat to senior leadership's commitment to deploy it at the front line and align its use at all levels of an organization.

Used correctly, experimentation, particularly in industries where the cost of experiments is low, provides a radically different engagement model for frontline workers. Rather than see their ideas rejected out of hand or arbitrarily taken away from them by higher-ups for implementation, employees can have a direct hand in crafting real-life solutions. In the process of solving problems, they learn about customers and the business, refining their judgment capability. Experimentation is also an antidote to the HiPPO problem, as it breaks down a leader's reliance on position power and gut intuition. Armed with hard data, employees at any level are able to demonstrate they can be just as smart and perhaps possess even more market insight than the managers above them.

6

BREAKING DOWN THE HIERARCHY

Being a doctor kind of trumps all the caregivers in the healthcare system according to the conventional, old school mentality. . . . The doctors and specialists come by, and they make their rounds, but the average patient is in their bed being assessed and monitored by a nurse. That's the sharp end of health care: that nurse at the bedside. They're held responsible; that's the first line of detection; the first line of protection when the patient's condition deteriorates. . . . But what if there's tension [between the nurse and doctor] about what's the right clinical decision? What's the process for those at the sharp end of health-care—our nurses—when the standard process isn't working?

—**Dr. Richard Zimmerman,**
associate professor of neurosurgery at the Mayo Clinic in Arizona

- **REDUCING HIERARCHY LIBERATES FRONTLINE CAPACITY**

  - Hierarchies proliferate rules and bureaucracy that bog down the front line.

  - Liberating frontline capacity provides more time for thinking and innovation.

- **HIERARCHIES DON'T DISAPPEAR OVERNIGHT**

  - The more entrenched the hierarchical mind-set, the more radical the action required.

  - The ultimate goal is creating meaningful collaboration at all levels.

I n 2003, Dr. Richard Zimmerman, then the hospital medical director for the Mayo Clinic in Arizona, began intensively reviewing data on patients dating back to its opening in 1998. The purpose of his inquiry was to guarantee that Mayo was doing all it could to provide the best patient care and ensure the highest probability of success. Health care, like any industry, is never perfect, but the Mayo Clinic in Arizona had some of the best performance statistics in the country, including very low standardized mortality rates. In fact, an examination of five years of data revealed few cases that suggested inquiry was necessary. Nonetheless, Dr. Zimmerman told us that he felt the need to "seek out opportunities for continuous improvement just in case in the future we could act a little earlier, get a bit more brain power, or bring even more knowledge to the bedside." After all, enduring success in health care ultimately rests on human judgment.[1]

Yes, doctors are schooled for years, many nurses have decades of experience, medical technology improves annually, and research statistics are plentiful. Still, no surefire algorithm exists for diagnosing a patient's condition or prescribing the proper protocol for recovery. Even some common killers that doctors see frequently are devilishly hard to detect. Take the case of sepsis, often referred to as "blood poisoning" in lay terms. This bacterial infection, which spreads throughout the body and frequently leads to organ failure, is reported to be one of the top ten causes of death in the United States by the Centers for Disease Control and Prevention. One in fifty hospital patients is diagnosed with sepsis, more than 750,000 each year, of whom nearly a third will die.[2]

Despite its frequency, sepsis is painfully hard to spot, particularly in its early stages. If patients are treated soon enough with antibiotics, they have a much higher survival rate. However, as Dr. Zimmerman told us, "sometimes the clinical picture makes it difficult to say for sure that the patient is infected or that this is the point when the infection has turned septic." Picking up on the clinical signs that a patient has sepsis is sometimes a matter of being around the patient frequently, treating symptoms, and accurately gauging the response.

Dr. Zimmerman explained, "We found that nurses sometimes would suspect something's wrong long before a physician, in part due to their increased frequency of interaction with patients." Sometimes this was the advantage of having firsthand observations of a patient over several hours. In other cases it was a matter of the nurse's experience being greater than that of the first call provider or on-call physician. After receiving fluids intravenously, for example, a patient with low blood pressure may stabilize, only to have their blood pressure drop again soon. "You do that two or three times and you realize it's not a lack of fluid; there's something else going on."

While the obvious solution for Mayo Clinic—and most health-care systems, for that matter—is to tap into the expertise and frontline observations of their nursing staff, breaking the hierarchy is no easy task. In the health-care field, Mayo is generally perceived as one of the most collaborative, team-based environments. Yet as is the case in most hospital environments, the status separation between doctors, with their lengthy education and deep specialization, and nurses with their often equally lengthy terms of service but less prestigious degrees, is clear and in most cases subtly nonnegotiable. As Dr. Zimmerman put it to us, "being a doctor kind of trumps all the caregivers in the health-care system according to the conventional, old-school mentality."[3]

In fact, as Eileen Oswald, the risk manager and patient safety coordinator for the Mayo Clinic in Arizona, explained, Mayo's history as a "physician-led institution," in which all doctors are equals and treated as partners in the practice, actually created a "hierarchy predicated on physicians being in the lead role with administrators supporting them."[4] In other words, while Mayo's culture has been much more open and cooperative, assumptions about doctors being at the top of the hierarchy remained embedded.

The Mayo Clinic's "Plus One" Protocol

In this chapter we discuss how organizations can systematically break down the entrenched hierarchy that obstructs frontline associates from utilizing their judgment. There are no singular solutions but there are many techniques that organizational leaders can employ, such as shifting organizational language and policies, eliminating unproductive work, soliciting frontline ideas more methodically, and promoting collaboration among workers at all hierarchical levels.

Mayo provides an interesting case example because societal and organizational assumptions about the roles of doctors and nurses are deeply ingrained. Clinically speaking, the problem with the conventional, old-school mentality that Dr. Zimmerman highlights above and which remains the status quo at many hospitals outside the Mayo system, is that it isn't always ideal for patient health. Encouraging nurses to speak up is more than simply a matter of imploring them to do their best for the patient. The reasons that some patients receive delayed treatment or nurses don't always share their opinions were embedded in organizational hierarchies and work processes. If a nurse disagrees with a physician or poses an alternative solution to a doctor's prescription, the nurse is perceived as challenging the doctor's knowledge and authority—something to which not many doctors take too kindly. To be sure, some nurses with superb communication skills can massage the situation and find just the right way to encourage a physician to explore other alternatives. But this type of solution assumes that the nurse was in communication with the doctor, that the doctor is uncharacteristically open to suggestion, and that the nurse and doctor collectively possess all of the knowledge required to solve the problem.

Dr. Zimmerman and Eileen Oswald knew that relying on perfect circumstances would never create a replicable, systemic solution. One of the biggest challenges, in fact, was simply getting nurses and doctors to talk to each other in a timely manner. It is not uncommon in the nursing profession for a nurse to call or page a doctor several times with no response. Critical time for patient treatment at Mayo was lost. This wasn't due to physician neglect. Doctors had other patients to see, were in surgery, were in the bathroom, and had a dozen other legitimate reasons for not responding as quickly as desired. The sheer volume of communication could also be overwhelming, particularly for new residents. One Mayo review noted that in a single surgical case the doctor received twenty-two communications in less than thirty-six hours. Multiply this by every patient a doctor is expected to see when making rounds, and the need for doctors to selectively filter communication becomes evident. Finally, there is the reality that doctors are human beings too—the person who responds to a page at 3:00 A.M. doesn't always have the same demeanor and thoughtfulness that they do during regular waking hours.

Such daunting complications left the Mayo physicians, nurses, and administrators wondering, as Dr. Zimmerman poignantly phrased the question, "What's the process for those at the sharp end of health care—our nurses—when the standard process isn't working?" The answer for Mayo came in the form of a new standard process dubbed Plus One. The program is an "empowerment process, an empowerment tool, an empowerment philosophy endorsed by our leadership up to the highest level in Mayo Clinic," says Zimmerman. More specifically, Plus One is a protocol that enables nurses to add one person to the patient-doctor-nurse relationship at any time.

Unlike traditional protocols in which the admitting or attending doctor is the implied authority, under Plus One a nurse, or any other clinical staff member, may elevate an issue up one level in the chain of command as he or she deems necessary. Whether the result of disagreement or an inability to contact the responsible physician, simply adding another clinician to the conversation ensures that different options are considered and the patient receives timely care. Dr. Zimmerman describes the process[5]:

> Let's say there is conflict when the doctor, who is a first-year resident, says, "Do A," and the nurse, who has twenty years' experience, says, "Maybe you

should do B" or "Maybe you should call for help." Now, the resident may not want to listen for different reasons. Maybe they feel the need to prove themselves or show that they know their stuff, or maybe they are afraid of how it will look if they ask for help. This Plus One process empowers the nurse to say, "Maybe you should call your attending," "Maybe you should ask a senior partner," "Maybe you should call a critical-care doctor to help with this." And, ultimately, Plus One empowers the nurse to actually make those calls when necessary.

While putting the Plus One program in place made sense, putting it into practice has meant facing some bumps in the road. Most significant, the program was deeply resented by a small but vocal group of experienced physicians, particularly when the new person added to the discussion confirmed the original doctor's diagnosis. Suffering through a number of "I told you so" moments, in which doctors confirmed that there was no need for the nurse to go above them, was one of the comparatively modest prices that Dr. Zimmerman paid for his leadership.

A deeper concern was the widespread fear that doctors would seek retribution against nurses or staff members who went up the chain of command and "around them." Oswald recalls, "We feared that in some cases, there might be an intimidation factor at work. Communication challenges had been recognized as a national health-care issue, and we also needed to look a little further into that. Hospital staffers were not always communicating up the chain of command as appropriate. A common illustration of communication issues is potential for wrong-side surgery. Think of the operating team as a group of sailors standing around the captain of the ship. The surgeon, who can be very intimidating, is about to perform surgery on the wrong side—maybe in a case of hip replacement—but starts the procedure with such confidence that the rest of the team is intimidated to speak up and say that's not the side to be operated on. We hear about these scenarios in our industry—it's akin to the copilot who's afraid to tell the pilot that the gas gauge is on empty."[6]

Communication issues in a hospital environment—much as in any organization with a strong chain of command—were not necessarily the result of something the doctor did that day to stifle open communication. It was equally likely that nurses or staffers might assume that doctors weren't receptive to their ideas so never spoke up in the first place. Even if a nurse hadn't faced intimidation from a particular physician, even one very negative experience from the past can result in what Dr. Zimmerman calls the "scar of intimidation, a lingering blemish that is never able to completely heal."

Of course, suspecting that there was some intimidation factor at work and actually knowing it were two different things. Recognizing that fear and intimidation stifle dialogue and dissent, Zimmerman and Oswald conducted "intimidation surveys" that assessed the extent to which the hospital created a "nonpunitive, just culture and environment." When staff members were asked whether there was potential for intimidation to affect patient safety, "nearly 20 percent of nurses indicated that it could occur."

"These statistics," Oswald flatly explains, "were alarming to us."[7] Since the implementation of Plus One, those numbers have been reduced by nearly 50 percent. Overall, there is no question that the program has been a success. Since implementation, the risk-adjusted mortality rate at the Arizona hospital has declined significantly faster than the U.S. average, while Eileen Oswald reports that "Plus One has had a major influence on decreasing unsafe circumstances for patients." In part, this is because every Plus One event, whether it results in changing the original doctor's recommendations or not, is reviewed after the fact and treated as a learning opportunity. Dr. Zimmerman and Oswald also describe a deeper cultural impact of Plus One.

First, the knowledge that Plus One is a legitimate option has bolstered the confidence of the nursing team, Mayo's first line of patient protection. Recognition of the program's effectiveness, Dr. Zimmerman believes, has encouraged nurses to more readily share their ideas and doctors to be more receptive to rethinking their initial positions if confronted. Ironically, with the program in place to encourage dissent, the number of Plus One events decreased from a baseline of forty per year when the program began to an average of between twelve and fifteen events per year today. Always fearful that less reporting may be a symptom of intimidation, Dr. Zimmerman relies not only on the annual intimidation survey but also on his frequent interactions with physicians and staff. In addition to acting today as chair of quality and process improvement for Mayo Clinic in Arizona, Dr. Zimmerman is the associate dean of all the clinic's graduate medical education residency programs.

The new generation of doctors and nurses coming to Mayo view Plus One very differently from how their predecessors viewed it. Rather than see it as an indictment of a doctor's judgment and experience, incoming residents view Plus One as a safeguard designed to help them. Assuming it is just part of the way of life at Mayo Clinic in Arizona, young physicians say the "presence of the program facilitates getting more help earlier and not to feel that, 'Oh, I can't call my staff physician or the chief resident because they'll think I'm incompetent.'"

Plus One has become so accepted as a conflict-resolution process that in some very rare instances physicians have even used it to improve nursing care. There have been instances when nurses became reticent or failed to comply with doctor's orders and the doctor called in another nurse who was able to help resolve the situation. "It's about one in one thousand when you have a physician that can't get the nursing help they need, but at least it shows that the Plus One system does go both ways and it's all about teamwork, not hierarchy. It is an enabling methodology that helps break through a communication impasse or teamwork barrier."[8]

Breaking Down the Hierarchy

Creating a front line–focused organization is difficult—as we outlined in our two opening chapters—because most corporate structures are designed along hierarchical principles that are throwbacks to the industrial factory era. Engaging the front line in problem resolution, innovation, and experimentation can have profound bottom-line benefits, but these may never materialize, and certainly won't endure, in the traditional organizational construct that assumes those at the top are smart and those at the bottom aren't. As Mayo's Plus One program demonstrates, deconstructing organizational assumptions about roles and where value is created requires process and persistence in the face of massive cultural, psychological, and institutional resistance.

The overwhelming majority of organizations, including most we have worked with, are founded on embedded assumptions about the role of hierarchy that date back to the early years of the twentieth century, or even earlier, as command-and-control hierarchies became the accepted model for all production. Starting in the 1960s, as concerns escalated regarding the alienating position of workers in such organizations and more recognition was given to their ability to create value for firms, a number of practices emerged to stimulate broader employee involvement. These included a wide-ranging menu of options, from cross-training employees to offering team-based incentives to putting more decision-making rights in workers' hands. However, these "participative organizations" or "team-based" structures, as they came to be known, often changed practices on the surface without fundamentally altering the hierarchy or power structures underlying those practices.

Academic research has shown, and our clinical practice has affirmed, that reframing the role of employees requires something far more profound and basic than the mere institution of a couple of new management practices. In fact, a debate continues as to how many changes are required to create a new organizational gestalt that begins to challenge command-and-control norms. Recently, some prominent academics have suggested that entirely new models of management and organization are required to undo more than a century of hierarchical management.

While we certainly cannot debate the appeal of wholesale change, experience tells us that this is an unlikely prospect for most organizations. The evolution of organizational structures, particularly in publicly traded companies, has historically happened in a stepwise fashion. Although we think this is part of the problem, we don't anticipate that large numbers of organizations will be willing to take the risks or confront the resistance associated with significant structural change. Most leaders who sit atop organizational pyramids, and most investors who support them, have experience only with hierarchical structures and question any departure at the first sign of trouble.

Take the case of the computer networking hardware giant Cisco, for example. In 2001, John Chambers, Cisco's longtime CEO, began moving the company toward a structure of collaborative management with councils that mixed employees of different levels and functional backgrounds. Chambers's goal was to stimulate growth at a time when the company's core business of Internet infrastructure networking had untapped potential, yet the aftereffects of the dot-com meltdown were putting cost pressure on the company.

While Chambers was convinced that the company needed to shift to a functional organizational structure that would optimize operational efficiency, he nonetheless worried that Cisco would fall into the typical organizational trap of isolating functions and diminishing the teamwork required to exploit growth opportunities to the fullest. Chambers's solution was to implement a new organizational structure that created employee "councils" and appointed a handful of senior leaders to each council aimed at ten-billion-dollar opportunities. To achieve these targets, members of each council organized "boards," or cross-functional groups, to work on specific growth projects with goals of a billion dollars or less. Operating committees assumed profit-and-loss responsibility, while enterprise-level councils were charged with establishing or disbanding councils aimed at specific growth markets. At one point, Cisco had more than fifty boards running across the company.

If this structure seems difficult to manage, it may be because it challenges our conventional notions and seems to fly in the face of traditional hierarchy. Chambers steadfastly defended the structure as a matter of necessity for achieving the firm's ambitious objectives, citing the council structure as the primary cause of the company's success in new markets such as telepresence video conferencing and advertising in sports arenas. Press stories extolled the virtues of the new structure, noting that more employees were engaged to share their ideas, resolve conflicts collaboratively, and combine their expertise.

Many scholars and pundits also cited Cisco as a potential model for a new organizational structure. However, in April 2011, shortly after Cisco missed earnings projections, some analysts began calling on the company to dismantle the structure and return to a more conventional organization. As they did so, reports leaked (ostensibly from internal sources) noting that there was "organizational fatigue" as employees attended the many meetings required by the elaborate structure of committees, boards, and councils. Likewise, some took aim at the lack of accountability in a collaborative structure and Chambers's seeming inability to pin the company's shortfalls on specific individuals. In early May, Cisco announced a restructuring plan that eliminated all but three of the councils.[9]

We raise the example of Cisco because it demonstrates the type of resistance, both external and internal, often generated by structural change. Certainly, other organizations have succeeded in rewriting the organizational rules around hierarchy, but those successes have happened in isolated cases and often in private or family-controlled businesses.[10]

As opposed to radical change, we believe that most organizations will adopt a slower yet still challenging path toward building a front line–focused organization. While we are intrigued by the possibility of new organizational models, practicality suggests that organizations will typically focus first on breaking down elements of the hierarchy in their existing structures. An example would be the Mayo Clinic in Arizona's Plus One protocol, which subtly challenged and reformed yet by no means undermined or fundamentally threatened the professional hierarchical governance structure of the hospital. Therefore, we focus our attention on how leaders in existing companies can create the correct organizational context, leadership roles, and employee expectations. In this chapter we will frame the specific actions that senior leaders can take to signal breaking down the hierarchy.

Changing the Organizational Context

By "organizational context" we mean the specific factors that influence the perceptions of frontline employees that they are (or are not) empowered to take action or make decisions and that help create the belief that their contributions are valued. While there are numerous individual factors that may play a role in generating this sense of power, we focus principally on the structure, processes, and organization-wide language or symbolism and the actions that senior leaders can take to change notions of how the organizational hierarchy operates. This process necessarily starts with senior leadership and the organizational CEO because, as former Harvard Business School professor Shoshana Zuboff has observed, "only top managers' values, behaviors, and publicly shared vision can free up the authority context of the organization enough to stimulate others to reflection and invention."[11]

One of the key issues is finding the right language to make the intent of the change clear to hundreds or thousands of people.[12] Over the years, we have seen numerous attempts to upend traditional notions of the organization using strong language and powerful imagery, such as "inverting the pyramid" or "if the customer is king, then our front line is royalty." The problem with catchphrases is that they are open to interpretation and imprecise about specific behavioral change.

For example, a large retailer we worked with invoked the "servant leader" mantra in an effort to get senior leaders to be more respectful and helpful when visiting associates in the field. The intent was that senior leaders should listen, make note of policy issues or organizational problems, and then follow through to provide help. The new language was emphasized during an annual meeting that involved all of the geography leaders, corporate operations teams, and the store managers. While no threats were levied, it was clear that "servant leadership" was the new model for succeeding at the company.

We heard innumerable stories from senior managers who were confused about their authority. Should they offer only positive comments? Could they take action against low performers? In short, the company had succeeded in breaking down notions of how the hierarchy operated but had utterly failed to be clear about what came next.

When companies talk about turning the organizational pyramid upside down, they rarely mean it in literal terms. We have yet to find examples where companies have completely ceded authority to the front line or dramatically changed their pay structures. Instead, they typically mean to say that they want to *diminish* hierarchy and eradicate the abuse of positional power.

Rather than using catchy slogans, we find that the companies most successful at empowering and enabling judgment at the front line tend to be very specific about the behaviors, policies, and processes they want to change. One key action is relating leadership expectations back to the Teachable Point of View[13] and specifically the organizational values. One retailer we worked with instituted "respect and humility," character traits that were easy to translate into front line–focused behavior, as core values. The company's leadership team invested time in outlining specific behaviors tied to the values that leaders needed to change, and then explained in clear language why:

The leader's humility invites others to play an active role in the business. By saying "I don't know" and asking for help, the leader encourages others to step up their contribution. Such leaders know that their role is to create an environment in which people feel valued and are positioned to make the greatest possible contribution. They also know that leaders who purport to have all of the answers or think they are the most capable to perform every task are delusory.

The company highlighted specific behaviors, such as saying "I don't know," delegating tasks, and focusing on building teams with complementary strengths. It also identified behaviors that would be disingenuous, such as asking for people's opinions only to ignore them or rudely interrupting others when the leader felt they might be sharing an idea without merit. While this was no panacea, leaders in this company weren't paralyzed by ambiguity or confused about the proper use of their authority.

In short, we advocate an evolutionary path that enables existing organizations, with all their flaws, to move toward freeing the intelligence and innovation capacity of their front line. This clearly won't happen overnight, but there are a few specific actions that nearly all firms are capable of taking, as outlined below.

Eliminating Unnecessary Work

One of the biggest challenges for frontline employees is the proliferation of seemingly mindless controls, policies, and procedures. While some are undoubtedly useful, organizations tend to create unnecessary bureaucracy as a by-product of their operations. As a rule of thumb, the larger the organization, the more layers of management, and the less connected the top managers are with the front line, the more likely unproductive rules and policies are to abound.[14] And, as a *Wall Street Journal* article noted, "line managers and employees occupied with operational issues normally don't have the time to sit around and discuss ideas that lead to cross-organizational innovation."[15]

It is not simply that this work is distracting, pointless, and disempowering for employees. The more pernicious effect is when frontline employees ask for policies to be changed only to have their pleas ignored, or when associates look to their managers for explanation only to hear stories about the "idiots at corporate." In some organizations, employees become trained to not question policy, avoid making recommendations, and keep their heads down.

One of the most powerful tools for simultaneously freeing up frontline capacity, signaling the importance of frontline work, and building employee confidence was created during General Electric's Work-Out process.[16] Abbreviated as RAMMP (pronounced "ramp"), it is a simple tool for employees to identify unnecessary reports, approvals, meetings, measurements, and policies. In other words, elements that prevent frontline employees from serving customers or doing meaningful work.[17]

RAMMP discussions usually take place in high-energy, two-hour sessions in which employees go through each of the categories to identify time-wasting work activities. The manager who oversees the key work activities for the team is present, and he is expected to make a decision on the spot on roughly 80 percent of the proposals. He either kills the unneeded work or engages in a dialogue with employees about why it is necessary and can't be eradicated (for example, Sarbanes-Oxley rules initially created new compliance requirements for many organizations that couldn't be ignored). In no more than 20 percent of the cases, the manager may agree to study the issue and respond to the group within one week.

Over the years we have been amazed at some of the solutions that have resulted from RAMMP. Involving frontline personnel has not only shed light on inefficient business practices but simultaneously given those on the front line a sense of increased control over their work environment. For example, at one former retail client, the RAMMP exercise revealed that the truck-unloading process on the two nights per week when stores received their largest shipments occupied nearly the entire store staff. The thirty-five-step inventory-receiving process required first moving all of the contents to a holding area, then filling out a series of forms, then moving products onto the floor for sale. When the company realized how many man-hours were being consumed by this process across dozens of stores, the leader for the area worked with store associates to redesign it so that it took less than half the time by enabling store employees to move product directly to the floor, eliminating the amount of space each store needed for warehousing, and freeing associates from hours of reports each week.

Making Time for the Front Line to Think

Another way to free up frontline capacity and demonstrate that leadership is serious about engaging employees in more meaningful work is to thoughtfully employ technology to simplify employees' work or seek their input. While many companies think of automating processes to drive cost savings, others use technology strategically to free their front line from manual work or menial aspects of their jobs.

Pepsi Bottling Group provides a great example. When Eric Foss became CEO of Pepsi Bottling Group (PBG) in 2006,[18] he knew the organization had problems with inventory, logistics, and field sales. PBG serves thousands of supermarkets, convenience stores, gas stations, and other retail outlets. Its customer representatives delivered nearly two hundred million servings of Pepsi products every day. "Our customers were saying in a pretty clear voice they wanted us to do four things,"[19] Foss told us. First and foremost, they wanted PBG to eliminate out-of-stocks, which sacrificed sales and irritated consumers. Customers also wanted PBG deliveries to show up on time. That included weekends, when 60 percent of Pepsi products are sold and PBG needed to have its best people on customer premises. Finally, customers told Foss that they didn't expect PBG to be perfect, but the company needed to resolve problems more quickly and with more communication.

To understand the root causes of PBG's challenges, Foss spent most of his first hundred days as CEO in the field visiting with customers and frontline sales representatives. He described what he found as chaos. During a trip to a retail outlet with a general manager, Foss discovered he couldn't carry on a routine conversation because the manager's cell phone rang continually. After several interruptions, Foss suggested a sit-down meeting with the sales and production teams back at a PBG warehouse.

Back at the warehouse, Foss couldn't get answers to seemingly routine questions about how many out-of-stocks the team had had the night before or how many trucks had been loaded without complete customer orders. "It was total chaos," says Foss. "After thirty minutes, we still had three or four different answers."[20]

Following his field visit, Foss shared the frontline situation with his senior team. Recognizing that the lack of structured sales processes, poor forecasting, and outdated warehousing technology were impacting the customer representatives' ability to do their job for customers, Foss mobilized cross-functional efforts to fix the situation. The company had several tests under way but hadn't tackled the problem in an integrated manner that recognized how the frontline employees and customers experienced the issues. Subsequently, Foss and team rolled together three separate pilots to build a holistic process that would fix the problem.

As a result, each of PBG's twelve thousand customer-service representatives were given a handheld PDA to electronically download customer information, including route schedules, service notes, and sales training videos. While in stores, they were able to upload information electronically so that headquarters could refine its sophisticated forecasting estimates, plants could develop production schedules (now planned at least two weeks in advance), and warehouses could use voice-automated technology to optimize inventory and delivery. Employee satisfaction hit all-time highs.

Customers were also impressed. In part, this is because PBG didn't use the technology merely to trim head count. Instead, Foss challenged customer representatives to use their newfound time—hours that were once devoted to managing the awful inventory process—to build relationships with their customers. While making deliveries on their routes, customer representatives could instead look for better display opportunities, talk to managers about product sales, and help to position company promotions. Foss told us that he believes that in addition to the customer-satisfaction boost that PBG realized, the new methods were critical to building long-term relationships and higher customer retention.

Getting Intelligence Directly from the Front Line

Many companies talk about how they wish they could get better customer intelligence to their product designers. It's an age-old problem: Corporate staff think they're calling the shots, so they don't listen to the people in the field. Typically the corporate staff has more concentrated power, since they are fewer in number and have direct access to a product vice president. Even if they are willing to listen, there is the logistical challenge of getting input from dispersed locations and hundreds or thousands of frontline employees and then making sense of it in a rational way.

Zara, the Spanish fast-fashion retailer, which overtook Gap as the world's largest fashion retailer in 2008, uses its approximately 1,700 stores in over seventy countries as the front line for spotting ever-changing fashion trends.[21] Unlike big competitors such as Gap or H&M, which may produce approximately four thousand distinct designs each year, Zara spits out more than ten thousand products. By one account Zara is twelve times faster than Gap while producing ten times more products, with the average product going from concept to store shelf in just fifteen days.[22] This enables the company to adapt quickly and stock stores according to local tastes.

Zara's sustained success, however, relies on a constant flow of information throughout every part of the company's supply chain. Every day store staff chat up customers to get feedback on current styles and understand what is selling. They may ask customers, "What if this skirt were longer?" or "What other color would you like to see this in?" All of the information is loaded into PDAs linked to the store's point-of-sale system, which captures actual customer purchase information. In less than an hour, every manager globally can send updates that include not only quantitative cash-register data but also qualitative customer insights and their own impressions.

To augment the data, store managers routinely speak with the market specialists and twentysomething designers to help them understand what is happening in the market. In fact, the company owes much of its success to a flat organizational structure, with few management layers between the product and the field staff and clear expectations that both field and product people think like business owners.[23] Everyone at Zara is expected to have an entrepreneurial zeal. As the job description for a store manager in a U.S. location read:

> We put our business in your hands. You will be managing an authentic fashion center, a model that doesn't exist with other companies and goes far beyond other retailers. Zara stores are real "fashion laboratories." Zara managers monitor how merchandise is selling and transmit this information directly to headquarters. Our customers tell us what they want to wear, we listen to their opinions and tastes and the store team passes it on to our in house designers. With this valuable information our product development team swings into action to offer our customers new items every week. [24]

Twice per week section managers in each store order approximately 85 percent of the product that will be on display. These store staff are responsible for identifying trends and selecting among nearly three hundred thousand items so their inventory matches the preferences of local clientele. Zara's policy of displaying products only if every size is in stock simplifies the job for store staff while ensuring that customers aren't frustrated by out-of-stock items. Section managers, meanwhile, are not only picking trends but also using corporate-generated forecasting data to help determine quantities to order.

In cases where sales are suffering or product and field people can't understand the sales data, the market specialists go directly into the field to talk with staff and customers alike. Market specialists don't show up to audit; they go into the stores and partner with staff to get the best possible data to understand consumer behavior. For example, in 2007 Zara introduced pencil skirts in bright colors to its stores. The items were not selling, but store staff couldn't put together a coherent explanation as to why based on their in-store surveys. Focused effort from marketing managers and store associates revealed that women couldn't wear their usual size in the slim-fitting skirt. Rather than purchase a larger size and incur any associated ego bruising, most women were willing to forgo the purchase of an otherwise appealing item. Based on this new understanding, Zara recalled the items and reissued the pencil skirts to the stores with new sizing. Sales exploded. This type of teamwork and constant communication has helped the fashion retailer limit failed product introductions to just 1 percent, while the industry average runs at 10 percent.

Rather than express concern about putting the business in the hands of the company's front line, Zara's CEO, Pablo Isla, notes that enabling thousands of people to make thousands of small decisions actually limits risk. Each small decision on a product or its quantity has a small impact on total sales, so no single manager is betting the store.

Promoting Collaboration at All Levels

In recent years, increasing numbers of organizations are using crowdsourcing and idea markets as a way to tap the knowledge of their employees. While not always aimed specifically at frontline employees, these efforts do help to demonstrate that a company is seeking the best ideas, regardless of where in the hierarchy they may originate.

IBM was a pioneer at using crowdsourcing efforts in what it refers to as an Idea Jam.[25] IBM's first Idea Jam was held in 2001 as a deliberate way of tapping into the company's three hundred thousand plus employees' collective smarts in order to improve how the company operated. Leveraging IBM's intranet infrastructure, employees used electronic bulletin boards and Web pages to share ideas and respond to questions such as "How do you work in an increasingly mobile organization?" or "How do we get IBM Consulting into the C-suite?" In the Idea Jam's first year there were approximately 52,000 posts. Perhaps most important, in addition to generating valuable ideas, it gave people a sense of participation and of being listened to that would be critical for future Jam events.

After Sam Palmisano became CEO in 2002, he utilized the technology to foster a three-day conversation with employees at all levels to come up with a revised set of corporate values. An estimated fifty thousand employees weighed in, posting more than ten thousand comments. While the initial tone of the online conversation was cynical, the comments eventually became constructive. Analysts pored over all of the postings looking for key themes. This enabled Palmisano and his team to announce new values in November 2003. Rather than resting on IBM's storied history, these values had the legitimacy of originating with the company's employees. As Palmisano would later note in a *Harvard Business Review* interview, the values were essential for engaging all of IBM's employees:

> You could employ all kinds of traditional, top-down management processes. But they wouldn't work at IBM—or, I would argue, at an increasing number of twenty-first-century companies. You just can't impose command-and-control mechanisms on a large, highly professional workforce. I'm not only talking about our scientists, engineers, and consultants. More than 200,000 of our employees have college degrees. The CEO can't say to them, "Get in line and follow me." Or "*I've* decided what *your* values are." They're too smart

for that. And as you know, smarter people tend to be, well, a little more challenging; you might even say cynical.[26]

With a new tone beginning to harmonize IBM's culture, Palmisano would again use the Jam in 2006 to engage employees to help move new products more quickly to market. With the stated purpose of promoting innovation, this Jam took place over two three-day sessions with around-the-clock participation coming from 150,000 employees in 104 countries. The first session, in July, asked participants to brainstorm new ways to use key technologies. The second session, in September, had participants working on separate sites with wikis devoted to building business plans. In the end, Palmisano pledged over one hundred million dollars to invest in ideas that originated from the Jam, including key technologies in IBM's growing environmental and health-care businesses.

While IBM has continued its tradition of Jams and even sells both the process and supporting technology to clients through its consulting arm, orchestrating such events is far from easy. It took fifty senior executives a week to review the output from the July session before they could ultimately synthesize the thirty-one "big ideas" that had resulted. Many of these ideas weren't entirely original, and it was more often the case that small ideas could be bundled into bigger business opportunities. While this meant that sifting and sorting the ideas couldn't be handled exclusively by a computer, the Jams enabled employees to articulate ideas to a much wider audience and create dialogue with IBM's senior leaders, who might otherwise have been inaccessible.[27]

Another form of crowdsourcing—idea markets—gives employees play money and encourages them to bet on outcomes such as sales forecasts, production volumes, or product launch dates. Applying market logic, the participants are encouraged to bet on outcomes. In other words, rather than rely on the judgment of a single manager, idea markets tap employees' collective knowledge in ways that have been proven to create more reliable outcome forecasts.

In the past, for example, HP has run prediction markets that forecast computer sales better than corporate departments did. Similarly, companies such as steel producer Arcelor, Microsoft, and Google have employed idea markets. Typically, employees win small prizes, T-shirts, or cash if they predict the actual result.

More recently, companies have forgone the event-based nature of Jams and the complexities of idea markets in favor of Web 2.0 or social technologies. For example, MasterCard has hosted webcasts open to all of the company's more than five thousand employees to review its strategy and offer innovation ideas.

Yet another retailer, Wal-Mart, conducted a blogging exercise focused on energy conservation. Among the six thousand posts, one idea was to remove the bulbs from the vending machines in store stockrooms. Rollin Ford, the company's chief information officer, reported, "As a result, our savings by taking that one light bulb out of machines was one million dollars aggregated across all our locations."[28]

A final way in which technology can be used to minimize hierarchy is to put employees in direct touch with one another and with customers. Historically, in many corporations, operation manuals and technical service bulletins have come from centralized functions whose job is to recognize problems in the field, aggregate solutions, and then broadcast them back out to employees. Increasingly, employees are maintaining their own technical Web sites through wikis or other Web-based media. This serves to put them in direct control of the content, which is typically both built and edited through voluntary participation in online communities. When organizations enable these conversations to happen by providing supportive technologies and managerial policies, it not only validates that employees have valuable knowledge to share but also provides them with a sense of control and expertise-based legitimacy. In turn, these build employee confidence, which fosters an environment in which frontline workers are more likely to challenge unhelpful policies or rules and more willing to share their ideas.

As we have seen through our own work, companies that put employees in control of one-to-one relationships with customers create even more sense of employee empowerment and can generate profound employee commitment. Charles Schwab, the investment company, has assigned direct telephone lines to customer-service representatives so that customers can build a relationship with an employee and follow up on a problem, rather than reach a randomly assigned service rep every time they dial the call center.[29] Again, such efforts diminish the hierarchy by demonstrating that employees are trusted to use their judgment in serving clients and in calling upon the company's resources as needed to solve problems rather than having communication routed and decisions controlled by automated logic systems.

By themselves, the use of these methods will not fundamentally alter how the hierarchy works in an organization. However, for companies that have invested in teaching employees about their business, developed problem-solving frameworks, and fostered a culture of innovation, employing one or more of these tools can be an initial step in demonstrating that a company is committed to enabling frontline associates to do meaningful, value-added work rather than wrestle with bureaucracy.

When Radical Change Is Needed

Breaking down a command-and-control hierarchy occasionally requires taking more radical steps. The more entrenched the mind-set, the longer-tenured the leaders, the more conditioned the employees, the more likely it becomes that revolutionary change will be needed. A dramatic example of transformative action that permanently altered an organization's hierarchy is the Providence Police Department (PPD).

In our research, we were intrigued by police departments because, like the military, they are predicated on a clearly delineated command-and-control structure to maintain order and discipline.[30] There are approximately seventeen thousand police departments across the United States, each with its own culture and each with a unique history of change and adaptation over the decades. When Colonel Dean Esserman took over the PPD in 2003, he found a department that was a throwback to the 1950s. As he describes it,

> it was a very strong pyramid here. It had no idea what was going on in American policing at all. It was disconnected from current American policing. It's one of the oldest departments in America and the second-largest in the Northeast. So its tradition was alive and well. I mean, old leather uniforms, snap to attention and salute, carrying blackjacks. A culture that really valued seniority more than anything.[31]

Shortly before Dean Esserman arrived in Providence, the department had been rocked by scandal. Providence's long-serving mayor, Vincent A. "Buddy" Cianci Jr., had just been convicted for turning local government into his personal criminal enterprise that allegedly exchanged tax breaks, jobs, and city contracts for hundreds of thousands of dollars in bribes and illegal contributions.[32] Corruption and bribery had become systemic in the PPD as well. It was well known that earning rank was based on favoritism and a pay-to-play promotion system in which everything from posts as senior command staff to slots for incoming recruits at the PPD Academy could be purchased. Crime had steadily escalated over a decade, and trust both among the public and within the department had been deeply compromised. Morale was low and coordination within the PPD was limited; police officers identified themselves principally as day- or night-shift workers with limited communication between the groups.

When Providence's new mayor appointed Esserman to the post of police chief, many department old-timers were skeptical. Esserman was a New

Yorker, the son of a doctor, an Ivy League graduate, and a former lawyer. However, he had also given up his law career to work with former New York City police commissioner William Bratton, whose innovative tactics were well known for incredible crime reductions. Following this, Esserman's leadership had been instrumental in turning around departments throughout the 1990s in New York and Connecticut.

Sensing that he had good people with poor leadership, Esserman immediately retired the former command staff. He then instituted a "return to our neighborhoods" campaign that rested on the values of community policing. As Esserman explained to anyone who would listen, the PPD had been depersonalized and lacked connection with the community it existed to serve. Values such as building personal relationships, knowing community leaders and local troublemakers, and having a visible presence in the community would be the new guiding principles for the department. The police force would become proactive problem solvers who could help defuse crime in troubled areas rather than playing catch-up after theft or violence had already occurred.

Esserman dismantled the centralized bureaucracy, installing district commanders whom he anointed as "police chiefs for their communities." This decentralization push put the district commanders in charge of everything from defining the borders of their districts to hiring personnel to selecting locations for community police stations. Esserman pledged the support of the PPD's resources and—even more precious—his trust to let them truly operate with more independence than had ever been seen in Providence policing. In turn, Esserman demanded only two things. First, he told them he didn't care about how hard people worked or how many hours they put in; he would watch only the results. Second, he said, "You can have great crime stats, but if the community hates you, you're in trouble."

One of the critical changes that Esserman introduced to drive accountability was the introduction of CompStat, a computerized system for tracking crime based on geographical information. In addition to providing a standardized language and tracking methodology, CompStat made it possible for police to track trends, display heat maps of crime incidents, and watch historical patterns. Each week Esserman opened up his weekly staff meeting to include community partners and neighborhood organizations, role modeling relationship-building efforts, to review the statistics and talk about new efforts.

These were far from public-relations events. In one of the operational meetings we observed, attended by seventeen police staff and twenty-three community agents, Esserman and team reviewed everything from an officer shot in the line of duty to the apprehension of a bank robber to the hunt for a thief responsible for four breaking-and-entering attempts in the past two weeks. District personnel were expected to know past offenders, talk about on-the-ground intelligence-gathering tactics, and explain their local strategies, such as increasing the number of foot patrols.

The combination of decentralization, new crime-tracking tools, and increased accountability actually pushed the PPD's leaders to seek more frontline information and engage patrol officers in innovative efforts. As Lieutenant Dean Isabella shared with us,[33] the efforts of a patrolman, Tommy Massey, enabled the PPD to build relationships with housing agencies and community builders to reduce crime in the Lepo Street area. One of the worst crime areas in Providence, Lepo was a brownfield site with a burned-down mill and few occupied houses that sat on just 3 percent of the area in Isabella's district but consumed 30 percent of departmental resources. Massey built a relationship with representatives of the nonprofit Ownerville Housing Corporation, which had taken an interest in reforming the area after the city said it would invest to build a park.

Massey worked with his sergeant and others throughout his district to expand the involvement of other nonprofit support groups,[34] including national organizations. Teaming together representatives of community agencies and not-for-profits, the PPD educated itself on designing public spaces, buildings, and properties to be more community friendly. Ultimately, through their combined effort, Lepo Street was transformed into a four-block area with two hundred affordable housing units. According to Isabella, "crime fell by almost thirty-five percent in the area, without displacing it to other parts of the city."

The Lepo Street effort—which has become the subject of national case studies and which Esserman was invited to explain to a Senate subcommittee[35]— is representative of how the PPD has changed its hierarchy. The effort was built on the initiative and good idea of a patrolman but certainly didn't stop with him. Before the PPD's transformation, there was limited motivation for senior leaders to try innovative methods and therefore less impetus to listen to the front line, but Esserman's emphasis on results, community relationships, and accountability compelled senior leaders to listen to any good ideas. The patrol officers who had the neighborhood relationships and local intelligence became indispensible in fighting crime. Isabella told us,

> Your business is your district. We've been given great freedom as lieutenants but also great responsibility. Years ago the job was basically you showed up for your eight-hour shift and then you went home. The responsibility of knowing everything that's going on in your district—it's actually strengthened relationships within the department.

The Lepo Street case is also representative of the impact that breaking down the hierarchy has had in Providence. From 2002 to 2009, total crime in the city decreased by 34 percent.

Summary: Tearing Down the Walls

The paradox of building a front line–focused organization is that it begins with senior leaders creating an organizational context in which frontline leaders feel valued and are engaged in valuable work without the burden of unnecessary bureaucracy. Yet the degree, endurance, and depth of change required largely depend on an organization's starting point. If, as in the case of the Providence Police Department, a hierarchy is firmly entrenched, more radical action will be needed.

Technology is a tremendous enabler for facilitating the flow of intelligence to and from the front line. As we saw in the case of Pepsi Bottling Group, intelligent updates can be delivered to frontline workers to boost efficiency and create more time for high-value work. Additionally, as in the cases of Zara and IBM, technology can be leveraged to solicit input and create conversations. In the best cases, these actions translate into actual relationships, such as when a Zara buyer teams with a store associate to dive deeper on fashion trends.

Ultimately, the goal is not to elevate the frontline workers at the expense of others in the hierarchy but rather to promote respect for them that diminishes the importance of titles, invites insight from employees at all levels, and encourages the use of data and the best intelligence when making decisions.

7

INVESTING IN FRONTLINE CAPABILITY

To have a candidate for a thirteen-dollar-an-hour job interview with fifteen people, that seems insane to a lot of people. It's really hard to do a spreadsheet ROI analysis, but as a company our number one goal has always been focused on hiring the right people. Everyone's committed, and it's why we and our culture keep growing.

—Christa Foley, senior HR manager, Zappos.com

- **RIGOROUS SELECTION AND TRAINING IS CRITICAL TO BUILDING COMMITMENT**

  - Failure to get the right talent will undo even the best efforts to create a front line–focused organization.

  - Up-front investment in hiring can break the cycle of employee turnover.

- **FRONTLINE SUPERVISORS CREATE LOCAL ENVIRONMENTS THAT RETAIN TALENT**

  - Frontline supervisors lead most of an organization's employees yet receive the least training.

  - Great frontline supervisors unleash employees and increase commitment.

Originally hatched as a concept many skeptics said could never work—an online shoe store—just as the dot-com bubble was bursting at the turn of the twenty-first century, Zappos has exploded over the past decade to become a purveyor of shoes, clothes, accessories, and much, much more. The Henderson, Nevada–based retailer sits on the sandy edge of Las Vegas's suburban sprawl and rings up sales in excess of one billion dollars per year—a top line that would put most of the showier casinos on the Sunset Strip to shame. At the heart of Zappos's explosive growth is a deliberate focus on customer service. Bought a pair of peep-toe patent pumps that just don't work for you? You can return them up to a year after purchase, no questions asked.

Largely as a result of the outstanding customer service provided by roughly four hundred people fielding five thousand calls per day, Zappos has become an icon of customer-centricity and was acquired in 2009 by Amazon for more than eight hundred million dollars. When employees are first hired by Zappos, most are admonished to forget everything they ever learned at their former employers. Their new job is to make customers happy, because at Zappos more than 75 percent of purchases are made by returning customers. At Zappos there are no budgetary parameters and few formal policies to guide customer-service reps. Instead, employees are told to think long term and create a service experience that will keep customers coming back, just like Tony Hsieh (pronounced "shay"), the CEO.

When mistakes happen, call-center employees field calls from disgruntled customers. Unlike at other businesses, however, these employees don't consult a playbook, reference rules, or pass problems on to a supervisor. Instead, they use their best judgment to fix the problem—the essence of a front line–focused organization.

Any employee at Zappos has the latitude to give the customer coupons for future purchases, discounts off their current product up to one hundred dollars, or a complete refund. As one call-center supervisor told us, the company doesn't do this willy-nilly. In fact, she added, most employees have to be encouraged to give customers *more*. "In the beginning, people are so protective of the company and our culture that they don't want to give the farm away. We have to push them to give twenty dollars instead of five."[1] Even the policies that are on the books, such as the one-hundred-dollar limit, are more guidelines than strictly adhered-to rules. Ultimately, employees do what they believe to be in the best interest of keeping long-term relationships with their customers. Hsieh has said,

At Zappos, we don't measure call times (our longest phone call was almost six hours long!), and we don't upsell. We just care about whether the rep goes above and beyond for every customer. We don't have scripts because we trust our employees to use their best judgment when dealing with each and every customer. We want our reps to let their true personalities shine during each phone call so that they can develop a personal emotional connection . . . with the customer.[2]

The personal connection that Hsieh speaks about is ultimately far more important to building customer relationships and driving consumer repurchase behavior than any financial remuneration that the call-center representatives can offer. One viral story circulating on the Internet tells the tale of a woman who sadly called to return a pair of boots ordered for her husband. He had never had the opportunity to wear the boots because he had been killed in a car accident. The customer representative not only accepted the boots but also sent her flowers with condolences from Zappos—an experience the woman shared at her husband's funeral.

This is hardly unique behavior at Zappos. First-time purchasers routinely receive handwritten cards in the mail from call-center employees. If a customer mentions that he or she is celebrating a special occasion such as a wedding, he or she shouldn't be surprised to get a card or small gift in the mail. While such stories are obviously touching, a more significant question is what separates Zappos from other vaunted paragons of brick-and-mortar customer service like Nordstrom or Disney. The biggest difference, we learned through our research, is the degree of trust and autonomy given to workers with relatively few boundaries. Zappos relies on a massive up-front recruiting and training investment in every employee to ensure that its front line is rooted in the company's customer-service culture and organizational values. This translates into an authentic desire to make customers happy that is not only infectious but also replicable and scalable. Employees tap into their own personality and creativity in building customer relationships. There are no templates for printing off cards, no standard gifts, and no required formulas for how much an employee should discount for a mistake.

Rather than rely on policies and procedures to direct employee behavior, Zappos finds and hires employees who actually want to help people and then gives them the tools and training to do so. Hsieh, the company's CEO, contrasted Zappos's approach with Disney's during an interview we held at a hangout near Zappos headquarters that serves as the company's informal social club. Hsieh had visited the famed Disney University and closely observed its celebrated training program. Like Zappos, Disney teaches and relies on a base of clearly articulated values to instruct new employees. However, Disney also enforces strict guidelines regarding everything from hair length to how employees should point when giving directions. The philosophy behind Disney's tightly wound matrix of rules is that guests enter a world of magical illusion when coming to a theme park; everyone from street sweepers to ride attendants are characters in what it refers to as "the show."

Yet impressed as he was by the Disney show, Hsieh came away convinced that Disney's rigid scripting provides employees rules and boundaries but little internal judgment for how to deal with unpredictable circumstances. In short, Disney's show is based on an implicit model of rule following, while Hsieh's Zappos is built on trust and autonomy.

Zappos's senior leadership is willing to give employees that trust—in fact, in some respects its long-term business model relies upon it—because it has rigorously selected, screened, and trained employees to use company values and good business sense when making judgment calls with customers. As Zappos's senior HR manager, Christa Foley, told us quite candidly, the company is "looking for people who are fun, willing to try new things, creative and inventive, and use respect with customers, because this is still a business." Everything from the application forms to the recruiting interviews is designed to screen for people who will fit the company culture.

The employment application, for example, maintains all of the essential questions that are de rigueur for labor-law compliance. However, mixed into the standard mind-numbing questions about educational background and assorted bits of legalese, applicants will find cartoons, a crossword puzzle (to occupy them while in the waiting areas), a pictorial guide to shoe types, and short and whimsical blurbs on the company history.

This fun-loving but still serious attitude carries over into the interview process, which is built around ten core values. Some questions are conventional, while others are designed to probe for similarity of values between the individual and the company. Typically, when posing questions about Zappos's "Deliver 'WOW' through service" value, an interviewer may ask a prospective employee, "What does great customer service mean to you?" Less conventionally, the recruiter may also ask the interviewee to talk about the most unusual person he or she has worked with and whether or not that person was successful in the individual's view.

Other questions are designed to gauge what Foley describes as "red flag" indicators. There are no right or wrong answers, but they provide the recruiter with insight into how the individual approaches life, rules, and work relationships. Some key takeaways come from asking employees to talk about a time they broke a rule at work. As Foley describes it, Zappos likes to hear from people who were deterred from doing what they wanted to do for customers by rigid work rules or supervision—and that they were bothered by this.

Since "create fun and a little weirdness" is one of Zappos's core values, off-the-wall questions not only are to be expected but also serve to break down barriers in interviews so recruiters can really get to know their prospective recruits. Foley recalls the time that an applicant arrived in a suit and tie and, realizing he didn't fit in with Zappos's casual-dress environment, clearly felt uncomfortable. The interview continued awkwardly until Foley asked him her favorite question: If every time you walked into a room a theme song played, what would it be and why? When the up-till-now rigid and reserved applicant responded with Justin Timberlake's "SexyBack," Foley had to apologize for laughing at such an unexpected choice. As Foley tells the story, however, the applicant laughed and finally relaxed, and she was able to get a better sense of his real personality from that point forward.[3]

Understanding who employees are beneath their shells is essential to Zappos's personalized brand of customer service and relationship building. As Rob Siefker, a director for Zappos's call-center team (known as the "Customer Loyalty Team" or CLT), has said, "We don't want people to hide who they are. We want them to bring that out because really allowing yourself to feel comfortable and confident in who you are as a person allows creativity and really enhances the environment."[4]

To get a sense of a candidate's authentic personality, Zappos has applicants work through two rounds of interviews. The first set of discussions is designed to assess functional skills. The second set is designed to assess the individual's character traits, background, and potential cultural fit as a Zappos team member. Before the process concludes, an applicant for any position is likely to see more than a dozen interviewers. As Foley told us, "To have a candidate for a thirteen-dollar-an-hour job interview with fifteen people, that seems insane to a lot of people. It's really hard to do a spreadsheet ROI analysis, but as a company our number one goal has always been focused on hiring the right people. Everyone's committed, and it's why we and our culture keep growing."

Even those who make it through the strenuous interview process and are offered jobs aren't necessarily guaranteed employment. Every employee, regardless of position or experience, begins at Zappos with four weeks of training, composed of days running from 7:00 A.M. to 4:00 P.M. Attendance—one of the top three reasons employees in the call center are fired—is nonnegotiable. If someone is late, they're out of the training. As Siefker explained to us, "Sometimes it's a valid reason, but no matter what the problem is, no matter how legitimate, even if it's a flat tire—they'll never be able to continue in the same class. But depending on whether we think the person's a good cultural fit, we may ask them to wait three weeks to join the next class."

The ranks of potential employees also thin out at the second milestone of the training. First, all recruits must pass a knowledge-based exam about the company's history and call-center procedures. Depending upon position, raw recruits must pass additional testing throughout the screening process. Prospective call-center employees, for example, must pass a grammar test, a typing test, and a Web navigation test. In fact, the grammar test is so difficult that, as the training manager observed, "there are a lot of people in higher positions in the company who might not be able to pass the test. I'm glad I don't have to take it."

Yet another seminal training event is the two-thousand-dollar offer. A brainchild of Hsieh's, every recruit who makes it two weeks into the training is offered two thousand dollars to quit. No questions asked—just hand in your resignation and receive your money to leave. As several Zappos employees told us, there is no judgment of those who take it. Zappos views it as motivation for a recruit to let the company know the fit isn't right, before the company invests more in training or puts the recruit in front of its customers. It's easy to see how this could be motivating to quit: For a call-center employee making thirteen dollars per hour, two thousand dollars is nearly a month's wages. Nonetheless, fewer than 2 percent of new recruits take the money and run.

Those who elect to stay will continue with additional training. As they finish the four-week program, they will be exposed to each company department to understand its role in customer service. They will listen in on customer calls and use real examples in class to discuss customer problems and Zappos's response. During one class, for example, they may listen to a recorded call with a VIP customer who placed an order of nearly five thousand dollars that included such top-shelf brands as Gucci but who ended up receiving the wrong product. The class of twenty or fewer will debate what to do to fix the problem. Is thirty dollars enough . . . or is that insulting? How about a coupon for 30 percent off the order value?[5]

After two more intensive weeks of training, most recruits will move on to training within their future departments. In fact, the call-center employees—who make the least in most companies—will apprentice for an additional three weeks after completing the new employee training. During this period, they will listen to calls, get feedback on calls they directly handle, and have "values days" in which one full day is devoted to talking about how a Zappos value is put into practice by the Customer Loyalty Team.

Those who successfully make it past the company's probationary hurdles—written application, twelve or more interviews, tests, and training—become part of the family. Walking the halls of the company, the culture and employees' commitment are readily on display. From the decorated work spaces and hand-drawn posters that cover nearly every wall of the company headquarters, it's clear that employees feel a sense of ownership, pride, and commitment. Those translate not only into outstanding customer loyalty and revenue but also into some of the lowest employee attrition rates in the industry. On the Customer Loyalty Team, for example, while typical annual turnover in U.S. call centers is 50 percent or more, Zappos averages 12 percent—and that includes internal transfers and promotions.

The Human Factor

In the previous chapter, we discussed many of the changes that senior leaders can control to break down hierarchies and encourage employee involvement. While all of these are critical steps on the road to constructing a front line–focused organization, top managerial exhortations are meaningless if local work environments don't support frontline employees in acting in the envisioned way.

We turn our attention in this chapter to the two variables that matter most to an employee working on the front line every day: the quality of one's coworkers and the behavior of one's immediate supervisor. Extensive research has shown that the most likely reason an employee will leave a company or, perhaps worse still, remain but be disgruntled, is their relationship with their immediate supervisor. As the old saying goes, it takes two to tango, so managing this dynamic is as much about the employees an organization hires as about simply building better bosses.

As Zappos demonstrates day after day and sale after sale, intelligent hiring is an important and controllable variable. Zappos begins by screening for good incoming talent that shares its value system and affable approach to building personal connections with customers. The company also invests heavily in training those employees. In doing so, much like the U.S. Navy SEALs' process discussed in chapter 4, Zappos is able to ensure a good cultural fit—weeding out any potential mistaken hires during the new hire training period—and provide training related to judgment skills, business basics, and technical capabilities.

Zappos's cohesive approach to hiring, training, and organizational induction reinforces the factors that both test for and amplify a candidate's commitment. More than three decades of organizational research has shown beyond dispute that there is a powerful psychological dimension to how employees experience their work. We use the "four C's" model, introduced in chapter 2, to summarize the principal dimensions that have been shown to impact an employee's sense of empowerment. Considering Zappos's recruitment and training processes, it is easy to see how the company's approach creates employees who feel empowered on day one (or perhaps better said, day thirty-one, since they will have had four work weeks of training prior to beginning their actual job). Zappos addresses each element in turn as it brings new employees on board:

• **Context:** Employees desire to connect their work to larger goals. Zappos's mission "to live and deliver WOW" customer experiences immediately connects employees to improving customers' lives. The recruiting process reinforces this by screening intensively against the company values, testing whether behaviors associated with these values play a meaningful role in the candidate's prior experience. The two-thousand-dollar offer to quit during the second week of training further reinforces this by ensuring that the candidate is motivated by Zappos's mission and culture, not just a paycheck.

• **Control:** The ability to make autonomous decisions and take action is fundamental to Zappos's mind-set and how the company prioritizes building long-term customer relationships. The recruiting process tests for a desire to act independently for the right reasons by asking candidates to share prior job experiences in which they were constrained by rules or tight supervision. The parameters for making good judgments are taught throughout training using case studies, observation, and real-time coaching.

• **Care:** In the time and energy invested in both recruiting and training, employees see immediate evidence that Zappos is concerned about their well-being. The screening process evaluates a candidate's competence, and then many weeks of training help the candidate to learn his or her job, unlike the "sink or swim" approach favored in many frontline positions elsewhere.

• **Creativity:** Self-expression is fundamental to Zappos's culture. While working in teams and as part of the larger Zappos family is constantly reinforced, there is a deep respect for each individual's uniqueness. The recruiting process enables candidates to express their personality and encourages tearing down the facade that most people erect when interviewing. Training provides an opportunity for individuals to experiment with ways of letting their personality shine through during customer interactions.

Overall, Zappos screens for recruits who feel good about themselves and are inclined to take action. These are characteristics that research has shown are correlated with more empowered and capable employees.[6] While less than scientific, Zappos asks questions designed to gauge a person's base-level sense of contentment and well-being. One such question asks applicants to rate themselves from one to ten based on how lucky they feel. Loosely based on academic research positing that people who view themselves as lucky actually tend to be more observant and more creative, Zappos listens carefully to see if employees have a positive outlook and sense of good fortune or tend to have a narrow, task-oriented focus and blame others or uncontrollable situations for any misfortune.

While companies may be leery of committing the resources to hiring and training frontline staff that Zappos does, senior leaders should consider the cost of turnover. We worked with an employee team from one well-known retailer to estimate the true costs incurred from its habitual cycle of hiring, firing, or losing employees at annual turnover rates that varied from 30 percent for outlet managers to over 100 percent for customer-service staff. The costs we considered included not only the expected price of recruiting, interviewing, hiring, and training but also the hidden costs of turnover, such as management time spent in interviewing, lost sales due to improper staffing as replacements were found, and the loss of productivity as people learned a new job. In total, the cost of turnover in this particular company exceeded $350 million per year.[7] More than half of that came from turnover in nonexempt part-time labor, which had churn of 107 percent.[8] An equally alarming observation of the study was that turnover among women employees was 12 percent higher than their male coworkers. This was occurring just as the company was pushing to hire more women in order to better reflect the demographics of its customers and communities. After this study, the company implemented a number of changes that included improvements to hiring and training. The net results was a 50 percent decline in overall turnover in five years,[9] demonstrating, just as at Zappos, that an up-front investment in frontline employees more than pays for itself.

Creating Supervisors Who Empower the Front Line

Investing in hiring frontline associates who match a company's desired culture and training them to be effective is only half the battle. Another variable cannot be ignored: the quality and temperament of frontline supervisors. Whatever actions are taken or rhetoric spouted by senior leaders, an employee's most direct and visceral experience of a company is the result of his or her relationship with his or her manager. Ultimately, each frontline employee requires a supervisor who creates an environment in which he or she can be successful. As Fred Hassan, former CEO and senior manager of several pharmaceutical companies and currently a partner with private equity firm Warburg Pincus, noted in a *Harvard Business Review* article:

Typically, [frontline managers] make up 50% to 60% of a company's management ranks and directly supervise as much as 80% of the workforce. It is the frontline managers who must motivate and bolster the morale of the people who do the work—those who design, make and sell the products or deliver services to customers. These managers are central to a company's business strategy because they oversee its execution.[10]

While we couldn't agree more, we find that in many companies these leaders receive limited training. Frontline supervisors are often plucked from the ranks of frontline workers based on their performance and perhaps interpersonal skills, but many have never managed before. Their only role model may be the supervisor whom they are replacing. Even those with genuine management experience under their belts may be new to the organization. Although they may lack the background or sufficient knowledge, these supervisors serve as the gateway to the company. In addition to handling basic managerial functions (communication, training, problem solving, disciplinary actions, interviewing, etc.), they are expected to answer employees' questions or help them find resources on topics ranging from health and safety issues to human-resource policies to payroll.

As a professorial colleague from INSEAD observed, tongue in cheek, many years ago, those at the front line must be exponentially smarter than senior company managers, because they are allocated minuscule sums per employee for training, while senior managers are provided budget-busting amounts. Many CEOs and human-resources executives rationalize this disparity by citing the complexity of senior-level jobs, the return on investment, or the unmanageable scale of the task of reaching thousands of frontline supervisors. As a result, those organizations that do train their frontline supervisors often opt for online courses or shorter one- to two-day programs taught by training staff. While these are better than nothing, we find that such experiences typically have sheep-dip superficiality and lack the opportunity for meaningful dialogue about how to solve difficult personnel problems.

Our own research has repeatedly demonstrated that if a work team trusts its direct leader, employees are more likely to feel empowered, and that can translate directly into performance improvement. Specifically, three sets of managerial characteristics are important for leaders as they manage their teams.[11] We will explore each of these and some of the behaviors that the best frontline leaders display.

1. Coaching, Informing, and Showing Concern for Employees

Trust is predicated on maintaining a healthy relationship. As we surveyed frontline leaders through both research and clinical work, we found that for managers to demonstrate continuous personal interest in their employees is vital to this relationship. Understanding employees' stories and circumstances—their backgrounds, their families, their living situations—enabled frontline leaders to better understand what motivated these individuals and helped connect them to their work. As in any relationship, the interest must be sincere and the connection real. Frontline supervisors who go through the motions or treat such intimate conversations as an analytic exercise can create distance and awkwardness in their relationships.[12]

Teaching is another critical skill for frontline supervisors rarely developed through experience working on the line. Supervisors become the conduits for execution of the strategy by ensuring that work is completed at a quality level and in a manner that is consistent with organizational goals. They are responsible for inculcating and integrating new employees and helping them adapt to the organizational culture while ensuring that they learn the skills necessary to do their jobs.

When issues arise with an employee's performance or behavior, frontline supervisors are the face of the organization. If they allow low quality or inappropriate behavior to persist in the workplace, this becomes the new norm, regardless of whatever more congenial state of affairs the senior leadership may aspire to. If they address performance but destroy morale in the process, they can create disgruntled employees and drive up organizational costs as the inevitable result of turnover.

In this way, frontline supervisors create pockets of organizational culture. If they are misinformed or misaligned, senior management's intent will not matter, regardless of how noble and empowering their organizational vision may have been. A frontline employee's experience—how he or she thinks about the organization and talks about it to friends and neighbors—is disproportionately dictated by his or her frontline supervisor.

The responsibility of acting as a frontline supervisor in an organization that seeks to become more front line focused is both empowering and taxing. One of the biggest challenges we have observed firsthand as a company moves toward greater empowerment, frontline problem solving, and experimentation is dealing appropriately with employees' innate creativity. When an employee brings an idea to a supervisor that he or she wishes to test, the frontline supervisor must coach the subordinate in a way that helps him or her refine the idea while maintaining the psychological ownership and emotional commitment. The frontline supervisor should never take ownership away from the employee who generated the idea.

Likewise, if an employee conceives of a potentially terrible idea, an effective frontline supervisor's coaching must incorporate a careful cost-versus-benefit analysis. Telling the employee that an idea is stupid or destined for failure sends a message that the supervisor is not serious about fostering employee input. Word travels fast among employees in such cases. However, if the idea is too costly or simply not well thought through, the supervisor must help the employee consider the obstacles that went unseen in the employee's planning. Such coaching often turns into teaching about customers or the business, so that the employee who generated the idea is armed with better information and, ideally, either concludes independently that the idea was ill considered or is able to propose creative alternatives.

2. Encouraging Goal Setting, Self-Management, and Ownership

As a frontline supervisor for a prominent athletic retailer once explained to us, an employee's ownership of his or her goals is critical to achieving high-quality frontline judgment because if goals are simply passed down from the supervisor, employees will never be fully committed to their achievement. The goal-setting process must therefore be oriented toward assisting frontline employees in tempering their frequent desire to overshoot while giving others the motivation to aim even higher. As he put it to us more succinctly, "sometimes you have to bring them back down to earth; other times you have to open their eyes so they look a little higher." This same supervisor described an effective process that we have seen replicated among the best frontline leaders. Assuming that an employee's goals are aligned with the company's objectives, an effective supervisor will focus the employee on specific goals that will improve the business, for example, improving sales of a specific product or achieving higher average sales per day. The supervisor first asks the employee to set a goal and define an action plan. During a one-on-one coaching dialogue, the supervisor reviews the goal with the employee. If the goal is inappropriate, the supervisor's responsibility is to probe to understand the employee's thought process and help him or her make adjustments to the goal that are aligned with the business goals. Even if the supervisor remains unconvinced that the employee will attain the goal, he lets the employee continue to try—provided, of course, that the objective is not completely unrealistic and the magnitude of likely failure so great that the employee may become disengaged. Likewise, if the employee sets a goal too low, the supervisor must encourage him to be more ambitious, leading him to a more acceptable goal without directly dictating it.

The supervisor is likely to do so by linking the frontline employee's goal to business benchmarks and the individual's personal desires. Assuming the supervisor knows the employee and has a sense of his or her career aspirations, he can help the employee set goals that simultaneously improve performance (and therefore career options) and help to drive personal learning.

3. Creating the Structures, Policies, and Practices to Empower Workers

Every frontline supervisor creates a local environment for employees. The supervisor makes choices about the extent to which corporate policies are pursued, when to make exceptions, and what the consequences are for employees if they break a rule. The supervisor also installs structures, practices, and norms that can impact teamwork, how frontline workers partner (or don't) with other company departments, and how employees spend their time.

If a supervisor doesn't create effective structures for employees to come together and share ideas, or doesn't make time for discussions about customer learning, then employees will be less likely to share ideas or build off other team members' thoughts. The supervisor controls the agenda, structure, and expectations about how people should participate during team meetings. A supervisor must be able to design a daily or weekly team meeting process that promotes a sense of solidarity, openness, and equality among people of diverse backgrounds, personalities, and education.

In sum, the frontline supervisor is expected to possess a broad array of skills for managing teams and individuals despite limited experience and training. In many organizations, these capabilities are learned on the job, most often through the observation of the supervisor's manager.

For this reason, we find that there is typically more than one level of frontline supervisor who serves as the key to an organization's success. Depending upon the company structure, people in positions one or two levels above the frontline supervisors impact the local work environment and strongly influence the behavior that is passed down to frontline workers.

For example, in a retail organization multiple levels will affect the frontline sales force. In addition to department supervisors who manage sales teams, the store manager and even district manager will have a profound effect on the floor culture. A store manager who disregards input from supervisors, places undue emphasis on company paperwork, or occupies workers with busywork can single-handedly shut down employees' engagement. Conversely, a store manager or district manager who encourages appropriate risk taking, uses employee input to grow the business, and spends time on individual employee development will see such behaviors cascade down to the floor.

Frontline Supervisor Development at Intuit

Developing the type of leadership behavior needed to sustain empowered, engaged frontline employees requires consistency at multiple managerial levels. However, many organizations that wish to transform their hierarchies begin the process with leaders who may have received little formal training, combined with significant variance in what types of behaviors are rewarded at lower levels.

The software company Intuit faced just such a challenge as it sought to improve the leadership at its call centers. Intuit operates call centers that not only offer customers basic application support for products such as TurboTax but also provides pay-for-service telephone and Web support for its more complex professional software packages, such as QuickBooks. Intuit's call operators deal with consumers who may have installation questions or relatively simple user-interface issues, in addition to professionals such as accountants, who require support related to specific tax laws and reporting processes. In the latter case, call centers actually became revenue centers, as they provided both support and cross-selling opportunities for other Intuit products.

Intuit embarked on its efforts to improve frontline leadership based on a few simple facts. First, it had found that engaged employees were 30 percent more likely to demonstrate high-performance behaviors and resolve customer issues. It had also found that such committed employees were five times more likely to stay with Intuit, even if offered a comparable position and salary elsewhere. Finally, it had determined through surveys and interviews that more than 75 percent of employee satisfaction was directly impacted by the employee's direct supervisor. When Intuit came to us seeking help, it had over 1,700 frontline employees who were managed by approximately 150 frontline supervisors, known as "coaches" internally.

The program we designed and implemented at Intuit, with our colleague Patricia Stacey, focused first on its frontline coaches. In our experience and Intuit's, training the front line directly had uneven results because some frontline supervisors would contradict the training and employees would quickly revert to old behaviors. Intuit's efforts, by contrast, were consciously focused on developing frontline coaches as leaders and teachers.

In a four-month process depicted on the next page, frontline coaches were expected to deepen their business acumen, develop individual behaviors consistent with organizational values, strengthen execution skills, build stronger teams, and improve their change leadership capability. Each of these skills related to specific expectations for how frontline coaches worked with their employees and drove results.

The process began with frontline coaches receiving 360-degree feedback, including qualitative responses directly from their employees. For most, this was the first time they had heard impressions of their management style directly from their team members, and not surprisingly, it was an eye-opening experience. On a personal level, coaches also considered

Frontline Leadership Development Program

	July–November			Ongoing
	Workshop I	Apply	Workshop II	
Apply Busines Acumen	• Company, BU, and FL team strategies • Diagnosis of team • Project—begin working some metrics	• Line of sight with manager on improvement project	• New skills for business acumen	• Execute individual development plans • L&D offerings for specific skill building
How We Behave as Individuals . . .	• Journey line • 360 feedback • I speak your language • Teaching Intuit values • Learn teach learn	• Action log commitments	• New skills for time management • Deeper dive into how leaders add value	• Use of operating mechanisms for continual development
Lead Change	• Vision exercise • Transformational leadership	• Implement improvement project	• Coaching on improvement project	• Continue to define and implement improvement projects
Build Strong Teams	• Coach development plan • Agent talent assessment • Agent development plans • Resolving tough isssues	• Execute action plan related to agent assessment	• Share learnings and best practices • Coaches coach one another • Work on difficult problems/conversations	• Coaches best practice clinic—sponsored by BU leader • New coach onboarding process
Execute Effectively	• Operating mechanisms • Process mapping • Work simple • Improvement project	• Implement improvement project	• New skills for process excellence	• Assessment of coaches based on leadership skills

Intuit™

how they related the organizational values to workplace behaviors and considered how they worked with different personality types.

To build better work teams, coaches learned tools for motivating individuals and groups and resolving conflict, both within their team and with other departments. Part of this was dealing with difficult issues. Some were performance related, such as the employee who clocked in on time every day but then disappeared to the bathroom for thirty minutes each morning. Others were team related, including a "loud talker" whose baritone voice boomed across workstations. Perhaps most difficult were cultural issues. In one case a top-notch employee had immigrated to the United States from a different country. Although nobody had confronted him on the issue, he had volunteered in casual conversation that bathing customs in his country of origin were quite different and he didn't understand Americans' preoccupation with showering so frequently. Unfortunately, due to a combination of his diet and lack of bathing, he had body odor that filled the room and quite literally left other employees feeling nauseated. While the case elicited the expected smirks and laughs as it was discussed in the program, it was quite evident that the coach had no idea how to address the issue. He didn't want to lose a good employee who had high integrity and was a great team member. Yet he had no idea how to raise the issue without risking permanently offending the person. Such situations were discussed and debated in the program in preparation for the coaches to return to work and provide personalized developmental coaching for each employee.

Coaches also developed operating mechanisms for their teams. They determined when teams would meet each morning, how meetings would be run to maximize participation and idea sharing, and how they would balance their leadership role with letting team members facilitate discussions about business performance. Some coaches took it upon themselves to set up special forums when their teams could meet to review specific topics such as customer feedback, improving organizational processes, or reviewing team performance indicators.

In order to relate their work to their business area, each coach identified an improvement project that he or she would work on with his or her team for approximately ninety days. These were typically quick-hit opportunities, such as improving customer-response times, increasing customer satisfaction scores, or raising cross sales of related products by more consistently offering services to customers.

Most important, coaches learned how to teach in the first workshop. Following their participation in the first session, they were required to teach their teams all of the content to which they had been exposed. Unlike in prior training programs, they didn't condense their three-day experience into three hours; they taught every element of the program in its entirety. Due to the nature of the work, some coaches broke the content into modules so they could teach in one- or two-hour increments over the course of several weeks. To assist them, each coach was given a kit of materials that included workbooks, slides, and videos that they customized to their part of the business.

After ninety days, the coaches returned to report on performance, share stories, receive additional coaching, and continue learning. Their business-analysis skills were tested with a deeper look at how operational actions and individual employee performance could impact financial results. They brought videos of meetings they had conducted so they could receive feedback on how to improve their facilitation skills. They also discussed how difficult issues were handled with employees—sharing what worked and what didn't—so everyone could learn from the collective experience.

All told, the projects created millions of dollars of benefits for Intuit. Perhaps most important, the strategic alignment created by having the coaches teach their teams directly drove improved performance. As one coach described it to us, the power of the process was having the coaches teach. This created an atmosphere of mutual accountability in which the coach had to follow up and employees couldn't say they were unclear about expectations. The process had raised the performance bar on everyone while fostering closer teamwork and better working relationships.

It wasn't surprising to us to learn that employee engagement figures among those who went through Intuit's process rose by double digits in less than one year.

Summary: Creating the Right Environment

Although companies may invest and senior leaders may sincerely desire to build an organization with a front line capable of caring for customers, problem solving, and innovating, the rubber ultimately hits the road when frontline supervisors and employees interact. Senior managers can support frontline leaders most critically by ensuring that a rigorous hiring process is in place for employees at all levels. This runs counter to the senior management pressure that results if leaders pay attention only to "staffing fill rates" or other measures that track the quantity of employees rather than the quality. This leads to frontline supervisor expressions that we hear too often and that seem to transcend industries, such as "Give me a warm body" (a retail favorite) or "I need butts in seats" (a call-center hiring mantra).

If the CEO and senior leaders are serious about building a front line–focused organization, they also need to cough up resources for training. Sending poorly equipped new hires to be trained by poorly prepared frontline supervisors leads to a staffing turnover cycle that is familiar to many companies. Even hiring new employees with prior industry experience is not a solution, as Zappos demonstrated, if you are attempting to use your front line as a competitive edge.

This holds true not just for the line workers but, even more important, for frontline supervisors, whom organizations rely upon to lead as much as 80 percent of the workforce. These leaders create local cultures that promote the desired employee engagement, creativity, and problem-solving behaviors. Despite this knowledge, many organizations fail to invest, as Intuit did, in their frontline supervisors. However, the lesson is clear: Those who accomplish this task well build organizational commitment, team performance, customer satisfaction, and better financial results.

A NEVER-ENDING PROCESS

None of this happens unless you have the right culture, the right trust, the right environment, the right training, the right guidance provided to the people on the team. We're going to—each of us—have to learn how to be more effective leaders than we are today.

—Brad Anderson, former CEO of Best Buy

- **THE FRONT LINE IS SUCCESSFUL ONLY WITH CEO SUPPORT AND DIRECTION**

  - If senior management fails to define a winning competitive strategy, the front line is set up to fail.

  - The burden of top leadership failure is felt most profoundly by those near the front line.

- **SUSTAINING A FRONT LINE–FOCUSED ORGANIZATION IS A NEVER-ENDING PROCESS**

  - Frontline disciplines require ongoing investment and development.

  - Communication mechanisms need to be structured to enable dialogue between the frontline and senior leaders regarding market or customer changes.

You may be wondering why Best Buy is a relevant benchmark for leadership judgment at the front line, particularly when the company recently closed its first quarter of 2012 with its share price down more than 60 percent from its 2007 peak, had just taken a $1.7 billion write-off as it planned to close fifty big-box stores, and its CEO had just resigned amid allegations of personal misconduct. Yet the story of Best Buy, replete with tragic flaws in leadership, is a modern parable demonstrating how quickly efforts to create a front line–focused organization may vanish without strong CEO support and guidance. Indeed, Best Buy highlights that sustaining a front line–focused organization must be a never-ending process that requires ongoing investment and senior leader diligence.

The depth of Best Buy's recent troubles became evident on the morning of April 10, 2012, when the company's board of directors announced the resignation of Brian Dunn as CEO, stating tersely in its press release that "it was time for new leadership to address the challenges that face the company." In the coming weeks, it was revealed that Dunn had an "inappropriate relationship" with a female subordinate, which founder Dick Shulze had failed to report to other board members, leading to his resignation as chairman of the board.[1] In many respects, the harsh spotlight on the company could not have come at a worst time given its steadily decaying business performance. As financial columnist Jim Fink noted on his widely read Web site, *Stocks to Watch*, "Ethical and moral lapses aside, as Best Buy's declining stock price attests, its current strategic direction is a road to nowhere."[2]

The turmoil the company faces at the time of this writing was neither sudden nor entirely unforeseen. Since early 2011, when Best Buy reported lower than expected earnings and a sharp drop in quarterly sales over the 2010 holiday period, analysts and journalists have been in search of the forces behind the company's financial descent. The consensus that emerged, and which is echoed ever more forcefully in analyst reports on the company, is that its business model is severely broken. Customers shopping at Best Buy have taken to "show rooming," or visiting the stores in order to compare products, play with them, ask questions of salespeople, and then buy elsewhere after searching for the cheapest online price at Best Buy's competitors. The company faces not only disruptive consumer behavior but is also squaring off with retail colossuses such as Amazon, Apple, and Wal-Mart. These companies not only compete more effectively on price but, as the trend toward digitization of content increases (largely fueled by Amazon and Apple), Best Buy is left with ever fewer products to stock on the shelves of its costly 50,000-square-foot stores.

Dunn's departure after a brief tenure of two years and nine months no doubt left the workforce of nearly 170,000 people—most of them frontline associates working in stores—wondering whether the company would survive or if they would soon join the ranks of the hundreds of Best Buy employees who had been laid off just weeks before. As consultants to Dunn's predecessor, Brad Anderson, from 2002 to 2005, we observed mounting analyst and journalist criticism with a feeling of genuine sympathy, mixed with a powerful sense of déjà vu.

Under Anderson, Best Buy had faced a comparably deep set of challenges in the bricks-and-mortar world with direct threats from Wal-Mart, which looked to make consumer electronics one of its core profit areas; Target's expansion into the sector; Dell's proliferation of new retail outlets; alongside the perennial challenge from a still competitive Circuit City. Anderson's stewardship had helped increase sales from $17.7 billion in fiscal 2002 to $40 billion in 2008, grew earnings at an average of 16.5 percent per year, and expanded from 600 stores to nearly 3,900.[3]

Although the challenges facing Best Buy today are particularly acute, the company has faced two near-death experiences that demonstrated its tenacity and ability to recreate itself. Indeed, Best Buy was born of reinvention after teetering on the edge of bankruptcy. After launching the chain in 1966 as a stand-alone stereo-components store called Sound of Music in St. Paul, Minnesota, founder Dick Schulze had fortuitously stumbled upon the big-box idea in the mid-1970s when a tornado wrecked one of his leading outlets. The sale of steeply discounted, salvaged goods he held under a rented tent drew thousands of wildly satisfied cost-conscious customers. Under Schulze, that warehouse served as the template for more than six hundred free-standing big boxes by the turn of the twenty-first century.

We entered the picture just as Brad Anderson was taking the reins from Schulze and the question that lingered over the company then—just as in 2012—was how long Best Buy's aging formula would last. Anderson's response was to foster a transformation from a product-centric business model to a customer-centric orientation that was largely reliant on the company's frontline associates.

As we will see, however, Best Buy's story is one of dueling narratives. With Anderson's guidance, the company installed many of the essential elements required to build a front line–focused organization. In its best moments, this unleashed tremendous energy and imagination, inspiring pockets of cultural change and contributing significant financial results that helped drive the share price to its peak in 2007. The bad news is that this transformation didn't stick when Dunn took the helm. The company's initial success—followed by the subsequent dissipation of its frontline efforts—provides instructive lessons for any leader wishing to make lasting change.

Never-Ending Process

In this chapter we will focus on the difficulty of maintaining a front line–focused organization. As we have noted repeatedly, ultimately it is the CEO who stands accountable for defining, aligning, and executing an organization's strategy for winning in the marketplace. Frontline employees can be both a major contributor to growth and innovation and an early-warning system if a company's strategy is off target. The CEO and senior leaders must use intelligence from the front line to adjust the overall strategy, in the process ensuring that frontline efforts remain pointed in the right direction. And should senior leadership fail them, those on the front line do not walk away with stock options or golden parachutes worth millions of dollars but are more likely to join the unemployment line.

The five-step process we have discussed throughout the preceding chapters must be a never-ending process in which leaders maintain mechanisms for open dialogue with leaders at all levels. Sustaining the benefits of a frontline investment requires keeping communication lines flowing with information back to top management. Otherwise, the process winds down and the company reverts to its initial steady state, as opposed to a continual process of self-examination and reinvention through frontline feedback.

During our work with the company from 2002 to 2005, Best Buy was able to engage its front line for growth and innovation to deliver stellar results. We will discuss Best Buy's past success and more recent stumbles to provide insight into not only how frontline employees can help to transform an enterprise but also the criticality of a company's top brass continuing to steadily engage with the front line to understand changes in customer needs and marketplace dynamics. Finally, we will examine how Best Buy's front line might yet help the company reinvent itself to confront an uncertain future.

Past as Prologue

In 2002, as Brad Anderson took over as CEO, Best Buy had just completed a five-year run that made it the top-performing stock on the New York Stock Exchange. While it seemed that the company—a retail darling of Wall Street investors—could do no wrong, Anderson saw storm clouds on the horizon. Anderson, who had joined the company in 1973 and lived through two near-death retail experiences, had enthusiastically embraced the idea that dramatic change would be required for the company to survive this latest competitive onslaught.

Intrigued by our clinical work, Anderson first asked Noel to meet with the founder and chairman, Dick Schulze, which led to a subsequent meeting with Best Buy's board of directors. It was during this meeting that the company's leaders discussed the importance of clarifying the strategy and establishing a shared enterprise-wide value system and a methodology that would mobilize and motivate thousands of associates to help the organization continue to change and grow.

The first step was to work with the top team to agree on the vision and values during a two-day workshop. At this session, Anderson and team also agreed to launch an "action learning" process that included evaluating strategic options such as acquisitions or geographic expansion.

In this six-month process involving thirty-six company officers, one team focused on capturing more share of the wallet from the high-end consumer segment. The team was introduced to our longtime colleague Columbia professor Larry Selden, who had a powerful methodology for helping companies define customer segments, develop value propositions, and drive customer-focused strategies. Based on our introduction, Selden subsequently worked with the action-learning team to help it define the high-end segment for Best Buy, which led to broader discussions with Anderson.

As the customer strategy began to take shape, it became evident that segmentation and localization of service and product offers would be a game changer for Best Buy relative to its competition. By October 2002, Anderson was convinced that a major transformation was needed, one that would involve everyone in the organization. We helped Anderson launch the first enterprise-wide effort to teach the new strategy and related values and prepare the top 160 corporate managers to define what the strategy meant for their part of the company. Gathering the group, along with the board of directors, in northern Minnesota for an offsite, Anderson started the meeting by screening a six-minute video that many in the audience found painful to watch.

The mini movie, which had been shot on sidewalks outside Best Buy stores by the company's internal communications department, featured real customers as they exited and shared their views of the shopping experience. One man in his early thirties, on his way out of a store empty-handed, caustically described the sales force he had encountered inside. When he finally attracted the attention of a salesman, the customer reported that he "felt as if he wasn't listening to me. He was happy to talk about everything on his mind, but he didn't show the faintest interest in why I was there or what I needed." Barely containing his frustration, the customer noted that whenever he asked a slightly technical question, "all he wanted to do was read me the box. Fortunately, I'm educated and I can also read." Another five minutes of visibly aggravated customers venting gripes about everything from the company's lackluster promotions to pushy salespeople to deceptive warranty offers followed.

Anderson used this brief exercise in cinema verité to create a burning platform for change. He knew that in doing so he would anger some of his top people. And he knew that this would be necessary to focus the company in a new direction. The retailer historically had been built with a mass-market strategy and strong centralization, with employees at the company's Minnesota headquarters setting strategy, selecting products, and passing down directions for the troops to follow. Its founding philosophy had been captured by early-day employees as "stack 'em high and watch 'em fly," an observation that implied that as long as Best Buy employees stacked the products (all of which were selected by corporate merchants at headquarters) in the aisles, consumers would help themselves and the company could virtually print money.

The new "customer-centric" approach flipped that equation on its head by acknowledging that Best Buy's customer offer had dimmed in contrast to Wal-Mart's potential for offering deep discounts or the brand loyalty demonstrated by Target's customers. The strategy that had enabled the retailer to dislodge Circuit City as the nation's largest electronics retailer and driven many smaller regional players out of business would not prevail against larger, more sophisticated competitors that had enormous purchasing power.

In the company's favor, consumer technology was growing more complicated by the day while customers were struggling with digital devices like never before. Customers not only had to install the products they purchased, but they now also had to get them to talk to one another. The big opportunity would be to provide a level of localized service and a customer experience that would make technology enjoyable again for customers—in much the same way that young audiophiles had once salivated over the latest amplifiers and turntables when Anderson first joined the company. The fact that Dell and Amazon enjoyed no physical presence and Target and Wal-Mart lacked specialization had to be turned to Best Buy's advantage: The way forward for Best Buy would be to create an in-store experience that would more closely connect the company's thousands of store employees with its millions of customers. Another way of defining this solution was to state that the new overarching strategy would be shaped less by pushing products than by deepening and enhancing the relationship to the customer.

Adopting this transformation from product-centric to customer-centric top to bottom would ultimately require a new product and service mix, new leadership in the stores, and an entirely new way of interacting with customers. "We're going to start listening to the customer," Anderson repeatedly declared to his increasingly motivated senior echelon and rank-and-file troops. His primary vehicle for achieving this goal would be to inspire and activate every frontline associate in every store. They—Anderson's "people"—would collaborate with him and his top team in crafting the company's new customer-value propositions, localizing the product assortments, and granting the front line sufficient autonomy to solve customer problems on the spot using their judgment.

Bringing Customer-Centricity to Life

While customer-centricity made intellectual sense, Anderson needed to connect this strategy with execution. He began by laying out a basic conviction:

> [Customer-centricity] starts with a belief that the company will create sustainable success by unleashing the creativity and energy of its 90,000 plus people. . . . The key to creating a constant flow of new growth platforms is to create a capability enabling the broadest number of minds (focused on what customers truly need) to contribute.

From the start, Anderson knew that a component critical to this transformation would be the evolution of an "owner/operator" business model in the company's stores. This would "enable individuals to contribute to the bottom line based on an understanding of actual financials," acting as a small business owner might. This concept lay at the root of his frontline-judgment-activation strategy, one explicitly designed to provide a vision, boundaries, and parameters framed from the top that would achieve the goal of unleashing "the power of the people" to experiment and innovate at the local level. These local experiments, designed to reach, touch, and embrace the customer segments targeted by the company, would over time achieve successful results that could be cascaded over the enterprise.

To make this happen, Anderson clearly articulated his Teachable Point of View on what would be required of employees to win with customers. First, power would need to shift from the central office to the field, enabling local leaders to alter their inventory mix, product selection, and selling strategies. This localized approach, enhanced by a platform of services, would enable Best Buy to create deeper relationships with customers than online or discount competitors. In order to make such judgments intelligently, Best Buy needed to unleash its people, showing more respect for those on the front line and giving them the tools and resources to learn from their day-to-day customer interactions. In sum, this new operating model would invigorate those in the stores as they became free to solve customer problems, contribute ideas, and mobilize staff to help reinvent the company.

Anderson's rhetoric of customer-centricity is commonplace today and even in 2002 needed some meat to back up the lingo. For Anderson and his top team, the first stage of the journey had to be developing a deeper understanding of Best Buy's customers before asking the front line to change how it worked. Ironically, many years earlier the company had invested several million dollars in a customer relationship management (CRM) platform, which had collected millions of potentially useful customer data points through its transactions and loyalty program. But over the years, Best Buy had failed to harness that trove of data and maximize its usable insights.

In January 2003, Anderson launched six teams of cross-functional high-potential executives tasked with combing through the CRM database to identify customer segments. Over a four-month period, the teams visited stores to observe customer behavior and assess how employees delivered the in-store experience. After a month, the amorphous data set buried in the CRM system began to take shape into distinct customer segments. By the end of this process, Best Buy had committed itself to six distinct customer groups and given each a name, such as "Barry," which comprised high-end male shoppers with big budgets. By far the most problematic was "Jill," which represented mothers typically shopping for other family members, for whom a dreaded visit to Best Buy was all too often a discombobulating experience.

Assumptions about each customer segment were tested through a series of "learning laboratories," starting with four stores in the Washington, D.C., area and then growing into more than one hundred as the tests expanded to involve Los Angeles, San Francisco, and Chicago. Store displays were changed and product assortments altered as each store attempted to home in on one or two target customer segments.

Getting frontline employees to embrace these cosmetic changes was conceptually simple, but changing their behavior proved considerably tougher. The "software" in the store needed to change. Employees had to learn to dialogue differently with customers, talking to them in a way that helped clarify what problem they were solving and what other technology they had in their home and finding new ways to interpersonally relate to what the company now realized were very different types of customers.

Changing Behavior on the Sales Floor

Certain assumptions were thrown out the window right from the start. Salespeople who thought they could read customers by how they dressed or spoke realized they were often dead wrong. The guy wearing blue jeans and a T-shirt shopping on a Saturday afternoon might be a "Ray" customer with an average income who would want to purchase using credit. Or he could be a "Barry" with a six-figure income who would write a check for a ten-thousand-dollar stereo system without blinking. The only way to truly "know" the customer was to have a genuine conversation to get to know him or her much better and to find out what he or she really needed.

The learning labs also confirmed that in order for employees to make better judgments, they needed to know how the business worked. The average employee was in his or her twenties and had limited business experience, and many associates were in school or had not completed college. These employees needed to understand the math behind the company's business decisions.

Retail might seem like a simple business, but there are numerous variables to contend with. At Best Buy, margins and profitability varied widely by product, with the company sometimes using loss leaders or low-profit items to drive customer traffic in stores. Moreover, every store had different lease terms and base investments. If the goal was to teach employees to act like small business owner-operators, then they needed to comprehend more complicated concepts, such as return on invested capital and weighted-average cost of capital, to determine just how much their box was earning for the company.

A few of the senior executives, particularly those who had spent their careers in the field, derided this approach as unnecessary. "Why does someone selling a refrigerator need to learn 'MBA math'?" they would ask with a scornful snort. "How are you going to teach a part-timer advanced financial computations?" But once in the field, we discovered that much of the criticism and bravado was actually cover for the fact that they struggled to do the calculations themselves.

Teaching business acumen began with a basic formula that our colleague Larry Selden identified and that made intuitive sense to anyone who had spent time selling on a retail floor. It started by noting that each store's performance was a function of its traffic multiplied by its close rate, or the percentage of customers who actually purchased after visiting Best Buy. The result, which showed the number of customers who bought something on a given day, could be multiplied again by the average number of items per transaction and by the average sales price per transaction.

This formula put simple math around a simple concept; namely, that most customers don't visit Best Buy just to hang out. Best Buy is a destination, so most shoppers enter the store to *buy* something. Not everybody buys, so the close rate multiplied by customer traffic explains the salespeople's success at converting customer visits into transactions. However, salespeople cannot only influence whether customers buy. They can also suggest additional products, or units, for the customer, for example, the memory card to go along with a new digital camera or the printer ink to go along with a new photo printer. Finally, selling higher-margin products was more likely to benefit the company.

This approach was dramatically different in two ways from what Best Buy had historically done, and many retailers still do. Salespeople were no longer pressuring customers to buy service plans or additional items because they had been given a quota. They started by asking what the customer was trying to accomplish. They suggested product bundles or services based on segment profiles (for example, "Ray" customers typically liked the in-store credit card and extended-warranty plans) and the individual customer's situation. For the first time, associates not only understood the numbers behind why it benefited the company to sell certain products, but they also had the freedom to sell based on what the customer wanted rather than worry about losing their job for failing to make quota.

The financial lessons didn't stop here. To teach the associates, there was a morning meeting for all employees in every store across the United States. In the first hour of their day, the store manager would personally review the financials from the prior day and work with employees to identify behaviors that needed to change with customers while brainstorming opportunities to sell more based on segment needs they were observing day to day. These were called "chalk talks" because they were modeled on the reviews football teams conduct the morning after every game. Each chalk talk also had short lessons on the math underlying the financial numbers. Over the course of six weeks, employees were able to absorb all of the concepts by practicing the calculations and reviewing store profit-and-loss statements.

It became apparent that understanding the business had become fun for employees when store personnel began finding creative ways to teach one another. In Los Angeles, for example, one store team came up with a chant that was repeated several times throughout the day. The store manager or chosen employee would ask the questions, reinforcing key financial concepts, and employees would shout back the answers.

Best Buy's Business Acumen Store Cheer

A Los Angeles store manager would begin each day with the team cheer below. The team's answers are underlined.

To start a business you need? Capital!

And with this Capital . . . We want to make a profit

And we call this? NOPAT

And NOPAT stands for? Net Operating Profit After Taxes

And the higher the NOPAT, the higher the? ROIC

And ROIC stands for? Return on Invested Capital

One of the employees in a San Diego store took this concept a step further and put together a *Business Acumen for Dummies* booklet, which was independently circulated to the employees so they would have facts and figures at their fingertips. (The title was later changed to the more sedate *Pocket Guide for Financials* to avoid any brand infringement on the "Dummies" book series.) Conversations percolated about profit margins and how to get a better return per square foot on the investment in the store. Employees were ready to begin experimenting, and small tests started to proliferate in all of the stores.

Best Buy's Experimentation Framework

Best Buy invested so much in teaching its people about the business because it was looking for local judgment and innovation at the front line. These goals, however, wouldn't be achievable if employees didn't understand the company's customer and financial goals and didn't have the tools to figure out whether each decision they made would lead to profit or collectively lead the company off the proverbial cliff. Where the company already had strong standard operating procedures (SOPs), it wanted to balance discipline and operating consistency with permitting employees to make changes that benefited local customers.

To teach employees how to innovate, a simple tool developed in collaboration with Larry Selden based on the scientific method linked investigative rigor to the customer and business disciplines that frontline employees were beginning to master on their own. The method changed internally over time as employees rendered it operational, but its essence remained consistent: Understand what you want to impact on the store P&L, link it to customer needs, then devise an experiment to test it.

Though employees were asked to assimilate quite a lot of discrete information by this method—customer-segment needs, business acumen, and the experimentation framework—they embraced it enthusiastically. Best Buy's core value, "Unleash the power of our people," became a mantra in the stores. Execution wasn't always perfect, but the opportunity to try ideas and fix problems was intoxicating for most of the employees. Experimentation became frontline employees' judgment and creativity put into action.

Best Buy's Scientific Method for Experimentation

What	How	Why
What are the results versus the plan? What is the trend (results versus last week)? For example: Net sales up 45K over last week Net sales down 15K from plan	How are operational metrics/drivers contributing to results? Quantify specifics Identify the degree of impact in order to determine where to focus the "Hypothesis" and "Test"	Why is this happening? Behavior driving the Value Proposition or Operating Model If the "Why" isn't known and verified with quantification, make a hypothesis, test and verify
Hypothesis	**Test**	**Verify**
What will you try? What are the expected results? Numbers needed for customer impact and financial impact There may be many hypotheses. Try one!	Specific work plan to execute the hypothesis What behavioral changes are required by whom? Communication/training plan Customer feedback loops Note: As you go through the test, learning may lead you to change your hypothesis	Reconcile actual results versus hypothesis Measurement plan with milestones

Local innovations flowed from the front line in a multitude of unexpected forms and were typically the brainchild of a genuinely enthusiastic employee who mobilized his or her coworkers to his or her cause. Some of the ideas were small, such as that of an employee who worked in the audio department and showed how certain alarm clocks could be tied to home theaters (the idea didn't test well). Other ideas were large, such as the weekend that workers at the Pasadena store spent ripping the linoleum floor out of the home theater department to install a parquet wood floor they had purchased at their own expense. The differentiated space for home theater and the rich look of the wood drew much more customer traffic and sales spiked almost immediately. (This was an important catalyst to eventually implementing a store-within-a-store concept at Best Buy, including the adoption of the Magnolia Home Theater brand, which occupies a corner of almost every location today.)

As the contributions from innovations became bigger and more visible, nearly every store had one or more stories to offer about changes it had implemented to great effect. Long Beach celebrated how Chris Applegate, a part-time associate, had spotted the emerging category of VoIP, Internet telephony. Working directly with his store manager, Applegate crafted his hypothesis that positioning the VoIP display closer to the store entrance would generate more customer sales. It didn't. Tinkering with the display didn't help much either. After a few iterations, Applegate decided to create a working demo of the product. The few weeks he focused on the product also helped him develop a clear explanation of the benefits and an ability to calm customer fears that they would be left without phone service. His next round of experimentation, in which he personally trained his sales colleagues on VoIP's benefits and taught them to maintain the demo, was an astounding success. Within weeks the store had more than quadrupled it sales of VoIP. Executives took notice as Applegate's experiment not only beat his store's sales targets but crushed those of every other store in the chain.

The list of successes went on and on. Whether it was Torrance, California, bragging about the low-cost flat-panel display in the middle of the store that had led to double-digit sales increases or Costa Mesa hyping its remodeled appliance department, the financial and customer-satisfaction results spoke for themselves. Customer surveys showed satisfaction rising steadily at the stores while the financial picture showed double-digit comps.

Breaking Down the Hierarchy at Best Buy

While the field was making investments and localizing the look and feel of many stores, those at the corporate headquarters were working hard to support the transformation. Part of the corporate work was driving efficiencies in order to pay for investments in new systems and store remodels. Another equally important contribution was corporate personnel's work to drive more decision-making authority and systems to the field as the organization decentralized some processes.

Anderson assembled six teams of corporate functional leaders who worked on everything from product merchandising to information-technology systems to supply chain. For four months these teams worked to redefine how their corporate function would operate with more field autonomy. Decisions and processes that had once been centralized and standardized—with little deviation from the prescription handed down by Minneapolis staff—now needed to be made by local employees to support local customers. For example, stores needed the capability to produce professional in-store signs and displays that featured the concepts they were testing without waiting three weeks for a corporate-approved vendor. Dozens of other changes were made, including granting stores more complete access to customer databases, creating new capital approval processes, and realigning field communication channels.

Operational changes demanded even more dramatic changes in how the central functions were staffed and organized. Departments were reorganized and head counts often decreased. For senior leaders, this meant uncomfortable changes and, in some cases, an unwanted loss of control. Monthly meetings and their combined work to oversee the remaking of the functional departments helped to ease tensions and better align functional work.

Creating the Right Environment

Change was no less challenging for many field leaders. Those at the top of the hierarchy, regional managers with large geographies and dozens of stores, often had decades of experience in retail. They were used to the operations of a command-and-control structure. Even those below them, district managers, knew their position in the hierarchy and had grown accustomed to telling stores what to fix and seeing a response in double time.

Significant time was spent training managers at all levels. Best Buy assembled a Transformation Leadership Team of specially assigned employees who lived in the stores, teaching store managers and working with field leaders to ensure that they understood the changes. Teaching employees about customer-segmentation schemes and ROIC seemed relatively easy when compared with getting managers to change how they set goals, visited stores, interacted with associates, and managed performance.

Getting It Right

When the pieces came together for Best Buy, it felt as though the company were creating magic in its stores—for both customers and employees. Senior leaders often visited the field. One story emerged in late April 2005 while six senior executives were each spending a week in California stores working side by side with employees to better understand the operational realities of customer-centricity.

Two of the executives met a frontline salesperson, Will, who shared the story of a customer, Stephen, who was looking to install a navigation system in his Mercedes. As he helped Stephen, Will asked him questions about how he spent his time, asked about his family, and inspected the vehicle. One of the first things Will noticed was a laptop and printer that awkwardly occupied Stephen's front seat. It turned out that Stephen spent most of his time in the car visiting customers and needed the ability to print files. As they spoke, Stephen asked whether the patchwork cabling draped across his front seats could be hardwired and hidden so that the machines would start when his car started. Will offered to look into it for Stephen.

By his own admission, Will was far from computer savvy, so he turned to his colleagues in the company's Geek Squad service area. After thinking it through, he wondered why the system couldn't be set up wirelessly, with the printer in Stephen's trunk and the laptop still easily removable. The printer could be wired to turn on automatically whenever the car was started, and Stephen wouldn't be burdened with a printer in his front seat. When Will presented the idea, Stephen remained hesitant but said he would think about it.

Will went to work installing the navigation system. Working under the dash in Stephen's car, Will realized that the premium sound system didn't work properly. After a quick call, Stephen confessed that he had paid two thousand dollars plus installation for the stereo system but it had never sounded good. "It's not the money that bothers me," he told Will. "I would have paid three times what it cost me. I just wanted it to sound right." Will told him he would fix it. Stephen's reaction was immediate and emotional. "Can you really?" he asked.

Will said that was the moment when Stephen first complimented him and the Best Buy team, saying this was a completely different experience than he had had at any store. Will and his colleagues installed the navigation system and fixed the audio system. When Stephen came back at 3:00 P.M. to pick up his car, he was delighted with the work. With a bit of hesitation he turned to Will, asking, "You know, is it too late to get that printer set up?"

As Will recounted the tale to the senior executives, he confessed that in the back of his mind he had hoped that Stephen would ask him to do the work while the car was still torn apart. Will shared that just a couple of hours from the end of his shift, he understood how important the work was for Stephen and how much it would help him do his job. He quickly agreed to do the additional work.

The relationship that Will sparked with Stephen not only converted a several-hundred-dollar hardware sale into a highly profitable job worth several thousand dollars. It also led to a lasting customer relationship and a personal bond between Will and Stephen. Will shared that Stephen kept in touch frequently. Once Stephen called Will while golfing in Hong Kong

LEARNING FROM WILL

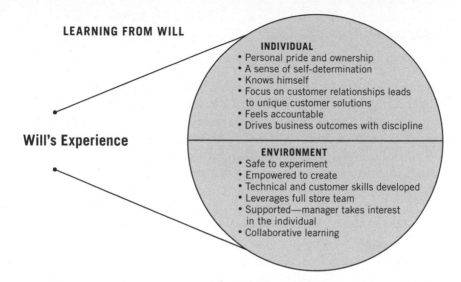

Will's Experience

INDIVIDUAL
- Personal pride and ownership
- A sense of self-determination
- Knows himself
- Focus on customer relationships leads to unique customer solutions
- Feels accountable
- Drives business outcomes with discipline

ENVIRONMENT
- Safe to experiment
- Empowered to create
- Technical and customer skills developed
- Leverages full store team
- Supported—manager takes interest in the individual
- Collaborative learning

with a senior government official because it reminded him of a conversation he had had with Will about golf.

What most impressed the senior executives talking with Will was the way he talked about his relationships with his colleagues and managers. Although Will ran point with the customer, this had been a team effort supported by multiple departments and celebrated by the store manager. The transformation process had created strong interpersonal bonds among frontline employees across the store.

Reinforcing the Framework

By the end of 2005, the structural reinforcement for customer-centricity was in place. Best Buy's transformation to customer-centricity had generated millions of dollars in innovation and cost savings in the span of just a few years. All the while, Best Buy's earnings, market value, and market share had continued to rise. The once-looming menace of Dell and other manufacturers moving downstream to enter the bricks-and-mortar world seemed like a distant threat.[4] Similarly, although Wal-Mart continued to work at the consumer electronics category, it had not repeated the pattern of sheer domination exhibited when the company had conquered the toy and grocery categories in earlier years. Best Buy had by no means perfected its new routines, but with nearly a hundred thousand employees operating across the country, it had achieved many of the fundamental changes that Anderson had first laid out in October 2002.

Confronting New Challenges

So let's flash forward to the media criticism of early 2012. With things seemingly going so well and the stock hitting its high in 2007, how did Best Buy run into trouble five years later? The lessons from Best Buy's experience provide insight regarding both how problems might have been avoided and a frontline path for the retailer to once again reinvent itself.

Let's first address the question of how the company's prospects dimmed in the eyes of Wall Street analysts. First, there is no question that Best Buy missed how technology was changing the consumer landscape. When Best Buy launched its customer-centricity initiative in a bid to fend off price commoditization and entry by new competitors, Amazon was just emerging as a serious contender in consumer electronics. At the same time, smart-phone penetration in the United States was less than 8 percent. Adoption rates have spiked in recent years, with an estimated 53 percent of Americans owning a smart phone at the end of 2011.[5] The ease of price checking and online ordering as a result of Amazon's ascension and the proliferation of smart phones—the very phones that Best Buy had been selling like hotcakes since the 2000s—has been turned against the company.

Best Buy further runs the risk of being "stuck in the middle," according to numerous industry analysts and observers. The company cannot compete on price alone, given the costs of carrying physical inventory in its stores. Meanwhile, it becomes increasingly difficult to monetize friendly service and technical advice for prospective buyers. In short, customers are free to take advantage of Best Buy's service associates, play with products, ask for help, and then order from whoever has the best price—often before they even leave Best Buy's parking lot.

Best Buy is equally challenged by the investment required to operate big stores. Not only do these create fixed costs that cannot be amortized across as many product categories as is possible at Wal-Mart, but the large-store format is today rife with dead space as once-hot products such as DVDs and CDs move increasingly to online consumption.

But more critical than the failure to divine seismic shifts in its competitive landscape has been the fact that Best Buy's frontline focus seems to have waned in the years leading up to the 2010 earnings miss. One account from a Best Buy executive noted that the company might have spotted the trend toward tablets and away from laptop consumers if it had paid closer attention to what was happening on the sales floor. Sales data and customer anecdotes from salespeople pointed to a purchasing shift away from ultra-portable notebooks toward iPads and similar devices.[6]

In our view, and with the benefit of hindsight, it appears that a number of these problems date back to 2007, when customer-centricity efforts took a backseat to putting wounded competitor Circuit City out of business. Although we were no longer working with the retailer, accounts shared with us by company insiders suggest that Best Buy marshaled all of its resources to focus on the flat-screen-TV business, which was one of Circuit City's last profit strongholds. The company reemphasized product as company leaders spent less time reinforcing the tenets of customer-centricity and frontline judgment. This lapse, although initially intended to be temporary, enabled some of the disciplines around customer segmentation and experimentation to slip. The effects were evident in January 2012, as Forbes.com contributor Larry Downes wrote, asserting that management had been focused on "improving some arbitrary metric from last quarter, even when doing so actually interferes with customers trying to buy something else."[7] (These comments are reminiscent of the disgruntled customer video Anderson shared with his management team in 2002.)

Charting a Path Forward

As Best Buy focuses on fixing its business model, it is looking at many changes, including once again building off frontline innovation to help it chart a new course. One such innovation came out of the company's Atlanta stores' local experimentation as they sought to improve their organic growth. Many of the stores in the area were at least fifteen years old, and many managers had accepted the mind-set that their market was mature, making it their primary mission to fend off competitors. That perspective was seriously challenged by Ramon Estevez, a store general manager, after a discussion he had with one of his employees.

Estevez approached one of his salespeople, Jun Yee, expecting to have a performance-management dialogue in which he addressed Yee's habit of taking what appeared to be personal calls. After Estevez asked Yee why he was interrupted at work so often and inquired whether Yee was facing a family issue, Yee clarified that these had not been personal calls at all. Yee had been burning up his mobile phone talking to many Korean customers who lived nearby, paying the extra phone expense out of his own pocket. "They don't speak English," Yee explained to Estevez, "so they're not comfortable coming into the store." Since Yee was fluent in Korean, it seemed that many of the eighty thousand Korean immigrants in the Atlanta area had designated his cell number as their personal tech hotline.

As Estevez spoke with Yee, he realized there was an enormous untapped market in his backyard—a customer segment that nobody was serving effectively. In fact, Yee explained, the Korean community felt disrespected by

Best Buy, which never spoke to it directly in its advertising and didn't carry a product assortment that reflected its unique needs.

Estevez moved quickly, engaging other company leaders and his own store associates to help. He organized roundtables with community leaders, businesses, and schools to better understand how Best Buy could cater to these customers' needs. The store staffed a new full-time position, a personal shopping assistant who was fluent in Korean. It also expanded its product selection, starting to carry high-end karaoke systems, rice cookers, and kimchi refrigerators. It even advertised a gaming night, to which Korean kids not only came but, reflecting differences in the ethnic community, brought their parents as well.

Ultimately, Best Buy expanded on Estevez's success by leasing space inside a supermarket in the heart of Atlanta's Koreatown. The store-in-store concept sat alongside restaurants, gift shops, and specialty food purveyors. At slightly over one thousand square feet, Best Buy's Korean destination was minuscule in comparison with its more typical sixty-thousand-square-foot boxes.

Best Buy has long operated small formats with less than one third of the floor space found in a typical store. However, while the company had managed to earn a respectable return on these investments, it had never been as financially strong as its older, larger brethren. The significantly smaller, highly local, low-overhead model developed by a suburban Atlanta store team seems to be pointing the way to entirely new growth opportunities in similar metro areas, such as Chicago, or with underserved customer niches, such as Brazilian tourists in the United States.

Summary: Lessons Learned

Nearly a decade after Brad Anderson assumed the CEO post and in the wake of his successor Brian Dunn's resignation, the company faces a strikingly similar challenge to reinvent itself as it did in Anderson's time. Whoever leads Best Buy after Dunn will face the challenge of implementing a business strategy that will fundamentally restore the chain to growth and profitability in the face of a marketplace that is no longer defined by traditional retail boundaries. As we have said repeatedly, the CEO's primary and essential job is to identify how the company can win with customers and against its competitors. Only then can frontline associates make their greatest contributions.

Best Buy's experience demonstrates the difficulty of not only transforming to become a front line–focused organization but also of remaining one. One transformation is rarely enough—continual transformation is a multiyear, even multidecade, effort to unleash the creativity and engagement of thousands of frontline associates. Sustaining such benefits, moreover, requires real-time communication returning in a continual feedback loop from the front line to inform senior leaders' judgments about customers, the market, and organizational strategy. To its great misfortune, Best Buy seems to have let a number of critical frontline disciplines lapse and failed to gather and make sense of the consumer behavior patterns that, in retrospect, many frontline associates must have recognized well before the key earnings misses of 2010 and 2012.

Best Buy faces a difficult road in the future. It will require resolving the strategic dilemmas of operating costly physical facilities in a digital world, maintaining its relevance as a product specialist while deepening and broadening its service capabilities, and ultimately learning to serve customers who wish to operate seamlessly across multiple channels. While not a panacea for the company's many ailments, a strategic solution will, we believe, ultimately involve leveraging Best Buy's front line, much as the company did successfully for a brief period before 2007, to look for differentiated advantage through its frontline people. Best Buy's interim CEO, Mike Mikan, seems to agree, telling analysts during a recent conference call that Best Buy stores once "wowed customers" but that the company's "customer experience is no longer unique, as it once was." Shortly before Best Buy announced that it would provide intensive service training to fifty thousand employees in an effort to personalize the technology experience for customers, Mikan added, "we have to invest in employees by giving them more training and better tools to maximize what they can offer to our customers." Concurrently, Best Buy is testing a store redesign that makes its large store format feel smaller, cleaner, and closer to Apple's retail experience. While these are positive steps, skeptics abound, including founder Dick Shulze, who completely resigned from the company and is reportedly considering making a bid for a controlling stake with a private equity partner.

As the company struggles to redefine its strategy and rediscover its frontline customer service capability, it is clear that recapturing its past success will be far from easy. "As the *Wall Street Journal*'s Justin Lahart noted in his "Heard on the Street" column of April 14, 2012, just days after Brian Dunn's resignation, "The future for Best Buy, if there is going to be one, may be very different: far smaller stores selling products customers absolutely want to check out, staffed by deeply knowledgeable (and therefore expensive) salespeople, offering prices that will get shoppers from the sales floor to the cash register. That is a hard trick to pull off."[8]

CORPORATE CITIZENSHIP ON THE FRONT LINE

Our most precious global resource, humankind, is vastly underutilized. There are about five billion people in the world at the bottom of the pyramid who are not part of the global market economy, and there's a lot the private sector can do to incorporate them. It makes good business sense and good sense, period.

—**Ricardo Salinas, chairman and CEO of Grupo Salinas**

- **ENGAGING IN THE COMMUNITY CAN TURBOCHARGE THE FRONT LINE**

  - Frontline associates learn by giving back and developing their leadership skills.

  - Participation in the community strengthens organizational commitment.

- **THERE IS A FRONT LINE OUTSIDE CORPORATE WALLS**

  - Progressive companies are turning citizens and social agencies into an extension of their front line.

  - Doing so is good for the individuals, companies, communities, and society as a whole.

On a hot summer day in 2011, Noel found himself in an urban park in the middle of one of the poorest neighborhoods of Mexico City. As he painstakingly picked over the mountain of refuse that had accumulated in the park—which clearly for years had served as a dumping ground for the ramshackle homes surrounding it—he separated what he could from the piles of mattresses, discarded tires, glass, and other miscellaneous pieces of debris that were too bulky or too dangerous to put in the large plastic bag he had been filling for the past three hours. Like the approximately five hundred volunteers he joined in the public park, his once-lily-white "Clean Our Mexico" polo shirt, baseball hat, and gloves were now darkly soiled from constant contact with decades-old dirt and grub.

The park was full of unpaid helpers that day, including Noel and a student team he had brought composed of University of Michigan medical and nursing students and West Point cadets, all working closely with hundreds of managers and employees, families, and friends of the large Mexican conglomerate Grupo Salinas, the corporate sponsor of this nationwide effort. Even Ninfa Salinas, the thirtysomething daughter of the firm's CEO, who serves not only as a senior executive in the company but also as a congresswoman in the national government, could be seen standing at the edge of the park side by side with other employees, filling her own plastic bag.

Regardless of their background or what had brought them there, everyone was engaged in backbreaking labor of some sort, whether collecting garbage or loading the overflowing trash bags onto the fleet of giant trucks provided by the local sanitation department. Toward the end of the day, volunteers began wielding shovels to dig hundreds of rows of shallow holes, planting tiny saplings in large numbers to replace the landscape of discarded waste.

This site was just one of hundreds spread across the entire country as part of the "Clean Our Mexico" campaign, in which Grupo Salinas mobilizes over 3.2 million Mexican citizens to join its fifty-thousand-person workforce to clean up their country by picking up garbage. This annual service activity is designed not just to motivate volunteerism but also to connect Grupo Salinas's front line directly with the communities that they serve. Many of the Grupo Salinas employees live and work in the neighborhoods that they clean up and labor shoulder to shoulder with their families, friends, and customers. The mixture of emotions on display—camaraderie, national pride, local sensitivity, genuine care—blend together to mask the exhaustion that most of the volunteers feel by the end of the day.

Citizenship on the Front Line

In this chapter we diverge from the five-step process for building a front line–focused organization to discuss one method for turbocharging the effort: engaging frontline employees directly in corporate-citizenship activities in their local communities. We also examine two less traditional methods that innovative companies are taking, expanding the boundary of their definition of "front line" to involve citizens and social agencies outside their corporate walls.

Far more companies are involved in corporate-citizenship efforts today than when Noel first began work in this area nearly thirty years ago. Over the years, we have worked with companies to collectively bring more than a quarter million corporate employees to work and give back to their local communities in more than eighty countries. Many of these have been frontline workers. Whether delivering food with an automobile factory employee or painting a halfway house with an oil industry engineer, each time we work with frontline associates in the community we are amazed at how profoundly such work impacts them and at the unanticipated benefits it brings in their relationships with their coworkers and employers. We see both great opportunity and tremendous benefits when frontline employees are able to represent their organizations in community service.

Corporate-citizenship efforts, as in the case of Grupo Salinas, offer an opportunity for frontline employees to partner directly with community members, who are often their customers. Working with someone on a volunteer project can create a more personal relationship than waiting on a restaurant customer, serving someone in a bank, or selling them a mobile phone. It offers the chance for employees to understand the thoughts, concerns, and lifestyles of some of their customers in an informal context, while also enabling customers to see frontline employees in an entirely different role.

Indeed, involvement in the community elevates the role of frontline workers and gives added dimension to corporate mission statements that encourage employees to help improve customers' lives. Such activity is typically meaningful to individual employees, who witness their company's dedication of time and resources to improving their community, and becomes a source of pride. As local ambassadors for their corporations, individuals may also be given the chance to champion personal causes that have touched their lives or impacted their families. In sum, community engagement can provide powerful reinforcement of employees' organizational commitment, making it not merely a reason for choosing a prospective employer but also a significant factor in the decision to stay with a company.

Citizenship activities also benefit individual employees by providing an opportunity to develop new leadership skills. In some cases, this may enhance their communication abilities as they interact with community members in untraditional circumstances. In others, they may be lending a skill to leaders in community agencies, showing them how to read a profit-and-loss statement or better manage their staff. The act of teaching and putting their skills to use in a different context reinforces what they know and challenges their coaching capability. Working with not-for-profits or social groups typically provides inspiration, as corporate employees see what the dedicated leaders of these organizations often accomplish on a shoestring budget with far fewer resources and trained personnel.

Finally, engaging frontline employees offers organizations the ability to exponentially increase both the scale and depth of their citizenship efforts. As we saw with the "Clean Our Mexico" campaign, by getting the word out through its employees, Grupo Salinas was able to mobilize sixty volunteers for each of its workers, a tremendous multiplier effect that cannot be achieved by billboards or television advertisements alone. Other citizenship efforts rely less on sheer numbers of volunteers but instead require people with access to those who need assistance. A frontline employee who is trusted by a customer may be a far more influential spokesperson and much better positioned to provide help than a corporate senior executive, social agency worker, or government employee. An example of such a case is the partnership between Grupo Salinas and Procter & Gamble to improve the quality of drinking water in Mexico's most impoverished communities.

Cleaning Up the Water in Rural Mexico

Grupo Salinas is a highly profitable electronic appliance, media, cellular phone, and financial services conglomerate that has grown by leaps and bounds since Ricardo Salinas inherited a small chain of fewer than fifty Elektra electronics stores from his father in 1987. Salinas's entrepreneurial leadership has shaped his family firm into a diversified multinational powerhouse that has also made him the second-richest man in Mexico and a perennial fixture on *Forbes*'s billionaire list.

Most Grupo Salinas companies serve the vast and intractably poor "base of the pyramid" customers who often lack traditional employment, stable incomes, and credit access, putting Salinas directly in touch with some of the least fortunate in his developing country. A short conversation, or even quick review of his Web site, reveals his sensitivity to their plight and the sense of personal responsibility he feels for employing his companies to help. He has written

Our most precious global resource, humankind, is vastly underutilized. There are about five billion people in the world at the bottom of the pyramid who are not part of the global market economy, and there's a lot the private sector can to do to incorporate them. It makes good business sense and good sense, period.[1]

The values that Salinas extols on his personal Web site include "contributing toward the creation of a solid middle class" and "returning the wealth created to society through social projects." Salinas's interests, however, are far greater than simply providing charity. He uses the financial, human, and political capital of his companies to engage multiple constituencies, whether government partners or other corporations, to join forces in citizenship activities with him. He said of the "Clean Our Mexico" effort:

We organized this campaign because we felt that our country urgently needed a change of habits, and we needed everyone's participation. As a group of companies, we are dedicated to action. However, we can't act alone; the government and most importantly society in general are essential participants. I am pleased to know that we are convinced about the need to clean up our Mexico. Now we must act.

Against this backdrop of strong social leadership and long history of multisector collaboration—both of which we view as essential to successful corporate citizenship activities—it was no surprise that Ricardo Salinas jumped at the opportunity to partner with Procter & Gamble (P&G) to improve rural drinking water.

Mexican health authorities link contaminated drinking water to the country's high infant mortality rate of seventeen deaths for every one thousand births. Although still utterly heartbreaking, this rate has actually declined from twenty-three deaths for every thousand births in 2003, a decrease almost entirely attributable to the fact that an additional 4 percent of the country's rural population gained access to clean water by 2010. Despite such modest advances, as many as ten million Mexicans still do not have access to clean water, making it the nation's single biggest public health problem.

While public health authorities have successfully encouraged all but the poorest Mexicans to stop collecting their drinking water from rivers, wells, or rainwater, the primary beneficiaries of this shift have been the suppliers of *garrafones,* or twenty-liter reusable water bottles delivered to clients' houses. Unfortunately, the quality and purity of water delivered by these private companies is unregulated by any governmental agency, and there have been numerous anecdotes of turbid or dirty *garrafón* water causing illness, mainly in infants and children.

The collaboration between Grupo Salinas and P&G was established to facilitate the low-cost distribution of a P&G product called P&G Purifier of Water, originally developed by Procter & Gamble in partnership with the Centers for Disease Control and Prevention in the United States. P&G Purifier of Water was produced to enable people anywhere in the world to conveniently and cheaply purify dirty water by pouring into it the contents of a Kool-Aid–sized packet filled with powder capable of turning up to ten liters of dirty, noxious water into clean, drinkable water. Using a chemical formula similar to that found in municipal water systems in developed countries, P&G Purifier of Water eliminates nearly 100 percent of bacteria, microorganisms, viruses, protozoa, and other pollutants commonly linked to intestinal illness and fatalities in adults and children.

P&G, under the direction of P&G Purifier of Water leader Greg Allgood, has created its own network of relief organizations, called the Children's Safe Drinking Water Program, which recently declared a new goal of saving one life every hour by 2020. While P&G has the product, social commitment, and a thirty-five-million-dollar pledge, what it lacks in some countries is an effective distribution channel. Although using P&G Purifier of Water takes just minutes and virtually no physical effort, its adoption relies on educated customers who understand the danger of unsanitary water and their willingness to change ingrained consumption behaviors.

As numerous social-science studies have proven, the most persuasive advocate for behavioral change is usually someone who is known and trusted and who is similar to the person being encouraged to change. For the base-of-the-pyramid customer in Mexico, there is perhaps no better representative than Grupo Salinas's employees who live and work alongside these people.

In fact, the collaboration between P&G and Grupo Salinas will depend on frontline associates at the conglomerate's retail electronics chain, Elektra, whose field credit agents visit customers' homes to distribute and market this socially beneficial product, which will be sold door to door. Elektra's frontline microcredit agents travel by motorcycle, visiting customers' homes weekly to collect loan payments. This microcredit business provides contact with nearly ten million base-of-the-pyramid customers, the vast majority of whom live in the poor rural villages that will benefit most from the widespread use of P&G Purifier of Water.

Both Elektra's roaming microcredit agents and the sales associates working the floors of nearly one thousand Elektra stores across Mexico have been trained to conduct demonstrations that include a brief summary of the health risks associated with drinking contaminated water, with an emphasis on its link to infant mortality. After the health risks are fully summarized, the presenter pours a packet of P&G Purifer of Water into a ten-liter bucket of visibly dirty water, which is both purified and consumed as part of the demonstration. These frontline employees are entrusted to represent P&G Purifer of Water and register customers, selling directly to them in their homes or in Elektra stores. Grupo Salinas is even offering added financial incentive to its microcredit agents to sell P&G Purifer of Water and conduct "Clean Drinking Water Days" in which they recruit important community members to participate in large-scale public demonstrations.

There is no question that the frontline employees engaged in this effort will help to save lives. They will also save their clients money, given that Grupo Salinas and P&G are selling the product at cost so consumers can purchase it for one-fifth of what they paid previously for less reliable *garrafón* water. But Grupo Salinas benefits as well. The salespeople and microcredit agents involved, some of whom now personally use P&G Purifer of Water, burst with satisfaction as they conduct the demonstrations, filling them with appreciation for their ability to have an impact as a result of Grupo Salinas's dedication to helping their communities.

Society's Front Line

The deep respect that Ricardo Salinas exhibits for the latent capability of people from all circumstances is representative of the view found in many front line–focused organizations. Just as these leaders see the potential for their frontline associates to inform and advise them, they see possibilities for many of society's least advantaged to contribute if given the opportunity. As a result, through both our clinical work and our research, we have found a number of benchmark organizations that have broadened their definition of the "front line" to include community members, often economically disadvantaged, who can become business partners, consumers, and future frontline employees if provided with the means.

One example is the Sustainable Cities Institute, a partnership between the Fundación Azteca, founded by Ricardo Salinas and run by Esteban Moctezuma, and the government of Chiapas, one of the most sparsely populated and poorest states in Mexico. Developed in 2007 in keeping with the United Nations' Millennium Development Goals, the first sustainable city prototype is Nuevo Juan del Grijalva, a planned community constructed from scratch in the province of Ostuacán. Populated by villagers who moved there from eleven extremely poor and highly dispersed villages in the countryside surrounding the new town center, the planned community contains public and private buildings, infrastructure, water-purification plants, public lighting, energy delivery, and garbage disposal. Today the community numbers over four hundred households and approximately two thousand citizens, with each household occupying a two-bedroom home solidly constructed in semitraditional style with adobe walls and concrete floors, indoor plumbing, electricity, and a safely ventilated wood-burning stove.

The practical purpose of what would seem at first glance a utopian pipe dream to revitalize impoverished rural Mexico is in reality a commitment to provide a new quality of life for the long-neglected rural poor. Each resident has enough private land to grow plants or raise chickens, and the community is provided services including a health clinic, a school with a computer, and an adult education center. Many of the town's residents have been trained through the consortium of businesses and government agencies and now run most of the various community businesses. A number of these entrepreneurial ventures, with the aid of corporate sponsorship, aspire to reach a scale in the next five years where they can supply produce or dairy products to some of the nation's largest companies. Just as envisioned, these once undereducated, subsistence farmers are demonstrating the ability to generate jobs, profits, and attractive goods, all while improving their quality of life in the process.[2]

The Agricultural Front Line

One of our more recent clients, the Charoen Pokphand Group, headquartered in a towering skyscraper overlooking busy Silom Road in the heart of Bangkok's bustling business district, has proven that these same principles are alive and well in Southeast Asia. Founded by Chairman Dhanin Chearavanont, one of Asia's richest billionaires and recipient of *Forbes*'s 2011 Asia's Businessman of the Year Award, the company constitutes a global conglomerate that operates in twenty countries with more than three hundred thousand employees, earning annual revenues in excess of eighteen billion dollars. Although the group today is made up of more than 250 subsidiaries in diverse industries such as telecommunications, retail, and real estate, the vast majority of its explosive growth has been driven by lessons learned from the seed and livestock sectors in its mainstay agricultural businesses.

The simple philosophy espoused by Chearavanont is called the "Three Benefits," the central tenet of which simply states that for CP Group to be successful, it must first ensure that the communities in which it operates will benefit also—a sentiment that might well have come straight from Grupo Salinas's Web site. By adhering to the Three Benefits, CP promises to provide quality products at reasonable prices, enabling people with low purchasing power to consume more and better goods. If they respect CP and choose to do business with the group, Chearavanont's reasoning goes, then the host government will provide support and encouragement for its people to use CP's products and services. If the government and people benefit, CP benefits as well.

"You need to give first in order to receive, and with that understanding we can achieve success," Chearavanont advised us in a recent interview.[3] These acts of giving are not charity, the chairman insists, but long-term investments, enabling thousands of subsistence farmers in Thailand, China, Vietnam, Myanmar, and Russia to modernize and grow their businesses, forming a broad-based supplier network for CP Group. The company partners directly with frontline farmers in these societies, providing them with investment capital, technology, and high-caliber raw materials that cash-poor farmers could never afford to purchase independently. Its longstanding policy of training farmers to use cutting-edge agricultural methods often more than triples their yield rates and dramatically increases their incomes.

As Chearavanont explained to us, he first put his philosophy into practice more than thirty years ago, when CP Group entered the livestock business with poultry farmers in Thailand. Chearavanont elected to give 240 households the chance to raise ten thousand chickens each. "I subsidized all expenses for them. I advanced them investment capital," Chearavanont said. While raising the young chicks would require an income of only 1,500 Thai baht (about thirty dollars at today's exchange rate), Chearavanont chose to give the farmers more than the minimum. "Fifteen hundred baht per month would have been enough in those days," Chearavanont explained, "but if a child became ill and doctor expenses were incurred, the farmer would have been forced to sell all their chickens to make ends meet." Foreseeing such risks and not wishing to put farmers in a precarious position, CP Group advanced the farmers an additional two thousand baht against their future earnings.

While many people inside the company ominously warned Chearavanont that his then-small venture would go bankrupt as a result of theft or lazy, uneducated farmers, Chearavanont replied that "the bad guys would be a minority. Some farmers even slept in their chicken coops because they were so afraid there would be theft." Working forward from this modest foundation, CP today operates the fourth-largest poultry operation in the world and has used similar techniques to become one of the world's leading producers of seed and animal feed. Indeed, governments across Asia have actively sought CP Group's investment and participation, recognizing what it can do to foster the technical abilities and production capability of their local farmers. CP Group shares in the profits produced by each farmer as a result of its investment, training, and technology. "You have to give first and improve their well-being," Chearavanont advises. "Then you can share the benefits."

CP Group was born from these humble beginnings but has not turned its back on its past. Chearavanont's most recent efforts include partnering with the base-of-the-pyramid farmers in China, where he is building a state-of-the-art cooperative with four hundred families that will be one of the largest and most modern poultry-raising operations in the world. CP calls the model for its new megafarm in China "Four in One" because it will integrate four primary components—farms for raising pullets and laying eggs, a feed mill, a processing plant, and a fertilizer factory—into a self-contained community designed around the simple principle of "boosting the farmer's income."

As CP pioneered in Thailand, the critical need when incorporating base-of-the-pyramid families into a social and industrial order is the provision of sufficiently stable financing over a long period of time so that the families are assured profitability while the company and the government assume a certain degree of the inherent risk of agriculture. With CP's operating company assuming the risks of credit commitment and legal guarantees, the age-old issues of property rights and income production are solved within the cooperative structure of the enterprise. CP offers these capable farmers the resources and education to fully enter modern society, making a substantial economic and social contribution to their local communities that will provide benefits for CP Group as they become frontline business partners and suppliers and certainly for many future generations of Chinese families.

Frontline Leadership in the Social Sector

As CP Group in Thailand and Grupo Salinas in Mexico clearly demonstrate, companies deeply committed to investing in building up the capabilities and skill sets of ordinary citizens who become their business partners and customers have refined a powerful growth formula. Is this altruistic or self-serving behavior? The answer, plainly, is both. This approach benefits the companies as well as the workers and the communities to which they belong.

The front line outside of corporations includes not just the Thai farmer or the Mexican housewife looking to set up shop in a rural village but also the not-for-profit and public sectors. Our work in these areas over the years has made it absolutely clear that the need for leadership judgment at the front line is perhaps even greater in social agencies than in the private sector. We have seen examples of this through our work in numerous nonprofit organizations, including with health-care clinicians in India, school principals in Brunei, and Boys & Girls Club leaders across the United States.

Indeed, making good decisions is arguably even more important for those in nonprofit organizations with limited resources because their choices can directly impact others' basic necessities, including food, shelter, and education.

Our engagement with the education sector in New York and Texas, for example, has confirmed the power of aligning frontline teachers and administrators to exercise judgment and innovate to improve learning. It has also shown that the school principal, really a frontline supervisor, is a linchpin position that can strongly influence a school's results, teacher engagement, and child performance.

This was even more evident in our work with Boys & Girls Clubs, the nonprofit organization that runs more than four thousand social centers serving over four million children each year in the United States. The clubs provide a safe place where, for just one dollar per year, children can spend time outside of school, often as an alternative to staying home alone or being unsupervised on the streets. In addition to offering help with homework, sports, crafts, and other activities that are designed to build skills and instill self-confidence, the clubs are managed by caring adults, many of them volunteers, who forge ongoing relationships with the children and set high expectations for their future success.

Each club is responsible for its own budget, ranging from a few hundred thousand dollars to in excess of ten million dollars annually, and the club leaders, designated chief professional officers (CPOs), must juggle the bevy of responsibilities that come with managing limited resources. Not only do they ensure staffing and training for the adults who look after the one hundred or more children who attend each club, but they also must oversee fund-raising, program development, facilities upkeep, communicating with the national Boys & Girls Clubs of America (BGCA) organization, and managing their local board of directors. Some regional club systems are also multiunit organizations, multiplying these demands across several locations.

Just as we described happening in the private sector in chapter 7, historically many of these club supervisors had been given their leadership roles with little direct training. Some had come up through the BGCA system, while others had been hired from the outside based on their prior not-for-profit, educational, or corporate experience. Many had little preparation for assuming their CPO role, a position that was further complicated by the necessity of managing volunteer employees and maintaining strong relationships with private donors in their communities.

Roxanne Spillett, president and CEO of BGCA, had long recognized the importance of fortifying the organization's leadership capabilities. In its recent past, BGCA had rapidly expanded geographically, more than doubling its locations. In Spillett's view it was time for BGCA to stop focusing on growing its reach and start growing its impact. Doing so would mean finding new measurements to understand how clubs were affecting youth and their communities. It would also mean focusing the agendas of local clubs on key issues that would maximize their impact. Funneling the clubs' disparate activities toward greater purpose would oblige club leaders to work more closely with their board members to ensure that everyone was on the same page. Finally, club leaders would need to reach deeper into the pockets of local donors, as government agencies had accelerated budget cuts, making it more difficult to guarantee even modest levels of centralized funding.

In 2007 we were asked to design and run a program that would develop club leaders' skills in these areas while building stronger leadership teams in the local organizations and providing them with the tools to engage their staff and volunteers in the transformation process. The program we launched, made possible through generous corporate donations, taught the club leadership teams skills for working with their frontline staff while setting clear objectives for the measurable impact their clubs would have. As a first step after returning from the initial development session at the University of Michigan Business School, each club leadership team was required to teach their staff team in a two-day clinic.

During this clinic session, taught directly by each CPO and key leadership team members, club staff learned about BGCA's new mission, reflected on how they could better implement the club values, identified unnecessary work that could be eliminated, and most important, were asked for ideas to help improve their local club. The focus of their helpful input was a project that each club team had defined and that was designed not only to provide tangible results but also to help energize the efforts of club staff.

One such project, framed by the team from Boys & Girls Clubs of Palm Beach County, set out with the mission to "create an environment that inspires all of our customers to become lifelong donors and advocates, enabling us to increase and improve services to our county's neediest youth." Simply put, the team aspired to build a lifelong connection with anyone affiliated with the club—children, parents, volunteers, staff, board members—forging a bond so strong that even those who left would someday return to volunteer or contribute. Soon dubbed "ADVODON," short for advocate-donor, the concept was embraced by the club's more than fifty staff members and board of directors.

After the initial training session, club staff began freely contributing ideas, leading to the implementation of monthly family nights, which were attended by dozens of parents. This was critically important for strengthening the club's impact because prior studies had shown that if parents reinforced the study habits and interests that children acquired during club time, those children were far more likely to succeed in school and go on to college. During these interactions with family members, and indeed with all community members, the staff actively proselytized, spreading the word about ADVODON. Staff members also began sharing daily stories about the results of their recruiting efforts, the most impressive of which resulted from a single donor who wholeheartedly embraced the idea.

The donor, a well-to-do individual deeply committed to helping the club's children, was so enamored with the ADVODON concept that she offered to pay for a block party equipped with amusement rides, games, and family activities that would draw members of the community and serve as a hunting ground for more recruits to the cause. More than one thousand children, parents, volunteers, and city officials turned out for the party, the same day that the donor also pledged the funds to build a new facility for the club.

Overall, the ADVODON campaign was successful in raising more than seven million dollars for Boys & Girls Clubs of Palm Beach County. More important, it strengthened the leadership team's skills and was a catalyst for culture change among club staff.

In all, BGCA supported such training for more than two hundred of its largest clubs, training over six hundred professionals and engaging thousands of club staff in less than two years. When the impact of the program was studied, BGCA found that nearly 90 percent of the clubs had reached or surpassed their impact target, increasing the understanding and commitment of their staff, board, and donors along the way. In fact, 85 percent reported that their board's effectiveness had increased as a result.

The study findings, later validated by a third party, led to an expansion of the program to cover hundreds of smaller clubs across the country. Our good fortune to help design and implement this effort, in partnership with BGCA's leadership development team, was the result of Spillett's leadership and the forward thinking of the corporate donors who recognized that, much as their own frontline leaders needed to be trained, the field staff of BGCA could accomplish much more if given the means and opportunity.

Focus: HOPE, a Model of a Front Line–Focused Organization

As we saw with BGCA, remarkable accomplishments are possible when corporations recognize the front line that lives outside their walls and provide the funding and other resources to unleash the latent potential that lies in these people. The best example we have found to date of such an organization sits just an hour away from us in inner-city Detroit.

Focus: HOPE is an oasis of its namesake emotion located in the blighted downtown of Detroit that has forged partnerships with government, business, universities, and other community-based agencies. Sitting on forty acres, it is a unique vocational-training and community-development organization that has blossomed into a major civic institution out of the wreckage of the 1967 Detroit race riots. It owes its founding to a quirk of television programming that led news coverage of the Nuremberg war-crimes trials in postwar Germany to be interrupted by live footage of violence against civil-rights protesters in Selma, Alabama. As a housewife, Eleanor Josaitis sat watching the juxtaposed images on her television of Nazi Germany and racial conflict in her own country, she immediately committed to take action. She recalled later, "You have to have the guts to try something, because you can't change a damn thing by sitting in front of the TV with a clicker in your hand."[4]

She partnered with a young priest, Father William Cunningham, whom she had befriended at the nearby St. Alfred Parish, and the two resolved to make a difference. Josaitis's first step was to uproot her family from a comfortable middle-class suburb on the outskirts of Detroit and relocate to the heart of the still-battle-scarred inner city. There, initially working out of a church basement, she and Cunningham would start a food program based on information from a study demonstrating that malnourished infants could lose up to 15 percent of their mental capacity. Pledging themselves to "intelligent and practical action," the duo reasoned that helping pregnant women, nursing mothers, and women with children ensure proper nutrition in their households would strengthen the foundation these kids had for entering mainstream society.

Not long after establishing the program, which quickly grew to feed more than eight hundred infants and mothers daily, Josaitis fielded a call from a woman seeking free food. After Josaitis elatedly described the program, the woman screamed a distressing question that rocked Josaitis. "I am seventy-two years old," the woman implored, "and you want me to get pregnant before you'll help me?"

This began a decades-long journey that would see the expansion of Focus: HOPE from a single food program to a broad initiative serving community members of all ages. Based on that fateful telephone call, Josaitis and Cunningham conducted a survey of food prices in Detroit shops, gathering precise data that revealed that inner-city residents were paying prices up to 40 percent higher for food than their more affluent suburban counterparts. Based on their findings, which resulted in public outcry and the normalization of prices, Josaitis and Cunningham expanded their food program to cover those of any age. However, this time they were beleaguered by a different question.

With the realization that feeding the hungry is more than just giving them food, they wondered what the underlying problem was that prevented parents from providing food for their children. The answer was unemployment. Conducting another survey, they determined that the best-paying jobs in the Detroit area, machinist jobs for the automobile industry, were closed to minorities. Of more than forty companies they surveyed, thirty-eight had never hired a minority worker.

Characteristically, Josaitis and Cunningham set their sights high, intent on producing not just average machinists but first-rate tradesmen. In 1981 they established the Machinist Training Institute. After realizing that many of their students lacked high-school diplomas and fewer than 10 percent could pass the equivalent of a tenth-grade math test, they also established Fast Track, a remedial academic program designed to take students from sixth-grade to tenth-grade math in just six weeks.

Their success in producing machinists led to funding for a state-of-the-art Center for Advanced Technologies (CAT), which today operates a 22,000-square-foot manufacturing and educational center that runs as a for-profit business. Competing on projects against commercial suppliers, CAT has manufactured products for all of the major U.S. automobile manufacturers, as well as the U.S. military.

Today, Focus: HOPE has also graduated more than ten thousand students into the workforce, serves more than 43,000 people each month through its food program—which subsequently became a model for a nationwide government program—and runs a 26,000-square-foot Montessori day-care facility open to both its employees and the public. While its accomplishments are mind bending, what is even more inspiring is that it does not simply turn out technical experts. Deeply embedded in the development experience of these future frontline employees is training on values, teamwork, and good judgment gained through hands-on experience working with colleagues and customers in Focus: HOPE's factories, children's center, food bank, and assorted other businesses.

Focus: HOPE instills a discipline and thoughtfulness in its students that isn't found at the average educational institution. All students learn to recite the mission statement by heart, committing themselves to "intelligent and practical action to overcome racism, poverty and injustice." They are taught to present themselves well, learning not just table manners but also the art of proper dress, good eye contact, and the value of a firm handshake. And most important, they are taught the discipline to resist the distractions and vices that took them off course in earlier years, so they remain committed to their education, families, and community.

In some respects, Focus: HOPE is the model front line–focused organization because it truly was built for those who work there. It aims to simultaneously develop its people and learn from them, because they are, after all, representatives of the community that Focus: HOPE aspires to revitalize.

Continuing a Legacy

In recognition of the leadership that Focus: HOPE has provided, not only as a civic institution to train the unemployed but also as a role-model organization that we have used to teach countless executives the importance of social action, the University of Michigan Global Business Partnership announced the launch of the Eleanor Josaitis Global Citizenship Initiative. Funded through a gift from Patricia Stacey, an alum, and Noel, the purpose of the initiative is to teach students how they can make a positive difference in the quality of life for the billions globally who are at the bottom of the pyramid. Students are placed on projects that serve the initiative's charter to "harness student diversity to deliver practical solutions to racism and poverty, with the Focus: HOPE mission statement, broadened to a global context." This mission has, for example, taken them to Bangalore to train rural health-care workers, to China partnered with 3M on occupational safety, and to Mexico working with Dow to reduce its carbon footprint. The hope is that the next generation of "enlightened capitalists" will develop sensitivity to the many global human capital and global environmental issues that may be solved by working directly with those on society's front line, much as CP and Grupo Salinas have.

Summary: Turbocharging Citizenship on the Front Line

In this chapter we have discussed three different models of corporate citizenship that engages the front line. The first is the conscious choice by corporations to deploy their front line in community service. As we saw with Grupo Salinas, involving employees provides both a scale and a depth to corporate citizenship activities that cannot be achieved through donations or by a small corporate team working in isolation. When companies involve their frontline associates in this way, service activities become a source of pride for the employee while also reinforcing their organizational commitment.

The second approach outlined broadens the definition of "front line" to include those who are outside company walls. It takes aim at the economically underprivileged and offers them the means and opportunity to engage in entrepreneurial activity. Whether a Thai farmer subsidized by CP

Group or a Mexican cheese producer living in a sustainable city sponsored by Grupo Salinas, the latent potential of these societal members is unlocked. In the process, they become suppliers, partners, and customers of the companies that assisted them.

The final approach highlighted is for corporations to directly sponsor the development activities of not-for-profit or community organizations. In some cases this may mean funding, while in others it may mean pledging staff to help teach and develop community leaders. As Boys & Girls Clubs demonstrated, a small investment in helping nonprofit leaders learn how to better utilize the talents of their staff can yield massive returns. Likewise, as we learned from Focus: HOPE, given the proper support, these organizations can help those who sit on the fringes of society to reinvent themselves, creating better employees and stronger communities.

10
CONCLUSION

Throughout this book we have asserted that too many organizations do too little to tap into the intelligence, creativity, and experience of their frontline workers. Our thesis—supported by looks into more than twenty organizations—has been that companies that have a sincere desire to maximize the contribution of *all* their employees need to invest in the development of good judgment among their people who occupy the frontline positions, where every organization most closely touches its customers and community.

From the first sentence of the first chapter, we set out to formulate a practical process for increasing that contribution by transforming the organizational dynamic from an increasingly outmoded hierarchical management style to one that fosters more trust and investment in frontline employees. We argue strongly that leaders who espouse customer-focused strategies must start by understanding what is required by those who are in the line of fire and interact daily with customers. Doing so requires reverse engineering the organization from the front line back to headquarters, creating systems, structures, and organizational roles that are designed to support those who serve the customer.

We further sought to maintain a pragmatic, evidence-based approach to these challenges rooted in decades of clinical experience helping senior leaders navigate the complexities of engaging thousands, or even hundreds of thousands, of employees. We certainly don't expect established companies to completely abandon hierarchical structures in favor of what for many would be radically different organizational models. While it is an appealing thought—and start-up companies may have the luxury of experimenting with such innovative organizational models—established companies face disruption to their existing business and the harsh criticism of skeptical investors if things go awry as a result of massive organizational changes.

Instead, we operated from the assumption that companies seeking to develop a frontline-judgment strategy embody the traditional organizational model, with a CEO who believes in the ability of associates at all levels to make meaningful contributions. Paradoxically, we began the process with the CEO and senior leadership team, because they ultimately exert the most control over the entire organizational environment. They typically have the ability to refocus their organizations on the frontline employee and customer experience, if they so desire. And as we believe we have demonstrated time and again in the book, CEOs who succeed in this quest typically succeed at the intimately correlated challenge of more precisely anticipating and meeting customer needs while simultaneously improving the morale of the staff.

If senior leaders wish to truly impact the front line, however, they must do more than spout rhetoric or take the occasional field trip to visit employees. They must be serious about investing in frontline capability. This process begins with training existing employees on the details of the business, customers, and frameworks for solving the problems that those on the front line are most likely to run into. The organization needs to teach everyone these concepts, eliminating MBA-speak while never assuming that employees are incapable of grasping the fundamentals required to run a business.

Armed with such knowledge, frontline employees can then begin to use their own liberated judgment to solve customer problems and improve business processes without escalating every important matter to a supervisor or relying on a script from headquarters. Customers today are savvy, possess many options, and are able to broadcast their dissatisfaction in a nanosecond when organizations let them down. Enabling frontline employees to solve problems in the moment, face to face, on the telephone or online with customers, makes good business sense, provided that the appropriate investment has been made to ensure that their judgment will be good.

Solving problems and improving processes is a significant step yet only one component of the contribution that frontline associates can make in most businesses. As companies increasingly favor tailored, localized customer solutions over mass-market offerings, we see a huge opportunity for frontline employees to innovate and experiment with their local customers. When the process is done well, employees are provided with a toolbox of techniques and frameworks for testing their concepts in the real world, measuring results, and deciding whether their idea will positively affect their business. Unleashing employee creativity in this way not only can boost business results but engenders deep commitment among employees as they see their ability to positively impact the customer experience.

Once a company embarks on this journey, it's likely to find that it is looking for a different kind of employee. The temptation to fill an empty slot with the first available body will vanish as the organization realizes its competitive advantage gained through the personalities and judgment of its employees. This also means investing meaningfully in developing capable frontline supervisors, since these positions most directly impact frontline employees. The misguided or untrained frontline leader who controls the daily work experience and local team environment for frontline workers can negate senior leaders' best intent and create high turnover after the organization invests heavily in frontline development. For this reason, it becomes imperative that the selection and training of frontline supervisors is not treated as a trivial matter left to the lower echelons of HR but is something that receives direct senior-management attention and concern.

Even for organizations that do all of these things, there is of course always a danger that the world will change, customers will become fickle, and competitors will gain ground. For this reason, we explain that building a front line–focused organization is a never-ending process in which senior leaders must frequently find ways of listening to and learning from the front line in order to adapt. The frontline employees and customers can be senior leaders' source of early warnings about shifts in the market, so that they may in turn exercise their own judgment about the organization's overall strategy.

Finally, we appeal to companies, which in many parts of the world have surpassed governments in their ability to support nonprofit organizations, to help develop the frontline community leaders in their own neighborhoods. We have worked with many resource-strapped not-for-profit organizations, educational institutions, health-care clinics, and other social enterprises where the basic tenet of building frontline capability is imperative for survival. For these organizations, often with limited staff, maximizing the contribution of every team member translates into the higher quality of a child's education, a patient's improved health, or a family being able to eat that night. Companies are able to develop this frontline capability, serving their community needs but also developing their own people in the process.

We hope that this book will serve as a useful and useable framework for leaders to unleash the talent and develop the judgment of their people. Our research and clinical experience have demonstrated that there is no singular method for doing so but that following the five-step process outlined in the preceding chapters increases the likelihood that organizations will develop their own successful solutions.

While we have profiled and extolled the talents of a number of CEOs who have grasped these lessons and put them to good use in their own organizations, from Yum! CEO David Novak to Intuit founder Scott Cook, Steelcase CEO Jim Hackett, Best Buy's Brad Anderson, Facebook founder Mark

Zuckerberg, and Amazon's Jeff Bezos, our hearts lie with those at the bottom of the organizational pyramid: retail clerks, call-center operators, bank tellers, and millions of others who possess both the ability and the desire to give more, to improve their daily work experience, and to make life better for the customers they serve. Like the simple idea of the pump maintenance worker from Royal Dutch Shell whom we introduced in the first chapter—which saved millions of dollars and hours of wasted employee time—countless other great ideas are lying dormant and untapped in the ranks of most organizations because, as he put it, "nobody ever asked."

More than simply asking the key questions, it is time for leaders to create organizational structures and systems that implicitly trust those at the front line—who often earn the least yet do some of the most difficult and frustrating jobs—to exercise good judgment, get closer to customers, and day in and day out, deliver great results for their organizations.

HANDBOOK FOR
Judgment on the
FRONT LINE

[SECTION ONE]

Introduction

In the United States alone, retail and service workers are estimated to total more than fifteen million people, or nearly one-fifth of the U.S. commercial workforce. Statistics and common sense tell us that the vast majority of workers are engaged in frontline positions—pharmaceutical salespeople, bank tellers, airline attendants, coffee-shop baristas, truck drivers, factory line workers, and the like. A former pharmaceutical CEO recently estimated that 80 percent of the employees in the companies he had led were workers and supervisors on his organizations' front line.[1]

Despite their overwhelming numbers, we don't read much about front-line workers in the press. Ignoring their indisputable impact on corporate bottom lines, we don't see many business books written about how to help frontline employees or managers be successful. And the prevalent corporate tagline about "people are our most important asset" notwithstanding, we don't see many company leaders prepared to tap into more than a tiny percentage of the knowledge, creativity, and judgment of their largest group of employees.

Not only are these workers smart and experienced, but they are also the face of their organizations to millions upon millions of customers daily. They interact with consumers, learning their preferences and spending habits. They square off against the competition each day, selling the relative merits of their organizations or executing processes that keep the company machinery running. They have insights into where that machinery breaks down—product defects, service slipups, inefficient corporate policies, ineffective customer campaigns, and much more. No organization can claim to be genuinely customer centric without being equally dedicated to getting the greatest insight and contribution from those who serve the customer.

THE TURTLE AND THE HIPPO

Because these workers sit at the bottom of the organizational pyramid, they rarely have the opportunity to share their insights or offer ideas for improvement. A centuries-old hierarchical, command-and-control corporate paradigm still separates the thinkers at the top from the doers at the bottom.

Although some companies have attempted to mitigate organizational limitations with initiatives such as open-book management, quality circles, or employee-engagement surveys, few companies have rethought their organizations to unleash the power of their front lines.

Our research and clinical work revealed two common reasons why organizations fail to tap into the capability of all their people. The first was explained to us by a retail store manager who gave us a biology lesson. He shared with us that if turtles are kept in confined spaces, they will grow only to a physical size that fits their environment. It turns out that while diminutive turtles are cute, confining them stunts their growth and impedes normal development. This manager, who had worked at several retailers, explained that the environment in a store or company is similar to a turtle cage: Managers often put constraints on how people act with rules and bureaucracy that limit their growth and contribution. It isn't simply restrictive policies that prevent employees from using their judgment in dealing with customers but also low organizational expectations, combined with little interest among senior managers in learning from their front lines.

We learned another lesson about the pernicious effect of hierarchy from Internet powerhouse Amazon. Internally, Amazon coined the term "HiPPO," which stands for "highest-paid person's opinion." The HiPPO rule notes that in most organizations, decisions are made by the most senior leader involved rather than through reliance on data or with multiple inputs. Amazon, by contrast, has fostered a culture of experimentation in which leaders at all levels are encouraged to test ideas in the marketplace and then let data—not senior leadership opinions—guide implementation.

WHY FRONTLINE JUDGMENT MAKES A DIFFERENCE

Those at the front line of your organization are more than just the customer interface. They are the best source of knowledge about how your organization is actually working, how customers and the market are changing, and whether your company strategy is being well executed.

Clearly, frontline employees are some of the best contributors for understanding whether your value proposition is working with customers. They know whether your products and services meet customer expectations. They can tell you about customer behaviors, customer segmentation, and how customers view your organization relative to the competition. When they listen closely, they can also tell you which customer needs are unmet and where opportunities for future growth may lie.

Additionally, those on the front line are the most consistent end users of organizational processes, policies, and communication. They can help you identify and correct communication breakdowns, customer-*unfriendly* policies, and inefficient work processes that consume employee time and company resources. They see not only waste and missed opportunity but also danger. Frontline workers often know where safety problems or crises are waiting to happen.

In sum, frontline employees are uniquely positioned to create value in three distinct ways:

1. Generate Ideas: Most organizations have an untapped reservoir of creativity and latent innovation in their thousands, or even tens of thousands, of frontline workers. These employees can offer new ideas for products or services based on firsthand dialogue with customers about their needs.

2. Solve Problems: No company is free of undesirable bureaucracy. Frontline workers not only see where the gears get stuck in serving customers as the result of organizational processes or policies, but they often know the solution. Additionally, when frontline employees are free to exercise their judgment to make good business decisions for the customer, they can solve problems on the spot rather than directing customers to supervisors or call centers.

3. Avert Crises: Frontline employees often know where danger lies on the job. They see if safety rules are skirted, hygiene standards relaxed, or security standards breached. If they feel they will be listened to, they are able to help companies avoid disaster by providing early warnings.

BUILDING THE FRONT LINE–FOCUSED ORGANIZATION

In this handbook we hope to provide practical applications to help leaders at all levels build a front line–focused organization, one that is free of turtle cages and overbearing HiPPOs and enables organizations to access the power of frontline employees' judgment. We draw upon best-practice research that looked inside more than twenty organizations and led us to institutions as diverse as Yum! Brands, the U.S. Navy SEALs, the Mayo Clinic, Zara, and Zappos. Our research has also been informed by a clinical perspective drawn from more than fifty years of collective consulting experience working with dozens of companies from the boardroom to the front lines.

The most successful organizations we researched and consulted with aligned the many variables affecting the front line's ability to deliver. They established clear strategies and customer-value propositions that were simply articulated throughout the company. Our benchmarks taught their frontline employees the business basics—problem solving, financial analysis, customer segmentation—so they could make good judgments. They gave them the latitude and leadership support to take risks, learn, and ultimately be successful. This included providing them with information systems, managerial policies, and work processes that enabled them to focus on customers and create value.

None of the companies that we researched, benchmarked, and consulted with have it all figured out. There are no singular answers to how to radically alter how companies operate, how to engage thousands of employees, or how to promote the free exchange of ideas. However, there were many best practices and common traits among the companies that we researched, particularly in contrast to typical command-and-control organizations.

[Characteristics of Front Line–Focused Organizations]

	Front Line–Focused Organization	Command-and-Control Organization
Strategy Development	Strategy is shaped and influenced to a large extent by knowledge from the front line. Strategy development and execution deliberately consider frontline delivery capability.	Strategy development is a top-down exercise that relies on the intelligence and judgment at the apex of the organizational pyramid. There is little consideration of frontline capability and an assumption that organizational leaders below the top will develop whatever is required to drive execution.
Execution Systems and Processes	Systems, processes, and centralized staff are designed to support those executing at the front lines. Policies are frequently designed or improved based upon frontline feedback. Frontline workers have access to complete customer data so they can make informed judgments.	Systems, processes, and centralized staff are oriented toward efficiency and central control. Policies are controlled by centralized staff who think first about minimizing corporate risk and expenses. Customer information is not readily available to the front line due to systems constraints or security concerns.
Hiring Practices	Frontline employees go through a rigorous values and skills screening before being hired. There are consistent standards, evaluation processes, and minimum requirements for hiring an employee.	Emphasis is placed on head-count controls, such as "staff fill rates," that emphasize quantity rather than quality. Hiring is decentralized and it is left to local managers to find the best available employees.

Continued on next page

Continued from previous page

[Characteristics of Front Line–Focused Organizations]

	Front Line–Focused Organization	Command-and-Control Organization
Training and Development	There are significant investments in training frontline employees and managers. Development includes teaching the front line business acumen and problem-solving skills. There is deliberate emphasis placed on developing frontline supervisors—those who have little prior management training but lead up to 80 percent of the workforce.	Training budgets are limited for the front line (if measured on a per-employee allocation), with disproportionate resources invested in developing senior organizational leaders. Business acumen and advanced problem-solving skills are considered too complex or not required for frontline employees to do their job. Frontline supervisors learn on the job after being promoted with little formal training.
Innovation	There is an organizational framework for solving problems and experimenting to test new ideas so everyone uses shared language, methodology, and data when making judgments. New ideas from the front line are tested so that data and experience can be used in innovation and resource allocation.	Innovation and problem solving are largely centralized, with most important decisions moving up the hierarchy for resolution. New ideas are evaluated by managers at each level of the hierarchy based more on their personal judgment and experience than on data or experimentation.
Organizational Learning	Senior leaders frequently spend structured time with frontline leaders to learn. There are formal and informal mechanisms for frontline workers and managers to interface with leaders at all levels. Technology is deployed to facilitate open discussion and knowledge transfer.	Senior leaders infrequently interact with frontline employees. Frontline workers perceive senior leaders to be intimidating. Dialogues feel hierarchical, with senior managers talking more than listening. Most communication from the field is directed back to the center; peer dialogue is not promoted.

ASSESSING YOUR ORGANIZATION'S FRONTLINE JUDGMENT CAPABILITY

Unless your organization is a start-up, chances are that it was built on traditional notions of hierarchy. Before trying to drive innovation and growth through frontline judgment, it is important to diagnose your starting point. Every organization has a different culture and history of working with the front line. Use the quiz opposite to assess the extent to which your organization is front line focused today. A score of 10 means that the item is always true, a 5 sometimes true, and a 1 never true.

Statement	Extent to Which This Is True	Explain Your Rating
Senior leaders always go to the front line to dialogue with customers and employees before setting strategy.	1 2 3 4 5 6 7 8 9 10	
Senior leaders carefully consider frontline execution capabilities and limitations, factoring them into strategy development.	1 2 3 4 5 6 7 8 9 10	
There is an open, nonhierarchical environment in which frontline leaders will gladly share all information with senior leaders.	1 2 3 4 5 6 7 8 9 10	
Frontline employees look forward to the opportunity to interact with senior leaders in the field.	1 2 3 4 5 6 7 8 9 10	
Our organization has multiple methods for tapping into the ideas and creativity of our front line.	1 2 3 4 5 6 7 8 9 10	
We trust our frontline workers and give them resources to solve big problems or resolve customer disputes locally, using their best judgment.	1 2 3 4 5 6 7 8 9 10	
We hire only the best talent for our front line, after a rigorous screening process.	1 2 3 4 5 6 7 8 9 10	
We invest significant resources so that our frontline employees understand our strategy, business model, and customers in order to make good judgments.	1 2 3 4 5 6 7 8 9 10	
We have structures and support systems to enable innovation by frontline employees.	1 2 3 4 5 6 7 8 9 10	
Our information systems, policies, and work processes are optimized to enable frontline employees to do their best work.	1 2 3 4 5 6 7 8 9 10	

Score Your Organization:

90–100 Front Line Focused
75–90 Some Work to Do
50–75 Untapped Potential
Less Than 50 Stuck in the Past

If you scored over ninety, your organization has already achieved a frontline focus that is rarely found. If not, there are opportunities for improvement that this handbook will guide you through. Before continuing, take a moment to note the major strengths and weaknesses in your organization's ability to tap into the judgment and capability of those on your front line.

Diagnosing My Organization's Starting Point
Our current strengths:
Our current weaknesses:

USING THIS HANDBOOK

This handbook is designed to provide an operational, step-by-step approach to the process laid out in *Judgment on the Front Line: How Smart Companies Win by Trusting Their People*. This five-step process is designed to help organizations become more front line focused:

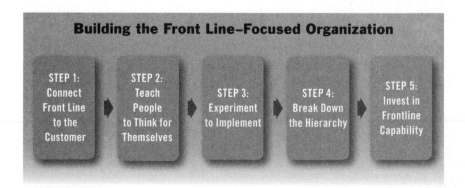

Building the Front Line–Focused Organization

STEP 1: Connect Front Line to the Customer → STEP 2: Teach People to Think for Themselves → STEP 3: Experiment to Implement → STEP 4: Break Down the Hierarchy → STEP 5: Invest in Frontline Capability

Many of the frameworks and exercises come directly from our clinical work and have been tested and used at all levels of organizational hierarchies. Our experience encompasses work in the United States, Asia, Europe, and South America with diverse companies and nonprofit organizations. We have found that the exercises are not culturally specific or necessarily related to certain industries. In fact, you are asked to define those characteristics that are unique to your organization, culture, employees, and customer relationships so that you can build the type of front line–focused organization that will succeed in your market.

The remaining sections of this handbook follow the five-step process for transforming an organization to be front line focused, with emphasis on providing a "how-to" explanation.

Section One: Introduction

- Why frontline judgment makes a difference
- Characteristics of a front line–focused organization
- Assessing your organization's frontline judgment capacity
- The five-step process for becoming a front line–focused organization

Section Two: Translating Customer Needs into Frontline Delivery

- Articulating your ideal customer experience
- Mapping your critical frontline-customer touch points
- Linking your frontline capability to customer needs

Section Three: Developing a Frontline Teachable Point of View

- Identifying your frontline success metrics
- Tying your organizational values to frontline delivery
- Energizing and recognizing your frontline teams
- Validating your Teachable Point of View with the front line

Section Four: Teaching People to Think for Themselves

- Understanding your most common frontline-customer problems
- Identifying opportunities for frontline problem solving
- Developing your organization's problem-solving methodology

Section Five: Innovation and Experimentation at the Front Line

- Defining who, where, and how the front line innovates
- Developing an experimentation methodology
- Assessing your organization's readiness for a culture of experimentation

Section Six: Breaking Down the Hierarchy

- Methods for breaking down the hierarchy
- Assessing your organization's readiness for change

Section Seven: Create the Right Environment

- Screening and hiring the best talent for the front line
- Developing supervisors who empower the front line
- Designing your frontline supervisor development experience

Section Eight: Citizenship on the Line

- Engaging your front line in the community
- Discovering society's front line outside your organization

Section Nine: The Never-Ending Process

- Preparing for ongoing change
- Staying close to the front line

[SECTION TWO]

Translating Customer Needs into Frontline Delivery

A mong academics and business pundits, there has been a long-standing debate about whether successful organizations begin by taking care of their customers or their employees. One side argues that without customers there will be no revenue, while the other side insists that dissatisfied employees will drive away customers regardless of how great the product or service. We view this largely as a pointless chicken-or-egg debate; businesses need both employees and customers to survive.

We start, however, with senior management's responsibility to define a clear customer strategy, because regardless of the starting point, the CEO and senior team are those who ultimately must connect frontline execution to customer needs. We won't delve into the science and art of customer segmentation and strategy development in this handbook but simply say that senior leaders must be clear about distinct customer needs, including where there are underserved customers and which customer groups offer the greatest profit potential. Senior leaders must also be concerned with ensuring that there is a simple and powerful customer value proposition that is compelling to customers while matching overall perceptions of the brand and organizational product and service capabilities. A deep understanding of customers may be gleaned from corporate databases, but true insight is more likely to come from watching consumers on the front lines or through anthropological observations of how they actually interface with the company, its employees, and its products throughout the usage life cycle.

BUILDING YOUR IDEAL CUSTOMER EXPERIENCE

Your customer strategy must address who your customers are, their unique needs, and the value proposition you have to offer them. Use the table below to summarize your organization's customer groups, including any segments that you hope to serve in the future. Label the customer needs and behaviors that distinguish each segment, as well as the differentiated value your organization can offer them.

Describe your customer segments, how they differ, and how you can serve them:

Who They Are	What They Want	The Differentiated Value We Can Offer

Once the essential value proposition has been determined, you must envision the ideal customer interaction you want to create at your front line. This includes breaking down that interface into key characteristics that are likely to influence the organizational capabilities required of your frontline people:

- **Complexity:** The more complex the product or service, the more help consumers are likely to require and therefore the more capable frontline employees will need to be in order to complete the sale, advise the customer, and build relationships.
- **Length:** If the sales experience is short—as in a convenience store or fast-food restaurant—there will be limited time for influencing the purchase process. Conversely, if the interaction with the front line is long, employees will have more opportunity to discern unique customer needs and differentiate the experience.
- **Interactivity:** Both the location and nature of the interaction need to be considered. If the frontline associate requires input from the customer to tailor a solution, it is far more likely that decisions will need to be made at the point of sale.
- **Predictability:** If transactions are routine and predictable, there will be fewer opportunities for frontline employees to differentiate the experience. On the other hand, if transactions are highly variable, then employees may need to make judgments on the spot to help customers.
- **Frequency:** Depending upon the industry and sales cycles, customers who seldom interact with an organization may provide fewer opportunities for frontline employees to get to know them.

The nature of the customer transaction will influence both customers' expectations and the degree of flexibility and judgment capability you're likely to need at the front line. For example, customer interactions that are simple, short, predictable, and infrequent are less likely to require much frontline interactivity or judgment. However, as one or more of these variables increases, a customer's experiences with your organization may be strongly influenced by the caliber of employee they meet. As the graphic below depicts, as transaction characteristics create expectations of a more fluid or differentiated customer experiences, employees must be able to innovate and exercise judgment during the customer experience, rather than relaying customer requests to other departments or managers.

In situations that are predictable and have limited variables, technology will be used to replace the employee completely or guide the employee through prescribed steps. In situations where employees need to have some autonomy to bend rules, offer pricing discounts, or make similar judgments, technology

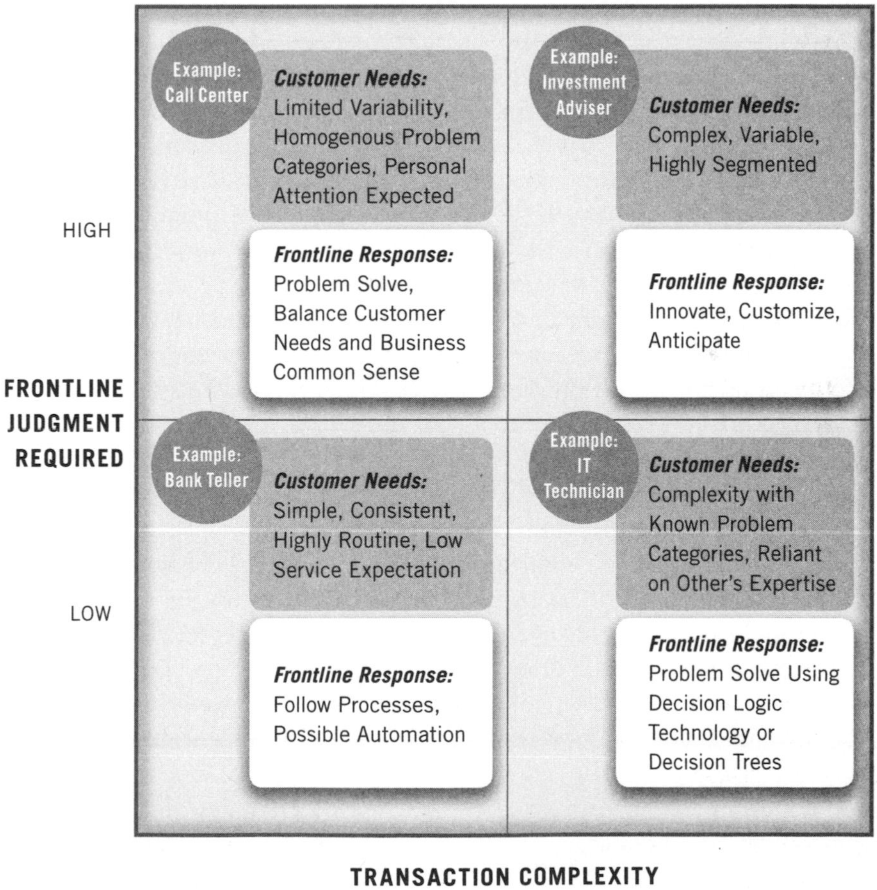
Example: Call Center
Customer Needs: Limited Variability, Homogenous Problem Categories, Personal Attention Expected
Frontline Response: Problem Solve, Balance Customer Needs and Business Common Sense
Example: Investment Adviser
Customer Needs: Complex, Variable, Highly Segmented
Frontline Response: Innovate, Customize, Anticipate
Example: Bank Teller
Customer Needs: Simple, Consistent, Highly Routine, Low Service Expectation
Frontline Response: Follow Processes, Possible Automation
Example: IT Technician
Customer Needs: Complexity with Known Problem Categories, Reliant on Other's Expertise
Frontline Response: Problem Solve Using Decision Logic Technology or Decision Trees
HIGH
LOW
FRONTLINE JUDGMENT REQUIRED
TRANSACTION COMPLEXITY

needs to provide easy access to information about the business, products, and customers that will inform employees' decisions. At the far extreme, in situations with highly differentiated customer interactions and the opportunity to innovate new products or services on the front line, technology needs to provide the infrastructure for employees to share learning and best practices, as well as collaborate with area experts and functional staff support.

WHERE IS YOUR FRONT LINE?

It may seem apparent that an organization's front line is at the point of customer interaction. For many companies today, there is actually more than one front line, as customers interact through salespeople, Web sites, call centers, and third-party channels. We also broaden the definition further to include key positions, particularly those that are entry level or low down in the organizational pyramid, that directly impact the customer experience. This may include software designers, merchandising specialists, product managers, or other roles that typically have limited authority but are essential for creating a positive customer experience.

It is often hard to pinpoint which employee group may most impact the customer experience, and we find through our clinical work that senior management's attention may shift over time. The first step is understanding the multitude of frontline roles and determining which have the greatest impact for your organization, given its customer value proposition and competitive environment. We often begin this process by working with organizations to build a customer journey map, or a simple process map that shows the complete customer experience. This may start with how customers gather information and gain an awareness of the organization, its brand, and its product or service offering. The customer journey map then flows from the initial point of customer interaction through the postsale service or follow-up contact that may result from warranty, consumables purchases, or simply repeat visits. Along the way, key contributions from various departments and personnel can be noted. For example, an apparel retailer cannot forget the contribution of the junior merchants who find fashionable products to stock store shelves, just as a consulting firm must remember how the insights of a new analyst who only recently graduated from college can generate a breakthrough client idea.

Building this is often an iterative process in which key elements and important contributors can be filled in over time. However, we find that even the most basic process map often yields insights for senior executives, who may not previously have understood the scope of operational detail or recognized the influence on the customer experience of key frontline roles.

FRONTLINE CUSTOMER TOUCH POINTS

A simplified approach to outlining your customers' experience is provided below. Using the chart below, select one of your most important customer segments and identify how they interface with your organization today. Identify the channels they use, the expectations they have at each purchase stage, and how your frontline employees engage with your customers today.

	Prepurchase (Awareness/ Research)	Purchase (Inquiry/ Comparison/ Decision)	Postpurchase (Use/Installation/ Service)
Channel			
Customer Expectations			
Frontline Experience (Today)			

CAPTURING YOUR IDEAL CUSTOMER EXPERIENCE

After outlining your organization's current customer experience and frontline interface, it's time to pull your thoughts together regarding the ideal experience that you want your customers to have. This requires consideration of what your frontline employees can do to provide differentiated value, through innovation and problem solving, for your customers. If your customer segments are highly differentiated, you may need to conduct this exercise for various customer groups. For now, select just one—your biggest or most profitable customer segment. Write this as a story that might appear in a magazine, taking the customer's point of view. In your story, describe the customer journey, including the sales process, how you were helped, how the people and the organization were different from the competition, and other details that make this feel like a specific, personal experience. Be sure to identify how your organization's frontline employees contributed to a spectacular customer experience, including any problems they solved or how they adapted to the customer's needs.

[The Ideal Customer Experience]

[SECTION THREE]

Developing a Frontline Teachable Point of View

In the last section you developed a narrative of the ideal customer experience you envision for your organization based on how your front line can better help customers. To realize it, you will likely need to teach and energize hundreds or thousands of people to ensure alignment of purpose and behavior. This will require you to have what Noel described in *The Leadership Engine* as a Teachable Point of View. In the context of building a front line–focused enterprise, this means that leaders must be able to clearly articulate four things:

- **Ideas:** How do we win with customers over our competitors? What role does the front line play in serving our customers' needs?
- **Values:** What are the values and leadership behaviors that will lead to successful execution of our customer strategy?
- **Emotional Energy:** How can we engage all of our people to ensure that our customer has a fantastic experience during any interface with our company?
- **Edge:** What are the judgment calls that those on the front line must make in order to ensure that our customers' needs are met, problems solved, and growth opportunities exploited?

We will take some time to explore each of these below in order to build your Teachable Point of View for frontline success.

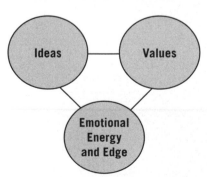

IDEAS

If you've completed section 2 of this handbook, most of your ideas about the customers and what it will take for the front line to serve them have already been articulated. Additionally, you need to consider how you align the organization around a set of metrics that will help you achieve your organizational strategy while remaining true to your customer value proposition and making your company a desirable place to work for your employees.

Metrics, because they are typically tied to compensation, are the most powerful statement of what an organization expects from its front line. A company's scorecard dictates where employees invest their time, attention, and energy. There are typically three problems we see with how metrics are defined in organizations:

- **Measure Everything:** If goals are too numerous, employees focus on nothing as they try to pay attention to everything.
- **Serve Many Masters:** If leaders above the front line don't have integrated and aligned goals, they will create schizophrenia at the front line by pressuring employees to focus on singular measures without recognizing the trade-offs and judgments that must happen.
- **Disconnect the Strategy:** If the operational measures conflict with the service expectations or types of customer relationships that employees are expected to build, they will ultimately disregard the company strategy in the quest to achieve local operational numbers.

These problems compel companies to think very carefully about what they will measure, particularly at the front line, where employees traditionally

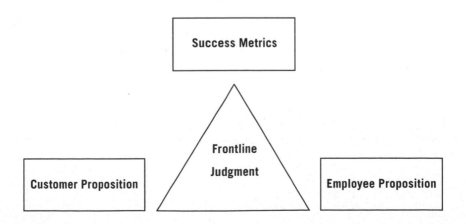

hear little about the overall strategy or receive messages relayed via e-mail or video or passed down the company hierarchy. Measurements of performance and success will dictate whether an employee feels he can confidently do the job, whether he is motivated to achieve a challenging but reasonable target, and whether he serves customers in the optimal way.

One of the retailers we consulted with had wanted to change its business model from what it felt was a short-term, transactional orientation to building long-term customer relationships. The company had taken the right initial steps by defining its overall strategy, outlining the characteristics of the long-term relationships it wanted to build with customers, and even noting how its culture would need to change so that employees would be supported by managers as they changed the sales model and results were not so easily measured. Unfortunately, the company had missed one crucial step: It had failed to fully realign its measurements and incentives. While managers hyped the new approach, stores and employees continued to be measured on their ability to meet budget numbers focused on high-margin products and services. The measurement system—a legacy from the company's past of high-pressure sales—inadvertently encouraged employees to continue their pushy ways.

As employees later told us, if senior management had simply changed the measurement scheme to align with the longer-term focus and placed more emphasis on the shopping experience, associates would have been quick to change. Ultimately, the company's efforts created deep frustration and residual cynicism among many sales associates, who were initially excited about the opportunity to meaningfully engage with customers but felt management was insincere about the change after their individual or team performance was criticized when they failed to achieve the budget numbers. After only a few months, the customer experience in many stores had reverted to the old way of doing business.

By contrast, when David Novak became chairman and CEO of Yum! (the parent company of quick-service restaurant megabrands Pizza Hut, KFC, and Taco Bell), one of his first moves was to align the measurement system with his emphasis on Customer Mania. Yum! had been created as a spin-off of PepsiCo, so Novak inherited what had essentially been standalone operations of three separate companies with little interface, cooperation, or synergy among them. Integrating the operations and cultures of these independent companies included aligning service expectations and setting operational standards that every restaurant would achieve. This meant that Taco Bell and Pizza Hut would no longer have different expectations about how many pieces of trash were allowable in the parking lot or how they defined friendly service.

Yum! instituted its CHAMPS program, which stood for "Cleanliness,

Hospitality, Accuracy, Maintenance, Product quality, and Speed." CHAMPS was designed to look at all customer touch points in a restaurant in order to create a great experience. It also became the standard measurement system with high expectations: Novak and team expected scores of one hundred on the CHAMPS customer surveys or during visits by an internal team committed to coaching stores on CHAMPS execution. CHAMPS helps to ensure that the fundamentals required for the ideal customer experience are in place in every one of Yum!'s more than 37,000 restaurants.

Identify Your Frontline Success Metrics

Think back to the ideal customer experience you described in section 1. How would you operationally measure this? What are the top five to seven metrics that would fairly assess how well frontline employees are performing? Use the space below to list your top success measures for the front line:

Success Metric	Process for Measuring This
1.	
2.	
3.	
4.	
5.	
6.	
7.	

VALUES

Once the customer needs, frontline delivery model, and success metrics have been defined, leaders at all levels of the organization must understand how results should be delivered. When a company defines values, they must encompass the entire organization, not simply the front line. However, it is imperative that senior leaders recognize that the company's values define how people work together, including how issues of power, hierarchy, and respect translate into the organizational environment. In fact, leaders must consciously define values that will create a workplace culture that leads to the creation of the right customer experience.

When companies define values such as "unleash the power of our people" or "recognize, recognize, recognize" or "coach and support," they signal to their people embedded beliefs about the value of each person's contribution and teamwork. Even more crucial, when they go the next step to define behaviors related to each value, they provide guideposts for how organizational members should lead and interact with one another.

Wawa, a regional chain of nearly six hundred convenience stores in six states along the United States' East Coast, demonstrates how values can create a culture and work environment that reinforce the work of those on the front line. The vast majority of Wawa's eighteen thousand associates work in the chain's nearly six hundred stores selling coffee, making sandwiches, or pumping gas.[1] Those associates are the face of the company's brand, which has achieved a cultlike following among its one million daily customers, who ring up four hundred million annual transactions. Wawa employees are typically local hires who are members of the communities in which they work. It is routine for associates to know every one of their regular customers' names and strike up conversations about sports, families, or local politics.

The company's six core values—"Value People," "Delight Customers," "Embrace Change," "Do the Right Thing," "Do Things Right," and "Passion for Winning"—are guiding lights for how associates build relationships with the communities and customers they serve, as well as how they work with one another. Values permeate nearly every activity, from hiring to in-store events to company picnics. For example, as one of the human-resources executives told us during a visit to the company's headquarters outside of Philadelphia, Wawa screens potential store managers first against the values of "Value People" and "Delight Customers." Regardless of results or their performance track record, nobody will be hired as a store leader, or even an assistant manager, if they don't prioritize investing in the development of people and caring for customers.

Similarly, the other values relate to how people do their daily jobs. "Embrace Change" is about being flexible, whether changing which shift you work or taking on a coworker's responsibilities if he calls in sick.[2] Meanwhile, "Do Things Right" encourages employees to follow processes and avoid cutting corners while "Do the Right Thing" is a reminder that Wawa is inseparably connected to its community members and employees. Wawa's

CEO, Howard Stoeckel, has said, "We have six deeply held values that guide almost everything we do in this business. If decisions embrace most of those values, they prove to be very, very successful decisions. . . . The values are at the heart of our success, they're what keeps our flock flying together, and always one wing ahead of the competition."[3]

Values, and the leadership behaviors they foster, are a constant focus at Wawa. Each year the company has "Values Day," a company-wide celebration in all of its stores that gives associates an opportunity to reflect on the chain's values. Posters of each value are on display and employees wear stickers to highlight the values. More important, living the values is recognized by coworkers. Through its "Big Six" program, Wawa invites associates at all levels to nominate anyone they see who exemplifies one of the values, whether in or out of the workplace. More than half of Wawa's associates may nominate someone for recognition in a given year, and more than 90 percent of those nominations will originate with a store worker. Those who are recognized receive a pin with an Olympics-like icon demonstrating that particular value, a handwritten letter from Stoeckel, or acknowledgment in the internal newsletter and Web site.

Additionally, as Barbara Ennis, the program director, told us, there are even bigger forms of recognition for living the values. In some cases, an associate may be invited to company headquarters. After being publicly celebrated for his or her achievements, the associate has lunch with Stoeckel in the company cafeteria, which is reset to create a top-flight gourmet restaurant atmosphere. In 2010, the program evolved and Stoeckel took to recognizing people—and even entire store teams—where they worked and brought the party on the road by visiting the stores. After store visits, he invited the associate or store team to be recognized, along with friends and family, to join him for dinner or lunch at a nice local restaurant. Such was the case for first year associate Glenn Vogel after he became the first person in company history to be nominated for demonstrating all six values.

On an even grander scale, Wawa has run its "Dream Maker" program for five years. This program attempts to make "dreams come true," Ennis told us, for associates who go above and beyond to help others. "This is Wawa's version of *Extreme Home Makeover* meets Make-a-Wish," she says.

In one case, Michael Porcella was recognized for selling the most charitable contributions in a company-sponsored benefit for the Children's Hospital of Philadelphia. Porcella sold more than 1,200 units each day, setting a company record. His prize: As a lifelong hockey fan—a fact that Ennis discovered after interviewing Porcella's friends and family—he was given personalized Flyers paraphernalia, Mario Lemieux's rookie card, four tickets to monthly Flyers games, the opportunity to watch a pregame warm-up from the Flyers bench, and a Zamboni ride during a game's intermission. Another employee, Samantha Eller, who worked as a parts analyst at Wawa's dairy, received the award after caring for a fellow associate who was hospitalized for three weeks following a serious car accident. In addition to visiting the woman daily, she acted as the liaison with her family, friends, and colleagues, helping the woman through an extraordinarily difficult period in her life. The reward for her kindness, courtesy of Wawa, was a deluxe salon and spa package, a new wardrobe, and a five-day Disney cruise for her family.

All of the attention that Wawa places on values is much more than theatrics. Stories of positive acts, big and small, become part of company lore and culture. The stories are told not just verbally but in newsletters and Wawa's *Living Our Values* annual publication. Stoeckel shared one such story, telling us of an employee who asked to be buried with his Wawa values pin.

By recognizing values in action, Wawa is constantly reinforcing the right way to build relationships with customers, community members, and coworkers. Each act of recognition is not just positive reinforcement for that single employee but also a reminder of what is expected and possible for everyone in that location. Peer reinforcement, with Stoeckel's public support and recognition behind it, sets local norms in each store, distribution center, or transportation depot that prevent the values from becoming empty corporate rhetoric. Everyone knows that his or her behavior is being watched, not by auditors or company managers but by the people he or she works and lives with daily. As Stoeckel told us, "you have to celebrate what you value and what you think is important. Value submissions come from peers, from bosses. . . . Anyone can send in values stories about anyone. It's not top down; if anything it's bottom up."[4]

LINKING YOUR IDEAS TO YOUR VALUES

The first challenge is to clearly define the organizational values required to build a front line–focused organization that delivers the desired customer experience. You must consider how the values relate to the frontline employees' ability to deliver value and what type of work environment is needed. At Wawa, for example, where community relationships and knowing individual customers are important, there is an expectation that store employees will greet regular customers by name. When you picture the ideal customer environment, what type of work environment is needed? What behaviors are on display as team members work with one another and serve customers?

Use the space opposite to define the key values that will create your envisioned customer experience and help employees achieve the success metrics:

Your Front Line–Focused Values
1.
2.
3.
4.
5.

Once you have identified the values, you must make them operational. You need to explain not only what they mean and why they are important but also the specific positive and negative behaviors associated with each value. Additionally, values often have embedded paradoxes, or moments when they seem to conflict with one another. A common example in many organizations is when employees are asked to value working with speed and efficiency while delivering quality output; when employees ask which is the bigger priority, the frequent answer is "both." Another example might come from Wawa. "Do Things Right" can mean not taking shortcuts and sticking to company processes and policies that are designed to safeguard customers or employees. Paradoxically, "Do the Right Thing" can mean exercising personal judgment and opting to go out of your way to help a coworker or community member. It might seem to some that if rules and procedures are locked in, associates won't have full freedom to stray from the path when someone needs their help.[5] Talking about this with frontline workers to ensure that there is alignment helps avoid employee cynicism and verifies whether the values can really be put into practice as imagined. For each value you identified above, use the table below to help you make it behaviorally specific for your team:

Value:	
What it means (your definition)	
Why it is important for your team's success	

Positive behaviors	
Negative behaviors	
Paradoxes	

EMOTIONAL ENERGY

Another component of the Teachable Point of View is engaging and exciting people. There are four basic elements that can boost frontline employees' desire to commit and contribute.

◆ **Context:** The Teachable Point of View must articulate how frontline employees' daily work and customer interactions are essential to the achievement of larger organizational goals. Understanding how one's work fits with the company's strategy and benefits customers or other organizational stakeholders gives a sense of meaning and importance to the work that frontline employees do. It is also important for leaders to recognize how interactions with those doing frontline jobs—which some may view as menial or simple in certain industries—are critical moments in a customer's life. Putting a smile on a customer's face, solving his or her problem, or providing fast and reliable service can be important moments for employees to connect with and help others.

◆ **Care:** The Teachable Point of View must also articulate how essential frontline employees are for long-term success and the organizational commitment to ensure that frontline employees have the opportunity to grow and develop with managers who will mentor and teach them. Leaders must reinforce the type of mutual dependence that exists with frontline employees. The organization can be successful over the long term only by helping them to grow and develop.

◆ **Control:** To engage frontline employees, senior leaders must consider how to give them the opportunity to make autonomous judgments (within boundaries) as well as to be listened to when they point out problems, broken processes, or ineffective policies.

◆ **Creativity:** Ultimately, the most engaging promise is when an organization asks people to provide their individual thought and creativity and invest their own personality in their work. A job can become energizing when someone feels that they are authentically engaged in the work rather than acting as an automaton who repeats scripts or tells customers why they can't break the company policy.

As an example, when David Novak began Customer Mania at Yum! he first addressed all of these issues for employees so the frontline cooks and cashiers were motivated to give their best effort.

Context	Putting a Yum! (or satisfied smile) on every customer's face became the personal mission for all employees.
	Novak declared the restaurant general manager position to be the most important in the company and dedicated all corporate employees to the service of those working in the restaurants.
Care	Yum! changed the job titles of managers so they became "coaches" with the mission to help employees develop and grow.
	Novak committed Yum! to building employees' life skills, such as customer relationship building and teamwork, so associates in this high-turnover industry would have capabilities that could translate to any job or industry. As Novak said, "I think people would rather come into a company that is committed to building life skills versus teaching you how to cook chicken for the rest of your life."[6]
Control	Yum! granted every employee a ten-dollar allowance to fix any customer's experience.
Creativity	Novak encouraged employees to have fun and bring their personality to work with their head up and a smile, rather than just work the cash register.

WHY FRONTLINE WORK IS ENERGIZING IN YOUR ORGANIZATION

Imagine that you are delivering your Teachable Point of View directly to a frontline employee. Based on the ideal customer interaction you described, explain why he or she should be excited and energized to come to work in your organization.

Context	
Care	
Control	
Creativity	

360-DEGREE RECOGNITION

One of the most important elements in creating an energizing work environment, particularly at the front line, is to create recognition systems. One example is Wawa's Big Six values program, which is laser focused on promoting the right behaviors. Yum! similarly has a recognition culture that comes directly from Novak. As CEO, Novak has pictures of himself shaking hands with or giving awards to employees around the globe. The pictures cover not only his walls but also his ceiling. As he likes to say, "there's nothing that people want and enjoy more than recognition. . . . Recognition says, 'I care about what you do. It matters.'"[7]

Recognition comes from both peers and managers at Yum! Employees at any level can hand a coworker a CHAMPS card in recognition of outstanding delivery of any of the operational elements described above. The CHAMPS card not only comes with a sticker the recipient wears but also includes entry into a regional lottery drawing in which employees can win prizes such as movie tickets.

Additionally, Novak requires every company leader to have an award that can be handed out to recognize employees. His first award, the much-touted "floppy chicken," was a rubber chicken that he autographed and gave to employees. After taking a picture with the associate and the chicken, Novak handed the employee one hundred dollars because, as he liked to say, "you can't eat a rubber chicken."[8]

Recognition is the cultural glue that encourages the behavior, teamwork, and organizational commitment needed to deliver on the organizational strategy. While recognition from one's manager is always welcome, peer recognition can ultimately be even more powerful for reinforcing the norms that are needed for local execution of company strategy or values.

Your Recognition Program

Consider one thing that your organization could begin or improve in order to better recognize the work of those on the front line. Think about the role not only of managers but also of coworkers in recognizing one another. Outline your program below:

What We Want to Recognize	
How We Will Do It	
Who Will Be Involved	

Role for Senior Leaders to Support or Participate	

TESTING YOUR TPOV

Developing your Teachable Point of View is an iterative process. Once you think you have it figured out, it is important to test it in the field. At Wawa, Stoeckel recently gathered 1,700 store personnel to test out the company's long-range plan to become the world's most appetizing convenience retailer. He told us, "We spent a day walking through our long range plan and getting their input as to what they thought we should do, giving them feedback, and then having them give us more feedback. It's their plan as well as ours."[9]

Equally important, we suggest that leaders, whether CEOs or frontline supervisors, actively test their Teachable Point of View by going directly to the frontline workers. The goal is to create a dialogue and get feedback so that those on the front line can offer insight about what may seem unrealistic or what key points you may have missed. It's important that you neither try to sell nor defend your Teachable Point of View at this point. The objective is to listen and learn. As you gather the feedback, thank people for their input and let them know that you'll be talking to many others to help you refine your view.

PLAN YOUR TRIP

Use the space below to identify how you will test your Teachable Point of View in the field. Where will you go? Whom will you talk to? What questions do you want to ask?

[SECTION FOUR]

Teaching People to Think for Themselves

I n the previous sections of this handbook, you considered how to align your envisioned customer experience with your organization's success metrics, values, and recognition systems. Next we turn to helping your front line actively engage with customers to solve problems.

Enabling your front line to make judgments requires anticipation of problems that your customers are likely to face in dealing with your organization. Problems can come in diverse shapes and sizes depending upon your industry and business model. Whether product shortages, delivery delays, or service failures, it is inevitable that organizations will face moments when they disappoint valued customers. However, as market research has reportedly shown, effective problem recovery can actually strengthen customer loyalty and repurchase intent.

A deep understanding of potential customer problems can come from numerous methods, such as reviewing customer complaints, conducting focus groups, using mystery shoppers, or speaking directly with frontline associates about the problems they feel ill equipped to resolve. It is important to understand that the moments of disappointment that may lead customers to your competitors are not always the result of a process or service failure; sometimes they are the consequence of restrictive policies, inflexible sales terms, or the inability to offer adjunct products and services. As a first step to outlining the problem-solving capability your front line must possess, identify the customer breakdowns that are most likely to occur. (You may want to revisit your analysis of customer touch points from section 2.) Review the data you have available and use the space on the next page to identify the ways in which your organization may most seriously disappoint valuable customers. Consequences may accrue to the customer or to your own people and business results.

Disappointments for Our Customers	Consequences

Protecting your customers from such disappointments will typically necessitate more boldly empowering your frontline employees to make judgments and providing them with better support to do so. It is the leader's responsibility to establish what we call the Judgment Playing Field. This describes the power, resources, and boundaries that employees have to make decisions and act autonomously. As the diagram below shows, it is the senior leaders' responsibility to provide the support systems that truly enable frontline associates to act. Regardless of what senior leaders may say,

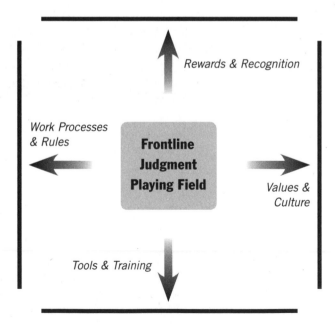

if any of the elements don't support the actions required to execute the ideal customer experience—or fix problems when things don't go smoothly—then employees won't be capable of exercising good judgment.

In the previous handbook section we discussed how two of the elements above (Values & Culture, Rewards & Recognition) can be used to create the right environment for employees to exercise their judgment. We will discuss Work Processes & Rules in a later section. For now, we will focus on how Tools & Training, particularly when focused on providing the business context needed for problem solving, can be used to enhance every employee's judgment capability.

Problems are diverse and highly dependent on business context. Training frontline personnel on how to think through complex problems, generate possible solutions, and make a business-savvy judgment call requires moving beyond simple protocols by teaching employees a thought process that relies upon contextual information to resolve knotty issues. Of course, the problem-solving capability required will depend upon the nature of the problem. In the diagram below, we identify three families of problem types that represent a progressive shift from recovery to resolution to reframing.

PROBLEM REFRAMING
- Problem definitions may vary or needs are unexpressed
- May require new designs, dilemma resolution, or cocreation
- Likely to require support of multiple constituencies

PROBLEM RESOLUTION
- Fixing more complex, unstructured problems
- Multiple possible solutions; requires novel approach or rule bending
- Likely to require support of multiple constituencies

PROBLEM RECOVERY
- Addressing customer complaints or fixing service defects
- Typically defined problems with few solutions; use of protocols helpful
- Most often solved among individuals

PROBLEM RECOVERY

Problem recovery requires fixing the situation for an already dissatisfied customer. Recovery skills are most likely to be needed under conditions of product or service failure, when customers don't receive the benefits promised and expected.

Yum! which has hundreds of thousands of frontline restaurant workers, uses the acronym "BLAST" to train employees for problem recovery. This step-by-step approach requires employees to begin by "believe the customer," not arguing or questioning their veracity. *L* stands for "listen to the customer," *A* stands for "apologize," *S* stands for "satisfy" (even if that means replacing an entire order), and *T* stands for "thanks," a constant reminder to every frontline employee and manager that the old-fashioned mantra "the customer is always right" can provide a reliable guide to present-day conduct at the customer interface. Frontline workers and managers are encouraged and trained to empathize with their customers and to take independent initiative to resolve customer problems and dilemmas.

The luxury hotel chain Ritz-Carlton utilizes a similar acronym for both problem anticipation and problem recovery. Through required training, Ritz-Carlton introduces "MR. BIV" to all of its more than thirty thousand employees. Rather than the process orientation used by Yum!, Ritz-Carlton favors a method to help employees identify problem categories in the hopes that they can spot issues before they create customer dissatisfaction. "MR. BIV" stands for "mistakes, rework, breakdowns, inefficiencies, and variations in work processes." In short, it is designed to help Ritz-Carlton associates recognize when things are outside of expected specifications so the employees can take immediate corrective action.

Consider your business and the types of customer complaints that you get most frequently. What are the customer issues that frontline personnel are most likely to face after the problem has emerged? Consider not only the problems but also how your front line can better assist in resolving issues. Too frequently organizations write rules and processes requiring employees to escalate. Instead of doing so, Yum! offers employees the latitude to spend up to ten dollars to solve any problem.

Likely Customer Complaints (after the breakdown has already occurred)	How Our Front Line Is Involved	What Our Front Line Should Do to Properly Resolve the Situation

PROBLEM RESOLUTION

Problem resolution encompasses a class of problems that share similar characteristics but are unique and personalized to a customer's circumstances. They tend to be more complex and ambiguous, relying on frontline employees to work out a tailored solution. The problem may be shared by multiple customers, but they may not articulate it uniformly, so it may be harder to define standard operating processes for handling these types of problems, since each scenario comes with its own twist.

For example, Ritz-Carlton empowers its employees to spend up to two thousand dollars to solve problems for its guests. In one case,[1] a family staying at the Bali property had carried special milk and eggs for their son, who had a rare food allergy. Upon arrival, they discovered that the milk had soured and most of the eggs had broken. The hotel's dining staff was unable to locate suitable replacements, but the hotel chef remembered seeing them in Singapore. With the hotel's funding, the chef's mother-in-law, who lived in Singapore, purchased the products and flew to Bali to hand deliver them. A problem that had the potential to ruin the family's vacation instead turned into a moment of delight that undoubtedly built customer loyalty.

Although guests who suffer from food allergies are hardly uncommon at Ritz-Carlton, the company could never write a standardized process for handling this situation. It required relying on the knowledge, ingenuity, and perseverance of its staff to create the right experience for the family. While the company spent money to do so, the lifetime value of a Ritz-Carlton customer is thought to be in excess of one million dollars, so this was truly a mutually beneficial outcome.

As you can see from this example, solving such problems typically requires engaging multiple people in the organization and calls for imaginative painting outside the lines of typical operating processes. Such problems require a mechanism for group dialogue and problem solving, a budget, and allowance for altering normal business operations to accommodate special customer needs.

It is important to note that while there are checks and balances in these organizations to ensure that people do not abuse the spending allowances, rather than mandate layers of approvals, the organizations rely principally on strong culture and values to guide employee decision making. Yum!'s mantra of customer-centricity makes it clear that employees must do right by customers, and the BLAST process reinforces this by starting with the faith that customers are honest in their portrayal of the problem. Similarly, one of Ritz-Carlton's values simply states, "I own and immediately resolve guest problems," making it clear that no employee can pass the buck or walk by a problem.

Use the work space below to think through how your organization may handle such problems by relying on frontline judgment. Since you will be unable to define specific solutions to such problems, focus instead on building a process approach at the front line with resources for execution, managerial support, and alignment with the values you defined in section 3.

Mechanisms to Promote Frontline Dialogue and Problem Solving	Resources/Budget for Problem Solving	Managerial Support/ Involvement	Alignment with Our Values

PROBLEM REFRAMING

The most difficult skill is problem reframing, which requires having the customer, or other involved parties, look at and analyze a given problem differently as a result of frontline workers helping them to see unrecognized needs or broadening the context in which they view the problem. Problem reframing is a deliberate attempt to change a customer's perspective regarding his or her needs and potential solutions, which may result from new ideas proposed by frontline workers or from cocreation with customers.

At furniture maker Steelcase, for example, a salesperson was asked to bid on a sizable deal to refurnish the offices of a *Fortune* 500 financial institution. From the conversation, he could tell that the customer viewed the product as a commodity that would ultimately be purchased on the basis of the best price. The salesperson had just been through intensive training at Steelcase's headquarters on how to use customer-research techniques to showcase Steelcase's differentiated offerings. Rather than succumb to the temptation of focusing on price or hardware, the salesperson put together a team of associates who fanned out across the country to visit branches, snap photos, and interview the customer's workers.

The insights gained as a result demonstrated that there were much deeper issues beyond replacing furniture. The photos shared with the client showed how ergonomically unsound many of the workstations were, with employees awkwardly contorted to use equipment or make notes. They further revealed how branding had become inconsistent across locations, with different fixtures and hand-drawn signage that muddled branch visuals. By the end of the discussion, the frontline salesperson and his team had convinced the client that the solution needed was much broader than originally conceived, and cost became one of several concerns rather than the customer's dominant decision criterion.

Problem resolution requires teaching frontline employees to change the way that they think about problems and engage in totally new problem-solving approaches. At Steelcase every newly hired employee, from senior vice president to entry level, was taught the "Critical Thinking Model," or CTM. This was a problem-solving approach created by Jim Hackett, Steelcase's CEO, to help employees carefully consider how to solve customer problems rather than default to discussions of product features or price. The model, elegantly simple in its approach, outlines a thought process for problem solving:

- **Phase 1:** Think. Individuals or teams must carefully consider different viewpoints, gather data, network, research, and visually represent their learning.
- **Phase 2:** Point of View. Data and learning from phase 1 is synthesized into a point of view that is represented by a single owner. The point of view is changed only if new evidence is presented.
- **Phase 3:** Plan to Implement. A plan for overcoming obstacles, enlisting support, measuring results, and contingency planning is developed before the action begins.
- **Phase 4:** Implement. Execution is the final result of CTM. Outcomes are measured, processes improved, and successes celebrated.

While it may seem unnecessary to teach such problem-solving basics, these are the foundation upon which the more advanced skills of problem resolution and problem reframing are built. Developing and scaling such a model also creates a shared organizational language and approach to problem solving that helps to diminish hierarchy and promote inclusion of diverse perspectives.

We do not advocate any single approach. Instead, we have found that it is most important that an organization uses a shared methodology and tool kit, whether derived from Lean Sigma, the A3 process, statistical methods, or any of numerous other approaches. Use the workspace below to consider the foundation for problem solving that you can build in your organization:

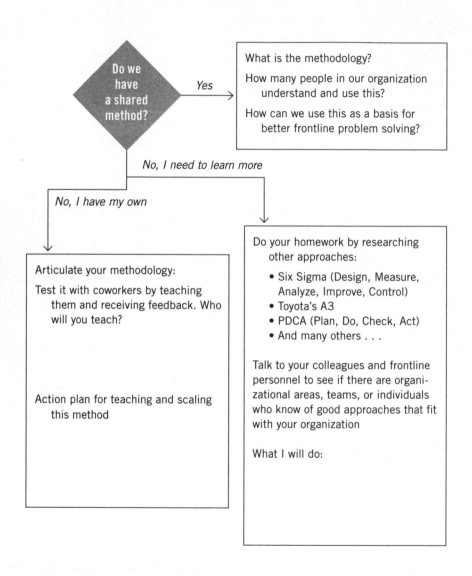

[SECTION FIVE]

Innovation and Experimentation
at the Front Line

In this section, we move beyond problem solving, with its emphasis on improving the business's status quo processes or service experience, and move to how organizations can actively tap into frontline creativity to generate innovation. Innovation, typically defined as the process for finding, making, and generating something new,[1] is pursued by virtually every organization as a necessity for staying alive in today's ever-changing world. It is the holy grail for many CEOs we meet, who often lament that they do not understand why their organizations have so little innovation when they employ so many smart people.

Organizational leaders face three principal challenges when involving their front line in innovation:

- Should the front line focus on improving products, business processes, or both? (*Innovation Area*)
- Where will innovation activities actually occur? Will the front line put ideas into practice or simply pass their ideas on to others, who will perform implementation? (*Activity Locus*)
- What is the methodology for screening and testing good ideas? (*Experimentation Methodology*)

INNOVATION AREA

When defining how the front line can contribute to innovation, it is important to identify whether there is the most potential for value creation through product innovation, business process innovation, or both. Product innovation is the relatively straightforward act of finding new products or services, combining existing products and services in new ways, or promoting products differently to address previously unmet customer needs.

Product innovation may be as simple as programmers at Facebook creating the video feature for users to share, an Amazon associate creating the shopping-cart feature, or an Oracle consultant creating a software module for a client that can be packaged and sold to other corporate customers. Business-process innovation is discovering ways to make front-end systems, policies, and procedures more efficient and effective. Frontline employees are knowledgeable about which systems work in practice and can often identify ways to reduce costs, speed processes, or develop alternative work methods. A simple example of business-process innovation occurred when a Chicago-based associate for Best Buy working in the company's computer-service division, Geek Squad, created a diagnostic software tool that could scan incoming customer computers in forty-five seconds instead of the prior six-minute benchmark. Multiplied across hundreds of stores and thousands of customer repairs, this amounted to an exponential productivity leap.

Take a moment to consider how your front line might contribute to both areas:

Potential for Product Innovation	
Potential for Business-Process Innovation	

ACTIVITY LOCUS

The next consideration is where you expect innovation to occur and how much discretion you will give those who are innovating. Famous innovation models from companies such as 3M and Google advocate giving individuals discretionary time—up to 20 percent of their working hours—to innovate in areas of their choice. This approach has led to revolutionary products such as 3M's Post-it notes and Google's AdSense. However, some leaders argue against the notion of letting a thousand flowers bloom by noting that the majority of energy invested in such free-form innovation amounts to few results and much wasted time. Instead, companies such as Facebook favor tighter constraints and more directive focus for innovation activities. Facebook uses twenty-four- to forty-eight-hour programming binges, known internally as hackathons, which provide a focused outlet for employee creativity. Special hackathons may have a theme, so that innovation efforts are pointed at improvement of specific features, while others are left open for the users to submit their ideas.

Decentralized		Centralized
	Individually Determined	
	Organizationally Directed	

As the diagram above demonstrates, if you are responsible for defining frontline innovation opportunities in your organization, you must determine the extent to which you are willing to expand participation to hundreds or thousands of people. Similarly you must determine whether you will define the innovation focus or leave it to individuals or teams to decide. The presumed trade-off is that the more centrally directed the efforts, and the fewer the participants, the more likely it is that the organization will miss a big idea generated by the rank and file.

In truth, the scarcest asset is management time to review and promote good ideas. If the resources and time required for innovation, or the dissemination of locally generated ideas to a broader user group, hinge on top management approval, organizations are far less capable of generating and disseminating ideas from the front line. Some organizations use intermediary bodies between the front line and senior management who act as conduits to screen, test, and spread new ideas.

Oracle, one of the world's leading enterprise software companies, deployed such an innovation board in Europe beginning in 2001.[2] The board's charge was to review ideas that were generated in the field as the company's developers, consultants, and salespeople worked with clients across Europe and the Middle East. The innovation board screened ideas that had been submitted, offering "Innovation Awards" to applicants with ideas representing the most potential for revenue or productivity enhancement. By 2005, the board had reviewed nearly 1,000 submissions, selecting 104 winners from twenty-two countries. Over three-quarters of these ideas were deployed, meaning that a minimum of three new countries adopted the innovations based on a clear business case. In this way, Oracle left client-centered innovation in the hands of its frontline staff, while balancing its commitment of organizational resources and management time to ensure that ideas with the most promise received investment.

Use the space below to identify how you can promote innovation at the front line:

Extent of Decentralization—the number of employees involved in innovation activities	0–100% _____%	Explain Your Answer:
Extent of Individual Determination—whether individuals can choose the area in which they innovate	0–100% _____%	Explain Your Answer:
How We Will Identify and Disseminate Best Practice Innovations from the Front Line:		

TEACH AN EXPERIMENTATION METHODOLOGY

Another consideration for building a frontline innovation strategy is determining the method for evaluating whether an idea is successful in the market. The more decentralized the idea screening process is and the more individual autonomy employees enjoy, the more difficult it becomes to screen the multitude of ideas via conventional management controls. When the scarcity of senior management attention becomes a bottleneck in the process, it becomes more likely that only *big* ideas will receive backing, while smaller, continuous-improvement efforts often become orphaned.

For this reason, pushing innovation to the front line requires giving employees a methodology to test their ideas, evaluate results, and determine how the idea might be improved or killed based on market feedback. Frontline workers who are trained on an experimentation methodology will be able to more nimbly adjust to customer learning, be better able to refine their innovations, and have a greater probability of success.

Just as there are numerous problem-solving methods, there are many different flavors of experimentation models. Some depend upon the industry. For example, companies such as Google, Microsoft, and Amazon have extensively used A/B testing, in which consumers receive different versions of a product or Web page (version "A" or version "B").[3] Programmers make subtle changes (often unnoticed by consumers) to things like the placement of a checkout button or the number of lines of explanatory text, to see how such changes impact variables such as the number of page visits or purchase amounts.

For those industries lacking the low-overhead cost structure of experimentation in the virtual world, the tried and tested scientific method provides a reliable alternative. The scientific method requires that the experimenter formulate a hypothesis based on information or observation, test the hypothesis in a reproducible manner, and then verify whether the results yielded were consistent with or refuted the hypothesis. When we have deployed this process with clients' frontline associates we ask them to begin by answering three questions:

1. *What* is the problem statement, in one or two sentences, that captures the unsatisfactory financial performance?
2. *How* are operational metrics affecting the overall financial performance?
3. *Why* are the operational metrics not where they need to be as a result of behaviors or processes?

For example, a manager at Best Buy worked with his team to develop the following answers to these questions based upon their analysis of the underserved market for consumer electronics on boats and other marine craft:

1. *What* is the problem? Answer: Missed revenue opportunity of over one million dollars in Miami store locations as a result of not effectively targeting marine customers.
2. *How* are metrics affecting store performance? Answer: Average sales price and units per transaction with the marine customer segment are lower than they should be.
3. *Why* are the operational metrics not what they should be? Answer: We don't recognize this segment when they come in the stores, fail to probe their marine needs, and don't carry the right product mix to serve them.

Once these questions had been satisfactorily answered, the team was prepared to construct an experiment. To do so, the team was asked to iden tify a hypothesis, test it, and verify the results. Typical guidelines for implementation include

- **Hypothesis:** Describe what you would do, over what time period, and the expected results.
- **Test:** Explain in detail who will do what by when in order to test the hypothesis.
- **Verify:** Detail the overall result expected at the end of the test, as well as the week-by-week milestones. Verification should be tied to the operational metrics highlighted in the "how."

1	*What* is the problem statement, in one or two sentences, that captures the unsatisfactory financial performance?	**4**	*Hypothesis:* Describe what you would do over what time period and the expected results.
2	*How* are operational metrics affecting the overall financial performance?	**5**	*Test:* Explain in detail who will do what by when in order to test the hypothesis.
3	*Why* are the operational metrics not where they need to be as a result of behaviors or processes?	**6**	*Verify:* Detail the overall result expected at the end of the test as well as the week-by-week milestones. Verification should be tied to the operational metrics highlighted in *How.*

As a result of their test, this Best Buy team was able to generate significant new revenue by creating product and service bundles, such as television and sound systems that could be installed on larger boats.

In order to teach and implement an experimentation methodology with your front line, you need to first experience it yourself. Use the space below to identify a test that you can conduct at a frontline location in your business. You may want to enlist the support of a small team of frontline associates to do so. Use additional paper if needed.

CREATING A CULTURE OF EXPERIMENTATION

When experimentation catches on with the front line, it has the power not only to drive remarkable business results but also to transform an organization's culture. Intuit, the California-based software company, has long been celebrated as one of the most innovative technology companies, but it only recently discovered the power of experimentation. Historically, Intuit had a customer-driven culture, deploying powerful techniques such as the "follow me home" anthropological studies of customer behavior that derived from founder Scott Cook's years as a Bain & Company consultant and

Procter & Gamble manager. Despite Intuit's tremendous success, however, Cook began to question his management philosophy while watching his son play Little League baseball.

As he shared with us, he realized that in Little League the coach never plays. The kids would throw a ball, catch a fly, or try to bat and receive feedback immediately. As he said, "In a single practice, every one of these kids would get multiple points of feedback on their own performance." Unlike in business, the coaches never tried to do the work for the kids. Cook realized that in business "the boss will sweep in and make the decision," depriving team members of the opportunity to grow their judgment capability through real-life experience and diminishing the sense of ownership that people have when excuting plans. Cook knew that people felt best about their work and were most committed to the organization when they had the power to act on their creativity. As a result of that moment, he committed to geometrically expand the number of experiments at Intuit.

"Our theory is that you should enable a lot of your employees—not just a small group—to invent business ideas or product features," Cook maintains, based on his own considerable experience. "If we build a great environment, a great place to work, and teach our people the skills of invention, only then do they create the kind of life-changing inventions that delight customers. And only in that way can we deliver the sustained profitable growth that delights our shareholders."

Cook's new approach has led to dramatic changes at Intuit. For starters, Intuit implemented an online idea-sharing system called "Brainstorm," which was created by two newly hired college graduates. Cook explained, "They looked at how we processed ideas and managed it inside the company and they said, 'That sucks, we can do better.' And they were right; they built something much better." Brainstorm generated thirty-two ideas that were incorporated into shipped products in its first year. By its second year, the system was responsible for the exploration of more than one thousand new ideas that had previously lain dormant in the company.

Experimentation also shaped the company's entry strategy in India. Cook shared with us that rather than build elaborate strategies and take months to evaluate the market, Intuit put a manager on the ground with a small team that ran experiments with live consumers. Within its first eighteen months, the team had tested thirteen different business models, three of which survived and have shaped the unit's future growth strategy.

Perhaps most profound, Cook noted that the approach to experimentation required deep changes in leaders' behavior, including his. The days of the imperial boss, whom Cook compared to Caesar at the Colosseum giving a thumbs-up or thumbs-down to every idea, have passed. Intuit's prior modus operandi, in which bosses would sift through reams of data and analysis prepared by a working team and then give them the answer on how to proceed, has been replaced by leaders who "champion a grand challenge" and encourage their teams to experiment their way to a solution. Rather than Caesar or wartime generals, Cook encourages his people to look to Thomas Edison as inspiration for their leadership behaviors.

Cook is convinced that to drive a culture of experimentation, leaders at all levels throughout the company need to be thoroughly trained in applying the scientific method, in building rapid prototypes, and in learning from actual user data. Cook is ready and willing to concede that such experiments don't always have the highest level of rigor or the greatest sample sizes. However, he is equally quick to point out that any level of experimentation with reasonable methodology offers a significant improvement over "zero experimentation, zero scientific method, no real learning. Compared to that desert of learning, a few drops of water are quite an improvement."

Use the space below to consider how prepared your organization is to build a culture of experimentation:

Leader's Role	1 2 3 4 5
	Boss's role is to Leaders encourage decide for the team experimentation so teams can find their own answers
Use of Data	1 2 3 4 5
	HiPPO Rules—Data always wins - Use of hierarchical power and position power is basis for most take a backseat to decisions test data
Resource Access	1 2 3 4 5
	Boss's approval is Resources for running required and resources tests are easily to experiment are limited accessed and not unduly constrained by manager approvals
Dealing with Failure	1 2 3 4 5
	Failure is to be Leaders recognize avoided at all costs failure from experiments as positive and required for learning
Celebrating Success	1 2 3 4 5
	We have no or few Leaders constantly ways to celebrate recognize individual small and large and team efforts local innovations

[SECTION SIX]

Breaking Down the Hierarchy

D espite leaders' best intentions, creating a front line–focused organization is difficult. Most corporate structures are designed along hierarchical principles that are vestiges of the industrial factory era. Engaging the front line in problem resolution, innovation, and experimentation can have profound bottom-line benefits, but these may never materialize, and certainly won't be sustainable, in a traditional organizational construct that assumes those at the top are smart and those at the bottom are not. Changing these assumptions often requires facing and ultimately overcoming deep-seated cultural, psychological, and institutional resistance.

Unless your organization is a start-up, it is likely that you will need to adopt a deliberate, stepwise path toward changing your culture to build a front line–focused organization. You will need to determine how to create an organizational context that has supportive leadership roles and clear employee expectations. As the diagram below shows, we will examine five interrelated approaches that leaders can take to break down hierarchy and encourage full-fledged frontline participation in their businesses.

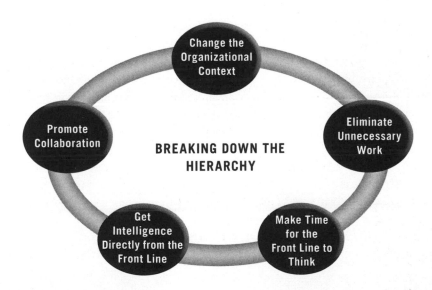

CHANGING THE ORGANIZATIONAL CONTEXT

By "organizational context" we mean the specific factors that influence the perceptions of frontline employees that they are (or are not) empowered to take action or make decisions and that help to create the belief that their contributions are valued. While numerous individual factors may play a role in generating this sense of power, we focus here principally on structure, processes, and organization-wide language or symbolism. Actions that senior leaders take in these areas have the power to change entrenched notions of how the organizational hierarchy operates.

Language is one of the most powerful tools available to managers, but we find that many leaders choose words that are imprecise or create false expectations. Over the years, we have seen numerous attempts to use strong language and powerful imagery to upend traditional notions of the organization, phrases, and sayings such as "inverting the pyramid," or "If the customer is king, then our front line is royalty." While this language, particularly the notion of turning the organizational pyramid upside down, is increasingly mainstream, the truth is that no organization means to confer blanket authority on its front line. Such imagery is useful for generating excitement but has little staying power and limited operational usefulness.

We advocate a focus on behaviors instead of catchy slogans. Cultural change is an outcome of widespread behavioral change, so it is critical that organizations clearly articulate the behavior expected of leaders. For example, one retailer we worked with instituted "respect and humility," character traits that were easy to translate into front line–focused behavior, as core values:

> The leader's humility invites others to play an active role in the business. By saying "I don't know" and asking for help, the leader encourages others to step up their contribution. Such leaders know that their role is to create an environment in which people feel valued and are positioned to make the greatest possible contribution. They also know that leaders who purport to have all of the answers or think they are the most capable to perform every task are delusory.

In addition to defining such behaviors, top leaders need to live them. An excellent role model is Wawa's CEO, Howard Stoeckel, who has deliberately emphasized informality in his frontline interactions to diminish the status gap between himself and line workers. Never taking himself too seriously, he insists that everyone call him by his first name, always correcting those who try to slip "Mr. Stoeckel" into conversation. He is also portrayed in company newsletters and publications as a cartoon character, lending his image to funny or informative anecdotes. While it may seem minor, his resolve to remain approachable despite being CEO serves as a powerful model for other senior leaders and helps to maintain Wawa's collegial culture.

Consider the behaviors of leaders at the top of your organization. Use the space below to capture the behaviors that your leadership will need to keep, kill, or add to support a front line–focused organization:

BEHAVIORS TO KILL inappropriate behaviors that emphasize hierarchy	BEHAVIORS TO ADD new behaviors needed to reinforce how leaders support our front line	BEHAVIORS TO KEEP things we do well and need to continue doing to support our front line

ELIMINATING UNNECESSARY WORK

One of the biggest challenges for frontline employees is the proliferation of seemingly mindless controls, policies, and procedures. While some are undoubtedly useful, organizations tend to create unnecessary bureaucracy as a by-product of their operations. As a *Wall Street Journal* article noted, "line managers and employees occupied with operational issues normally don't have time to sit around and discuss ideas that lead to cross-organizational innovation."[1]

One of the most powerful tools for simultaneously freeing up frontline capacity, signaling the importance of frontline work, and building employee confidence was created during General Electric's Work-Out process.[2] Abbreviated as RAMMP (pronounced "ramp"), it is a simple tool for employees to identify unnecessary reports, approvals, meetings, measurements, and policies. In other words, elements that prevent frontline employees from serving customers or doing meaningful work.[3]

We have used RAMMP very successfully with numerous organizations to bust bureaucracy and free the front line from unnecessary work. Just a few of the examples we have noted over the years:

◆ Tellers in a large European bank who spent nearly two hours on paperwork for each new loan application. The process was reduced to less than fifteen minutes.

◆ Line workers in a European manufacturer were able to add steps to the production process with only the approval of their team leader. In order to simplify work processes, however, the approval of the business's manufacturing director was needed. The seven managerial levels in between killed virtually all suggestions. The policy was changed so that production supervisors, or in limited cases plant managers, had approval authority to implement all frontline ideas.

◆ Sales personnel at a retailer noted that company policy required stores to keep all Apple products in plastic shells that were connected by wire and locked to an in-store display. Policy prevented sales personnel from removing the phones from the shells in order to reduce theft concerns. Customers frequently complained because they couldn't get a real sense of a phone's weight and certain features were blocked from use by the protective casing. Based upon frontline input, the corporate merchants relented and allowed salespeople to remove the products. Sales went up by double digits with no increase in the products' theft.

The best way to experience RAMMP is to assemble a group of frontline workers from your organization and use the tool with them. Use the process below to identify low-value work that may be unnecessarily consuming your frontline capacity and distracting people from taking care of customers.

RUNNING A FRONTLINE RAMMP MEETING

Step 1: Organize a small team from one or more of your frontline locations.

Step 2: Share your desire to eliminate wasted time and increase the available hours they have to help customers.

Step 3: Teach RAMMP. It is a tool developed to identify unnecessary reports, approvals, meetings, measurements, and policies.

Step 4: Ask individuals to fill out the RAMMP matrix below, noting their ideas for activities in each category that could be eliminated without adverse impact on the customer or the company's performance.

	Activities Under Our Team's or Manager's Control	Activities Under Corporate Control
Reports		
Approvals		
Meetings		
Measurements		
Policies		

Step 5: Ask people to team up in small groups to review each person's ideas and select the top ideas in each category.

Step 6: Go through each element of the RAMMP matrix, calling on each group to share its ideas for work that can be eliminated.

- If you agree that the work can be eliminated and it is under your control, then agree to stop it.

- If you agree but it is not under your control, then agree to enlist support of other stakeholders.

- If you are unsure, commit to review the issue in more detail and respond to the group in one week.

- If you disagree because stopping the activity will cause harm, explain your position. Chances are the individual or team will not have recognized the activity's importance.

As a rule, try to give an answer on 80 percent of the ideas, leaving no more than 20 percent of the recommendations that require study.

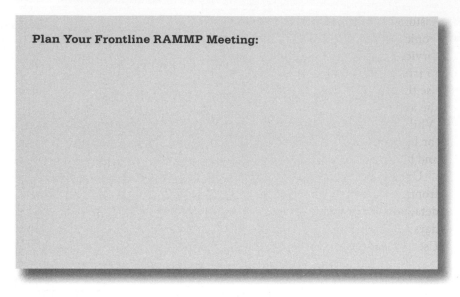

Plan Your Frontline RAMMP Meeting:

Making Time for the Front Line to Think

Another way to free up frontline capacity and demonstrate that leadership is serious about engaging employees in more meaningful work is to thoughtfully employ technology to simplify frontline work. While many companies think of automating processes to drive cost savings, others use technology strategically to free their front line from manual work or menial aspects of their jobs.

Pepsi Bottling Group provides a great example. When Eric Foss became CEO of Pepsi Bottling Group (PBG) in 2006, he knew the organization had problems with inventory, logistics, and field sales. PBG served thousands of supermarkets, convenience stores, gas stations, and other retail outlets. Its customer representatives delivered nearly two hundred million servings of Pepsi products every day.

Foss spent most of his first hundred days as CEO in the field visiting with customers and frontline sales representatives. He described what he found as chaos. During a trip to a retail outlet with a general manager, Foss discovered he couldn't carry on a routine conversation because the manager's cell phone rang continually. Foss couldn't get answers to seemingly routine questions about how many out-of-stocks the team had had the night before or how many trucks had been loaded without complete customer orders.

Recognizing that the lack of structured sales processes, poor forecasting, and outdated warehousing technology were impacting the customer representatives' ability to do their job for customers, Foss mobilized cross-functional efforts to fix the situation. Each of PBG's twelve thousand customer-service representatives were issued a handheld PDA that electronically downloaded customer information, including route schedules, service notes, and sales training videos. PBG didn't use technology merely to trim head count. Instead, Foss challenged customer representatives to use their newfound time—hours that had once been devoted to managing the awful inventory process—to build relationships with their customers. While making deliveries on their routes, customer representatives looked for better display opportunities, talked to managers about product sales, and helped to position company promotions.

Understanding how technology or process redesign can be used to free frontline capacity will require living in the field, just as Foss did. Although detailed job analysis is helpful, we suggest starting by setting aside several days when you can truly live in the field to see how people spend their time. Use the guide below to plan your visit:

PLANNING YOUR FIELD VISIT

Preparation

1. What are the most significant challenges facing your front line? (For example, Foss identified inventory, logistics, and field sales.)
2. What is the best field location to observe the processes and activities related to these challenges?
3. Whom should you observe and speak with while in the field?

Visit

1. What are the root causes of the problems you see?
2. What are employee ideas for how to fix the problems?
3. What cross-functional or cross-departmental support may be required that frontline associates do not recognize?
4. What is your action plan for fixing processes and using technology to free frontline capacity?

Follow-up

1. Identify how you will periodically review progress and get field input.
2. Plan your follow-up date to visit the field to assess progress.
3. Recognize early success and develop plans for transferring technology, processes, know-how, and people across locations to continue scaling the new work approach.

Plan Your Visit

GETTING INTELLIGENCE DIRECTLY FROM THE FRONT LINE

Another way to elevate the status of frontline personnel is to use their input for strategic insights. Zara, the world's biggest fashion retailer, has built its business in part on trend spotting by frontline associates.

Every day store staff chat up customers to get feedback on current styles and understand what is selling. They may ask customers, "What if this skirt were longer?" or "What other color would you like to see this in?" All of the information is loaded into PDAs linked to the store's point-of-sale system, which captures actual customer purchase information. In less than an hour, every manager globally can send updates that include not only quantitative cash-register data but also qualitative customer insights and their own impressions. Store staff are responsible for identifying trends and selecting among nearly three hundred thousand items so their inventory matches the preferences of local clientele.

In cases where sales are suffering or product and field people can't understand the sales data, the market specialists go directly into the field to speak with staff and customers alike. For example, in 2007 Zara introduced pencil skirts in bright colors to its stores. The items were not selling, but store staff couldn't put together a coherent explanation as to why, based on their in-store surveys. Focused effort from marketing managers and store associates revealed that women couldn't wear their usual size in the slim-fitting skirt. Rather than purchase a larger size and incur any associated ego bruising, most women were willing to forgo the purchase of an otherwise appealing item. Based on this new understanding, Zara recalled the items and reissued the pencil skirts to the stores with new sizing. Sales exploded. This type of teamwork and constant communication has helped the fashion retailer limit failed product introductions to just 1 percent, while the industry average runs at 10 percent.

Consider whether your organization can more nimbly or effectively respond to customer preferences based on frontline insights:

Untapped Customer Information We Can Get from the Front Line	How We Will Get the Information (technology, video chat, other media, etc.)	How We Will Use the Information	Other Parties Who Should Work with Frontline Associates to Understand the Market

PROMOTING COLLABORATION AT ALL LEVELS

Elevating the status of frontline workers doesn't need to be done at the expense of the respect given to those in more senior positions. In fact, one way for senior leaders to appreciate the perspective of frontline associates is to foster more opportunities for frontline workers to publicly share ideas and to encourage collaboration across employee groups as those ideas are developed for implementation.

In recent years, increasing numbers of organizations are using crowdsourcing and idea markets as a way to tap the knowledge of their employees. While they are not always aimed specifically at frontline employees, deploying these tactics helps to demonstrate that a company is seeking the best ideas, regardless of where in the hierarchy they may originate.

IBM was a pioneer in using crowdsourcing efforts in what it refers to as an Idea Jam.[4] IBM's first Idea Jam was held in 2001 as a deliberate way of tapping into the company's three hundred thousand plus employees' collective smarts in order to improve how the company operated. Leveraging IBM's intranet infrastructure, employees used electronic bulletin boards and Web pages to share ideas and respond to questions such as "How do you work in an increasingly mobile organization?" or "How do we get IBM Consulting into the C-suite?" In the Idea Jam's first year there were approximately 52,000 posts. Perhaps most important, in addition to generating valuable ideas, it gave people a sense of participation and of being listened to that would be critical for future Jam events. Idea Jams have since become a frequent occurrence at IBM, and the company has packaged its system for sale to other companies.

Another form of crowdsourcing, idea markets, gives employees play money and encourages them to bet on outcomes such as sales forecasts, production volumes, or product launch dates. In other words, rather than rely on the judgment of a single manager, idea markets tap employees' collective knowledge in ways that have been proven to create more reliable outcome forecasts. In the past, for example, HP has run prediction markets to forecast computer sales that had better forecast reliability than corporate departments. Similarly, companies such as steel producer Arcelor, Microsoft, and Google have all employed idea markets.

More recently, companies have forgone the event-based nature of Jams and the complexities of idea markets in favor of Web 2.0 or social technologies. MasterCard has hosted webcasts open to all of the company's more than five thousand employees to review its strategy and offer innovation ideas. Similarly, Wal-Mart conducted a blogging exercise focused on energy conservation. Among the six thousand posts, one idea was to remove the bulbs from the vending machines in store stockrooms, resulting in one million dollars in savings.[5]

Your options for building collaboration and encouraging the free flow of ideas across hierarchical levels will depend upon the technology infrastructure your organization has developed. However, there are a number of low-tech ways to engage viewpoints across hierarchical boundaries, including town-hall discussions and multilevel work teams. Some rules for designing your process are below for consideration.

BUILDING COLLABORATION AND ENCOURAGING IDEA FLOW ACROSS HIERARCHICAL BOUNDARIES

1. Open participation to as many people as possible.
2. Make the rules clear with emphasis on respect and valuing multiple perspectives.
3. Have an editor who can ensure that everyone plays by the rules.
4. Organize conversations across functions and hierarchical levels to stimulate creativity.
5. Ensure that the process for adopting or investigating ideas is clear to all from the outset.

ASSESS YOUR ORGANIZATION'S READINESS FOR CHANGE

This section has offered different ways in which, as a leader, you can diminish hierarchy and elevate the status of frontline workers. Before undertaking this challenge, it is important to look realistically at how firmly embedded your organization's hierarchy is today:

Is This Your Organization?	1 = not at all true; 5 = very true
There is a clear status divide between managers and our frontline workers based on hierarchy.	1 2 3 4 5
There is little discussion or public recognition of the important role played by our frontline workers.	1 2 3 4 5
There is little interest among senior leaders in hearing ideas from the front line.	1 2 3 4 5
There is little consideration given by senior managers to how frontline workers do their jobs or how to make their efforts more efficient.	1 2 3 4 5
There are few opportunities for senior managers and frontline workers to work side by side.	1 2 3 4 5

The more embedded notions of hierarchy in your organization, the more likely you will face great resistance requiring you take bold, dramatic action to ignite change.

[SECTION SEVEN]

Create the Right Environment

In the last section we examined how to break down organizational hierarchy and encourage employee involvement. In this section, we look at the local work environments created as frontline managers and workers interact with one another. Managing this dynamic requires carefully screening the employees who enter your organization, as well as adequately preparing the frontline managers who will engage with them daily.

Zappos, the online retail specialist acquired by Amazon in 2009, demonstrates how significant up-front investment in hiring and training ensures that frontline recruits enter with a great attitude and the right skills. Hiring for every position, including call-center representatives, requires multiple interviews that focus on the candidate's values, sense of autonomy, and desire to help customers. As Zappos's senior HR manager, Christa Foley, told us, it isn't unusual for an applicant to see fifteen people before being offered a job—for thirteen dollars an hour. "That seems insane to a lot of people," Foley observed. "It's really hard to do a spreadsheet ROI analysis, but as a company our number one goal has always been focused on hiring the right people."

Once new hires clear the interview hurdle, they are required to take a minimum of four weeks of training. Attendance at the daily sessions, which begin at 7:00 A.M., is mandatory, and no excuses are accepted for being late. To get through training, employees must not only pass tests on grammar, typing, and Web navigation but also rotate through different departments to understand the customer experience. They are also exposed to company history and values, which they put into application as they debate real-life customer cases on topics such as handling unusual requests, offering discounts for delivery problems, and dealing with out-of-stock situations.

Most companies are leery of committing the resources to hiring and training frontline staff that Zappos does. However, our analytic work with a number of clients has revealed that organizations with large workforces that suffer from high turnover habitually underestimate—by a factor of up to ten—the hidden costs of repetitively hiring, training, and then firing or losing employees. When all of the costs are considered—recruiting, interviewing, hiring, training, lost sales due to improper staffing, lower productivity during induction times for new employees, etc.—the costs of turnover are in the tens of millions for many companies.

Take some time to consider your company's situation and what you can do to better prepare the frontline employees you are hiring:

Our annual turnover rate for frontline positions	
Our annual cost of turnover when all variables are considered	
How we can better screen our employees for values, skills, and cultural fit	
How we can better train our incoming frontline recruits	

CREATING SUPERVISORS WHO EMPOWER THE FRONT LINE

Investing in hiring frontline associates who match a company's desired culture and training them to be effective is only half the battle. Another variable cannot be ignored: the quality and temperament of frontline supervisors. Whatever actions are taken or rhetoric spouted by senior leaders, an employee's most direct and visceral experience of a company is the result of his or her relationship with his or her manager. Ultimately, each frontline employee requires a supervisor who creates an environment in which he or she can be successful.

We find that in many companies these leaders receive limited training. Frontline supervisors are often plucked from the ranks of frontline workers based on their performance and perhaps interpersonal skills, but many have never managed before. Although they may lack the background or sufficient knowledge, these supervisors serve as the gateway to the company. In addition to handling basic managerial functions (communication, training, problem solving, taking disciplinary action, interviewing, etc.), they are expected to answer employees' questions or help them find resources on topics ranging from health and safety issues to human-resource policies to payroll.

The software company Intuit faced just such a challenge as it sought to improve the leadership at its call centers. Intuit operates call centers that not only offer customers basic application support for products such as TurboTax but also provide pay-for-service telephone and Web support for its more complex, professional software packages, such as QuickBooks. Intuit's call operators deal with consumers who may have installation questions or relatively simple user-interface issues, in addition to professionals such as accountants, who require support related to specific tax laws and reporting processes.

Intuit embarked on its efforts to improve frontline leadership based on a few simple facts. First, it had found that engaged employees were 30 percent more likely to demonstrate high-performance behaviors and resolve customer issues. It had also found that such committed employees were five times more likely to stay with Intuit, even if offered a comparable position and salary elsewhere. Finally, it had determined through surveys and interviews that more than 75 percent of employee satisfaction was directly impacted by the employee's direct supervisor. When Intuit came to us seeking help, it had over 1,700 frontline employees who were managed by approximately 150 frontline supervisors, known internally as "coaches."

In a four-month process, frontline coaches were expected to deepen many skills while engaging their business teams on projects that produced real financial and operational benefits. Some of the skills they developed included

◆ **Business Acumen.** The Intuit coaches learned how to connect their area's operating metrics to their business unit's operating dashboard and the company's overall financial results.

◆ **Teaching.** Frontline supervisors were given tools and practice opportunities so they could teach employees more effectively on any topic. They began by running a workshop with their team—without the help of trainers or consultants.

◆ **Building Teams.** Intuit's frontline leaders developed the ability to organize and mobilize their teams, recognizing the unique capabilities and work style that each individual brought.

◆ **Creating Operating Mechanisms.** Many leaders had no methodology for systematically reviewing results, getting input from their team, and discussing operating issues. Not only did the coaches develop operating routines, such as weekly meetings, but many also created special forums for reviewing customer feedback, improving operating processes, and dissecting team performance.

♦ **Performance Management.** Leaders were taught how to address difficult topics with employees in a productive and clear manner, whether dealing with performance issues, dress code, or personal hygiene.

While these may seem like business basics for anyone managing people, many frontline supervisors receive little or no coaching on how to perform their core leadership responsibilities. Lacking training, these supervisors take a limited view of their job and fail to see themselves as representatives of the company culture and spokespeople for the front line.

Our research has repeatedly demonstrated that if a work team trusts its direct leader, employees are more likely to feel empowered, and that can translate directly into performance improvement. It wasn't surprising to us to learn that, in addition to the business results accrued through the projects, employee-engagement figures among those who went through Intuit's process rose by double digits in less than one year.

Consider what you should teach to better develop your frontline supervisors' capability and align them with the front line–focused organization you are trying to build:

What do we need to teach our frontline leaders?	
What is the process for teaching and better preparing them?	
Action plan:	

[SECTION EIGHT]

Citizenship on the Line

O ur discussion of how to build a front line–focused organization has focused so far on elements of the five-step process introduced in section 1. In this section, we'll diverge from that task to discuss one method for turbocharging frontline efforts: engaging frontline employees directly in corporate citizenship activities in their local communities. We also examine two less traditional methods that innovative companies are taking, expanding the boundaries of their definition of "front line" to involve citizens and social agencies outside their corporate walls.

Far more companies are involved in corporate-citizenship efforts today than when Noel first began work in this area nearly thirty years ago. Over the years we have worked with companies to collectively bring more than a quarter million corporate employees to work and give back to their local communities in more than eighty countries. Many of these have been frontline workers. Whether delivering food with an automobile factory employee or painting a halfway house with an oil-industry engineer, each time we work with frontline associates in the community, we are amazed at how profoundly such work impacts them and the unanticipated benefits it brings in their relationships with their coworkers and employers.

DIRECT ENGAGEMENT

The most traditional model of corporate citizenship that engages the front line is the conscious choice by corporations to deploy their frontline associates in community service. One example of such an effort is the "Clean Our Mexico" campaign annually supported by the influential business conglomerate Grupo Salinas and the Fundación Azteca and sponsored by Grupo Salinas's chairman and CEO, Ricardo Salinas. This effort to clean the country's public spaces mobilizes Grupo Salinas's fifty thousand employees—who in turn mobilize more than three million others—for one day of voluntary service picking up trash and planting trees. This initiative is designed not just to motivate eco-friendly volunteerism but also to connect Grupo Salinas's frontline workers directly with the communities they serve. Many Grupo Salinas employees live and work in the neighborhoods that they clean up and labor shoulder to shoulder with their families, friends, and customers. The mixture of emotions on display—camaraderie, national pride, local sensitivity, genuine care—reveal how profoundly impacted some people are by the experience.

While engaging frontline employees offers organizations the ability to exponentially increase both the scale and the depth of their citizenship efforts, it simultaneously carries multiple benefits for frontline employees:

♦ **Partnering with Community Members.** Working with someone on a volunteer project can create a more personal relationship than waiting on a restaurant customer, serving someone in a bank, or selling someone a mobile phone. It offers the chance for employees to understand the thoughts, concerns, and lifestyles of some of their customers in an informal context.

♦ **Increasing Frontline Organizational Commitment.** Involvement in the community elevates the role of frontline workers and gives added dimension to corporate mission statements that encourage employees to help improve customers' lives. Such activity is typically meaningful to individual employees, who witness their company's dedication of time and resources to improving their community, and becomes a source of pride.

♦ **Frontline Leadership Development.** Formal and informal skill development occurs as frontline workers interface with others in the community. Based upon the experience, frontline associates may deepen abilities in areas that include communication, teaching, relationship building, negotiation, and coaching.

Consider how you can bring your frontline associates into the community. If you or your organization haven't done this before, you may want to start small, with one team and one community agency. If you have experience, look for large-scale projects with deep impact, as in the case of Grupo Salinas. Here are some guidelines for designing the experience:

DESIGNING YOUR FRONTLINE COMMUNITY EXPERIENCE

◆ Find an agency that addresses a significant social issue, preferably one that has a direct relationship to your business. Ask your frontline associates about issues in the communities in which they work.

◆ Before committing to engage your team, visit the agency and meet with the director. Ensure that there is a committed agency leader who will take charge of organizing your visit and ensure a positive experience.

◆ Determine how you can work with the agency and its members to both learn and add value. Find projects that require side-by-side work and facilitate one-on-one personal interaction. Some examples include mentoring students, painting, building playgrounds, and cleaning up a neighborhood.

◆ Be sure to take any appropriate health or safety precautions.

◆ Structure your visit and confirm your agenda with the agency. A good visit will consist of introductions, an overview of the agency and its social agenda, a minimum two-hour experience, and a dialogue between agency leaders and your team to better understand the agency and the community members it serves.

◆ Ensure that you have a plan for how to marshal any resources that may be needed to complete the work you are doing.

◆ Prepare your team for the experience, their role in it, and the expected benefits.

◆ Never commit future support, involvement, or resources unless you are fully committed to deliver!

The frontline team I will engage

The agency or community group with which we will work

How we will contribute

What we will learn

When this will happen

Actions I will take to make this happen

ENGAGING THE FRONT LINE OUTSIDE COMPANY WALLS

Through both our clinical work and our research, we have found a number of organizations that have broadened their definition of "front line" to include community members, often economically disadvantaged, who can become business partners, consumers, and future frontline employees if provided with the means. Charoen Pokphand Group, headquartered in a towering skyscraper overlooking busy Silom Road in the heart of Bangkok's bustling business district, has demonstrated how such a model works in countries across Asia.

Founded by Chairman Dhanin Chearavanont, *Forbes*'s Asia Businessman of 2011, the company constitutes a global conglomerate that operates in twenty countries with more than three hundred thousand employees, earning annual revenues in excess of eighteen billion dollars. Although the group today is made up of more than 250 subsidiaries in diverse industries such as telecommunications, retail, and real estate, the vast majority of its explosive growth has been driven by lessons learned from the seed and livestock sectors in its mainstay agricultural businesses.

The simple leadership philosophy espoused by Chearavanont is called the "Three Benefits," the central tenet of which simply states that for CP Group to be successful, it must first ensure that the communities in which it operates will benefit also. By adhering to the Three Benefits, CP has promised to provide quality products at a reasonable price, enabling people with low purchasing power to consume more and better goods. If they respect CP and choose to do business with the group, Chearavanont's reasoning goes, then the host government will provide support and encouragement for its people to use CP's products and services. If the government and people benefit, CP benefits as well.

"You need to give first in order to receive and with that understanding, we can achieve success,"[1] Chearavanont advised us in an interview. These acts of giving are not charity, the chairman insists, but long-term investments, enabling thousands of subsistence farmers in Thailand, China, Vietnam, Myanmar, and Russia to modernize and grow their businesses, forming a broad-based supplier network for CP Group. The company partners directly with frontline farmers in these societies, providing them with investment capital, technology, and high-caliber raw materials that cash-poor farmers could never afford to purchase independently. Its long-standing policy of training farmers to use cutting-edge agricultural methods often more than triples their yield rates and dramatically increases their incomes.

By looking beyond its own employees, CP and many other companies have found capable and committed entrepreneurs among the economically underprivileged, whose latent potential can be unlocked. In the process, they become suppliers, partners, and customers of the companies that assisted them.

Consider those on the societal front line whom you might discover, enable, and enlist for your organization's success:

Potential partners—the people with whom we can engage	
How we can engage and prepare them for partnership	
Benefits for this group	
Benefits for our organization	

DEVELOPING FRONTLINE LEADERS IN YOUR COMMUNITY ORGANIZATIONS

The front line outside of corporations includes not just the Thai farmer or the Mexican housewife looking to set up shop in a rural village but also not-for-profit and public sectors located in communities worldwide. Our work in these areas over the years has made it absolutely clear that the need for leadership judgment at the front line is perhaps even greater in social agencies than in the private sector. We have seen examples of this through our work in numerous nonprofit organizations, including work with health-care clinicians in India, school principals in Brunei, and Boys & Girls Club leaders across the United States. Indeed, making good decisions is arguably even more important for those in nonprofit organizations with limited resources, because their choices can directly impact others' basic necessities, including food, shelter, and education.

The final approach we highlight is for corporations to directly sponsor the development activities of not-for-profit or community organizations, such as school systems or Boys & Girls Clubs of America. In some cases support may mean funding, while in others it may mean pledging staff to help teach and develop community leaders. This latter approach is particularly powerful, for it often combines the benefits of directly engaging frontline associates in the community, as described above, with the positive results that come from transferring private sector know-how to public-agency leaders.

Use the space below to reflect on the community agencies with which you work and how your frontline staff can contribute to their development. If you are unsure, spend time with not-for-profit and community agencies to better understand their needs.

Not-for-profit or community agency that would benefit from our support to develop its frontline leadership skills	
What we could teach or provide	
Who would be involved from our organization	
How we will do it	

[SECTION NINE]

The Never-Ending Process

This handbook has attempted to guide you through some of the initial steps of building a front line–focused organization. Our thesis—supported by looks into more than twenty organizations—has been that companies with a sincere desire to maximize the contribution of *all* their employees need to invest in the development of good judgment among their people who occupy frontline positions, where every organization most closely touches its customers and community.

We hope that our central arguments have been simple and straightforward to follow:

- Too many organizations do too little to tap into the intelligence, creativity, and experience of their frontline workers as a result of increasingly outmoded hierarchical management styles.
- Leaders who espouse customer-focused strategies must start by understanding what is required by those who are in the line of fire and interact daily with customers.
- Top leaders must have a "Teachable Point of View" regarding how frontline workers contribute to customer and organizational success through their daily actions and behaviors.
- Serious investment is required to train existing employees on the details of the business, customers, and frameworks for solving the problems that those on the front line are most likely to run into.
- Armed with such knowledge, frontline employees can begin to use their own liberated judgment to solve customer problems and improve business processes without escalating every important matter to a supervisor or relying on a script from headquarters.
- As companies increasingly favor tailored, localized customer solutions over mass-market offerings, we see a huge opportunity for frontline employees to innovate and experiment with their local customers.
- Once a company embarks on this journey, it's likely to find that it is looking for a different kind of employee and a much more skillful frontline manager.

Even for organizations that do all of these things, there is of course always a danger that the world will change, customers will become fickle, and competitors will gain ground. For this reason, building a front line–focused organization is a never-ending process in which senior leaders must frequently find ways of listening to and learning from the front line in order to adapt to changing environments. Frontline employees and customers can be senior leaders' source of early warnings about shifts in the market, so that they may in turn exercise their own judgment about the organization's overall strategy.

As a final step, consider your ongoing mechanism for staying close to the front line, learning from frontline associates, and continuing to adjust your leadership approach based on the lessons you learn through this process.

Staying Close to the Front Line

My mechanism for ongoing learning from the front line:

How I will continue to challenge and upgrade our frontline capability:

Acknowledgments

We have many people to thank for their profound help and support throughout the process of writing this book. First among them have been our editors, Adrian Zackheim and Emily Angell, who patiently worked with us through the more than two years required to finish. Our colleague Stephen Fenichell has also worked steadfastly with us throughout the process, offering invaluable insight and editorial help in reworking the manuscript.

We owe a tremendous debt of gratitude to old friends and new who provided us with access to their organizations, generously spent time with us to explain how their organizations have achieved success, and openly shared challenges and failures from which they have learned: David Novak, Sam Su, Scott Cook, Ricardo Salinas, Dhanin Chearavanont, Tony Hsieh, Richard Zimmerman, Eileen Oswald, Shari Ballard, Eric Foss, Ed Staros, Kevin Williams, Adam Curtis, Jim Hackett, George Wolfe, and Dean Esserman. We are also very appreciative of the colleagues, particularly Michael Brimm, Don Pryzgodski, Ida Faye Webster, and Brian Hyman, who selflessly gave their time to read drafts of the manuscript and to challenge our point of view.

Finally, our work on this book was possible only with the loving support of our families, who tolerated many nights away from home for clinical work and research trips and stolen weekends so we could complete our effort.

Notes

[Preface]

1. Statistics are taken from the United States Department of Labor Bureau of Labor Statistics Web site (http://www.bls.gov/oco/ocos121.htm#emply). For example, the total number of employees as of 2008 in the "Retail" and "Leisure and Hospitality" sectors of the U.S. economy was approximately 17.8 million.

[Chapter 1: The Frontline Innovation Factory]

1. See http://glinden.blogspot.com/2006/04/early-amazon-shopping-cart.html.
2. Ibid.
3. Ibid.
4. George Anders, "Inside Amazon's Idea Machine: How Bezos Decodes the Customer," *Forbes*, April 23, 2012.
5. Ibid.
6. John Thrasher, interview with the authors, October 2008.
7. Ronny Kohvai, Practical Guide for Controlled Experiments on the Web: Listen to Your Customers, Not to the HiPPO, June 6, 2007, http://exp-platform.com/Documents/controlledExperimentsHippoEbay.pdf.
8. Similar facts have been presented in numerous studies in recent years. For several examples see Joyce L. Gioia, "Employee Engagement: Your Key to Bottom Line Profitability, Declining Motivation, Commitment and Loyalty Play out in Decreased Creativity and Productivity," *IndustryWeek*, February 29, 2012.
9. We owe our thinking about this to Clay Shirky, who uses the notion in a different context. Clay Shirky, *Cognitive Surplus: Creativity and Generosity in a Connected Age* (New York: Penguin, 2010).
10. Vanessa O'Connell, "Stores Count Seconds to Trim Labor Costs", *Wall Street Journal*, November 17, 2008, p. A1.
11. Ibid.
12. YouTube.com, "Why Bank of America Fired Me," http://www.youtube.com/watch?v=a5E0WNO7e_Q. Arthur Delaney, "Jackie Ramos, Bank of America Employee, Fired After Helping Customers," *Huffington Post*, March 18, 2010.
13. Note that we don't condone Ms. Ramos's behavior. It would have been better for her to quit than to lie. However, needing a job in the middle of a recession, she felt her choice was to either lie to corporate or become detached from customers. The solution, in our view, would have been for Bank of America either to create

an escalation center where frontline employees could have sent difficult customer cases for more specialized negotiation and settlement or to invest heavily in teaching branch customer advocates how to do this type of credit negotiation.

14. Mark Bly, ed., Deepwater Horizon Accident Investigation Report, September 8, 2010, p. 118. This report was compiled by an internal BP investigation team. It may be viewed or purchased at http://books.google.com/books?id=oJnW9R4m _3sC&pg=PA118&lpg=PA118&dq=Then+all+of+a+sudden+the+degasser +mud+started&source=bl&ots=nWqNWeI_sP&sig=tqTzgVD9hXKoX FVHs5FbOXATeZo&hl=en&sa=X&ei=KImaT8iYC8Kg6QHStrjmDg&ved =0CEUQ6AEwAg#v=onepage&q=Then%20all%20of%20a%20sudden%20the %20degasser%20mud%20started&f=false.

15. "BP at Fault for 21 of 35 Factors in Gulf Spill, Panel Finds," MSNBC.com, September 14, 2011.

16. "BP E-mails on Well Safety Don't Jibe with Engineer's Testimony," CNN Wire Report, June 16, 2010. The article can be found at http://articles.cnn.com/ 2010-06-16/us/gulf.oil.disaster.documents_1_bp-mails-e-mails?_s=PM:US.

17. "BP's Investigation of Oil Spill: Several 'Warning Signs' Were Ignored," Washington Post, May 26, 2010, p. A7.

18. Suzanne Goldenberg, "Gulf Oil Disaster: BP Admits Missing Warning Signs Hours Before Blast," Guardian, September 8, 2010.

19. Rowena Mason, "BP Oil Rig Explosion: Technician 'on Cigarette Break Missed Warning Signs,'" Telegraph, December 8, 2010.

20. Energy and Climate Change Committee, House of Commons, "Examination of Witnesses: Dr. Tony Hayward, Group Chief Executive, BP Plc, Mr. Bernard Loomey, Managing Director, BP North Sea, and Mr. Mark Bly, Group Head of Safety and Operations, BP Plc," September 15, 2010.

21. Steve Mufson and Anne E. Kornblut, "Lawmakers Accuse BP of 'Shortcuts,'" Washington Post, June 15, 2010, p. A1.

22. Goldenberg, "Gulf Oil Disaster."

23. Rowena Mason, "Shell Attacks BP over Oil Well Safety, as US Lifts Ban on Gulf of Mexico Drilling," The Telegraph, October 12, 2010.

24. Gary Steele, interview with the authors, December 8, 2010.

25. At the time of writing, BP had submitted a settlement proposal of more than two thousand pages that, without admitting liability, proposed settlement with some claimants for an estimated $7.8 billion. The U.S. federal judge overseeing the case had not yet ruled. Even if the settlement is accepted, BP will still face tens of billions of dollars of potential claims by the U.S. government, individual U.S. states that were affected, and its business partners. BP has reportedly set aside $37 billion to cover costs associated with the spill. See Miguel Llanos, "Judge: Leaning Toward Approving Huge BP Settlement in Gulf Oil Spill," msnbc.com, http://usnews.msnbc.msn.com/_news/2012/04/25/11376457-judge-leaning -toward-approving-huge-bp-settlement-in-gulf-oil-spill?lite, April 26, 2012.

[Chapter 2: Building the Front Line–Focused Organization]

1. Undercover Boss, 7-Eleven CBS, Season 1, Episode 3, CBS, original airdate of February 21, 2010.

2. Judy Neuman, "Heart. Does Undercover Boss Have It?," August 31, 2011, http:// www.heasleyandpartners.com/heart-does-undercover-boss-have-it.html. This is just one example of articles or commentary.

3. These are part of the leader's Teachable Point of View, which we explain in more detail in chapter 3.

4. Our research and clinical work, described in more detail in later chapters, have been measured by corporate clients and shown to provide double-digit engage-

ment increases with corresponding improvements to customer satisfaction and measurable financial improvements. A European bank with which we worked was able to improve engagement by approximately 11 percent, streamline customer processes, and produce significant cost savings. For an example of academic research linking employee involvement, customer loyalty, and financial value, see, for example, *The Service Profit Chain* (reference below).

5. James L. Heskett, W. Earl Sasser Jr., and Leonard A. Schlesinger, *The Service Profit Chain* (New York: Simon & Schuster, 1997).

6. For examples see John P. Meyer et al., "Affective Continuance, and Normative Commitment to the Organization: A Meta-Analysis of Antecedents, Correlates, and Consequences," *Journal of Vocational Behavior* 61, 20–52 (2002) or Mee-Yan Cheung-Judge, "The Main Drivers of Employee Engagement," *Training Magazine*, February 20, 2012.

7. There has been in recent years a surfeit of academic and executive debate about whether the customer or the employee needs to come first when building an organization. We view this dispute as largely irrelevant, since the last time we checked a successful business needs both. We start our discussion with the customer, however, because fulfilling customer needs is the ultimate purpose of the front line. Until the senior leadership clarifies the organization's target customers and how they expect to be served and can build a profitable delivery model, the front line stands little chance of focusing its actions or executing successfully.

8. The term "Teachable Point of View" (TPOV) was used in Noel M. Tichy with Eli Cohen, *The Leadership Engine: How Winning Companies Build Leaders at Every Level* (New York: HarperCollins, 1997).

9. Laurie Brannan, "Upfront: 'Turning Strategy into Action,'" *Business Finance Magazine*, July 1, 2002. The article can be found online at http://business financemag.com/article/upfront-turning-strategy-action-0701.

10. Jeri Clausing, "Hervé Humler, Ritz-Carlton," *Travel Weekly*, January 10, 2011.

11. See http://corporate.ritzcarlton.com/en/about/goldstandards.htm.

12. Robert Green, "Baldrige Award Winner Profile: The Ritz-Carlton," *Quality Digest*, August 2000.

13. "How the Ritz-Carlton Is Reinventing Itself," *Gallup Management Journal*, October 12, 2006. The 23 pecent figure comes from two sources: Joseph A. Michelli, *The New Gold Standard* (New York: McGraw-Hill, 2008), p. 115, and Jennifer Robison, "How the Ritz-Carlton Manages the Mystique," *Gallup Management Journal*, December 11, 2008.

14. "Fresh Service Strategies: Connect with Customers on a New Level," *Success Magazine*, August 4, 2009.

15. "How the Ritz-Carlton Is Reinventing Itself."

16. Ed Staros, telephone interview with the authors, August 31, 2011.

17. Ruthanne Terrero, "Interview: Hervé Humler, president and COO of the Ritz-Carlton Hotel Company," *Hotel Management Asia*, April 19, 2011.

18. Bruce Schoenfeld, "Reinventing the Ritz-Carlton," *Travel + Leisure*, June 2008.

19. "Customer Service Champs," *BusinessWeek*, March 5, 2007.

20. Joseph A. Michelli, *The New Gold Standard* (New York: McGraw Hill, 2008), p. 36.

21. As Ed Staros pointed out to us in an interview (April 2012), Ritz-Carlton's twelve Service Values were introduced after the company had spent many years ingraining twenty rules dubbed the "Ritz-Carlton Basics." In Staros's view, these twenty rules provided a behavioral foundation for consistent service that enabled the more contemporary, flexible approach embodied in the Service Values to succeed.

22. See http://corporate.ritzcarlton.com/en/about/goldstandards.htm.

23. The Ritz-Carlton, Sarasota, "2008 Recipient Florida Sterling Council Governor's Sterling Award," http://www.floridasterling.com/08BoardOnlyFiles/RitzSterling Powerpoint.pdf, pp. 15–16; and Michelli, p. 97.

24. Ibid.
25. Ed Staros, interview with the authors, April 23, 2012.
26. Carmine Gallo, "How Ritz-Carlton Maintains Its Mystique," *BusinessWeek,* February 13, 2007. Also Richard Maxwell and Robert Dickman, "The Elements of Persuasion" as quoted by Shawn Callahan, "Imbuing Your Workplace with Stories," posted June 8, 2008.
27. Michelli, *New Gold Standard*, p. 178.
28. National Institute of Standards and Technology, http://www.nist.gov/baldrige/ritz.cfm.
29. Michelli, *New Gold Standard,* p. 112.
30. Bill Lampton, "Show and Tell: The Ritz-Carlton Hotel," *Expert,* December 1, 2003.
31. Carlo Wolff, "The School of Horst," *Lodging Hospitality,* January 2006, p. 45.
32. Michelli, *New Gold Standard,* p. 103.
33. Patrick Mayock, "Top Lists: Innovators: Ritz-Carlton," HotelNewsNow.com.
34. Mila D'Antonio, "Inside the Ritz-Carlton's Revolutionary Service," *1to1,* February 27, 2007.
35. John C. Timmerman, "A Systematic Approach for Making Innovation a Core Competency," *Journal for Quality and Participation,* January 2009, p. 5.
36. Ibid., p. 10.
37. Rob Cross, Nitin Nohria, and Andrew Parker, "Six Myths About Informal Networks—and How to Overcome Them," *MIT Sloan Management Review,* Spring 2002.
38. Melanie Nayer, "Ritz-Carlton Hong Kong: 7 Days Until Opening," *Huffington Post,* October 1, 2011.
39. See http://corporate.ritzcarlton.com/en/Careers/YourOpportunities/Hiring Process.htm.
40. Ed Staros, interview with the authors, April 23, 2012.

[Chapter 3: Starting at the Top]

1. Rahul Sachitanand, "KFC to Focus on Innovation; Targets Youth to Build Brand Loyalty & Fight Competition," *Economic Times,* January 18, 2012.
2. Ben Golden, Yum! public relations officer, e-mail message to the authors. The figure cited is from the date of spin-off to March 1, 2012.
3. Ken Blanchard, Jim Ballard, and Fred Finch, *Customer Mania! It's NEVER Too Late to Build a Customer-Focused Company* (New York: Free Press, 2004), p. 17.
4. "Why the Customer Is So Important to David Novak," *QSR,* May 2010.
5. See chapter 2 for further explanation of the matrix.
6. David Novak with John Boswell, *The Education of an Accidental CEO* (New York: Three Rivers Press, 2007), p. 230.
7. We have written extensively elsewhere about the role of a Teachable Point of View in aligning and developing leaders. For additional information regarding the definition and use of a Teachable Point of View, please see *The Leadership Engine* by Noel M. Tichy with Eli Cohen (New York: HarperCollins, 1997), *The Cycle of Leadership* by Noel M. Tichy with Nancy Cardwell (New York: HarperCollins, 2002), or *Judgment* by Noel M. Tichy and Warren G. Bennis (New York: Portfolio, 2007). "Teachable Point of View" and "TM" are registered trademarks of Tichy Cohen Associates.
8. Yum! company document, "Our Founding Truths."
9. YUM! 2009 Annual Report, "Dynasty Growth Model," p. 12.
10. The "how we Win together" statement has been updated in recent years and is shown as HWWT^2 today in internal documents.
11. YUM! 2010 Annual Report, "how we Win together," p. 13.
12. David Novak, interview with the authors, December 8, 2008.

13. Frances X. Frei, Amy C. Edmondson, James Weber, and Eliot Sherman, "Yum! Brands, Inc: A Corporate Do-Over," *Harvard Business Review,* September 21, 2005, p. 4.

14. David Novak, interview with the authors, March 2008.

15. Ibid.

16. Yum! Brands, 2009 Annual Report, "A Famous Recognition Culture Where Everyone Counts," p. 10.

17. Adam Bryant, "At Yum Brands, Rewards for Good Work," Corner Office, *New York Times,* July 12, 2009.

18. Frances X. Frei and Amy C. Edmondson, "Yum! Brands, Inc: A Corporate Do-Over," Harvard Business School, Case 9-606-041, January 9, 2006, p. 9.

19. Tricon Global Restaurants, 2001 Annual Report, p. 3. See sections titled "The Journey: Customer Mania" and "Teaching Life Skills."

20. Novak, *Education of an Accidental CEO,* p. 167.

21. Sam Su, interview with the authors, August 18, 2011.

22. David Novak, interview with the authors, May 24, 2011.

23. Kathy Gosser as quoted by Frances X. Frei and Amy C. Edmondson, "Yum! Brands, Inc: A Corporate Do-Over," Harvard Business School, Case 9-606-041, January 9, 2006, p. 7.

24. Dina Berta, "Yum!'s 'Customer Mania' Program Seeks to Add Passion to Service," *Nation's Restaurant News,* June 10, 2002.

25. Eric Chester, *Getting Them to Give a Damn* (Dearborn, MI: Dearborn Press, 2005),pp. 196–97.

26. David Novak, interview with the authors, December 8, 2008.

27. Online interview with Roger Eaton provided to CEO Forum Group, "Customer Mania," http://www.ceoforum.com.au/article-detail.cfm?cid=8501&t=/Roger -Eaton--Yum-Restaurants-International/Customer-mania/, 2006.

28. Ibid.

29. Ibid.

30. Ibid.

31. David Novak, interview with the authors, May 24, 2011.

32. David Novak (with John Boswell), *The Education of an Accidental CEO: Lessons Learned from the Trailer Park to the Corner Office* (New York: Three Rivers Press, 2007), p. 176.

33. Sam Su as quoted in David E. Bell and Mary Shelman, "Yum! China," Harvard Business School Case 9-511-040, December 16, 2010, p. 3.

34. Sam Su, interview with the authors, August 18, 2011.

35. Ibid.

36. David E. Bell and Mary Shelman, "Yum! China," Harvard Business School Case 9-511-040, December 16, 2010, p. 11.

37. Sam Su, interview with the authors, August 18, 2011.

38. Ibid.

39. David Novak, interview with the authors, March 24, 2011.

[Chapter 4: Teaching People to Think]

1. This story was relayed to the authors during a visit to the U.S. Navy SEALs' training base at Coronado, California, and through subsequent interviews with Kevin Williams.

2. Adam Curtis, interview with the authors, November 2008.

3. "A Historic Year for Harvard Admissions," *Harvard Gazette,* online edition, http://news.harvard.edu/gazette/story/2010/04/a-historic-year-for-harvard -admissions/April 1, 2010.

4. An additional thirty weeks of training and drills cull the herd by another 1 percent to 2 percent.

5. Kevin Williams, interview with the authors, November 2008.
6. Adam Curtis, interview with the authors, November 2008.
7. Kevin Williams, interview with the authors, November 2008.
8. Ibid.
9. Ibid.
10. For one example, see Sophia Scott, "Team Performance and the Problem Solving Approach," *Journal of Industrial Technology,* vol. 23, no. 4, October–December 2007, p. 2. Historically, the Meyers-Briggs Type Index and Kirton Adaptation-Innovation Index have often been used to describe varying cognitive styles that guide individual problem-solving approaches that can improve or impede team communication.
11. Brian Shapland, interview with the authors, November 2, 2009.
12. Ibid.
13. Jim Hackett, interview with the authors, August 20, 2009.
14. Please see chapter 2 for more detail regarding IDEO's role in helping Ritz-Carlton to localize scenes at its hotel properties.
15. Catherine Fredman, "The IDEO Difference," *Hemispheres,* August 2002, p. 54.
16. Mark Greiner, interview with the authors, January 29, 2009.
17. IDEO's design process was shared with us by Mark Greiner. More information can be found in numerous publicly available, online sources including http://rapidbi.com/deepdivebrainstormingorganizationaldevelopment/ and www.ce.umn.edu/~smith/docs/MSPE-IDEO-ho.ppt
18. George Wolfe, interview with the authors, July 22, 2009.
19. George Wolfe, interview with the authors, February 4, 2009.
20. Jim Hackett, interview with the authors, August 20, 2009.
21. Ibid.
22. Ibid.
23. James P. Hackett, "Preparing for the Perfect Product Launch," *Harvard Business Review,* April 2007, p. 3.
24. Interview with the authors, February 4, 2009.
25. Hamid Khorramian, interview with the authors, November 12, 2009.
26. Mark Greiner, interview with the authors, January 29, 2009.
27. Ibid.
28. Ibid.
29. Ibid.
30. George Wolfe, interview with the authors, February 4, 2009.
31. Brian Shapland, interview with the authors, November 2, 2009.
32. Ibid.
33. Following the teaching of the Critical Thinking Model, Steelcase introduced Think 2.0 in 2009. Aimed at all employees, this was a supplemental course designed by Steelcase's leadership team with input from the Illinois Institute of Technology and the University of Toronto's Rotman School of Management. The course focused on resolving two questions frequently heard from employees: "How do I know when I'm done thinking?" and "What does a good point of view look like?" The model detailed the steps of formulating a central question to be solved, scoping a project, and then using tools and frameworks to generate insight. One of the key points of learning was that simple problems could often be solved in a linear fashion, moving from step to step, while more complex judgments required iteration and movement among the steps in the model.
34. George Wolfe, interview with the authors, July 22, 2009.

[Chapter 5: Experiment to Innovate on the Front Line]

1. The actual competition was streamed live at http://apps.facebook.com/facebook live/ and available in the company's online video archives. Written accounts of the

event can be found on several Web sites (see, for example, http://cs.illinois
.edu/news/2010/Nov12-1 or http://www.insidefacebook.com/2010/11/12/facebooks
-camp-hackathon-competition/ or http://www.dailyillini.com/index.php/article/
2010/10/ui_students_hack_for_facebooks_new_product_ideas).

2. In response to the question "Who brought hackathon to Facebook?" on the
    Quora Web site, former employee Scott Marlette responded on April 2, 2010,
    that he had had a conversation with Zuckerberg and others at Gordon Biersch
    (see http://www.quora.com/Who-brought-hackathon-to-Facebook). Another
    respondent identified Marlette as the "main spearhead" behind the effort.

3. "Mark Zuckerberg, Moving Fast and Breaking Things," video interview and
    transcript by Henry Blodgett on *Business Insider*, October 14, 2010, http://www
    .businessinsider.com/mark-zuckerberg-2010-10.

4. Eddy Junarsin, "Managing Discontinuous Innovation," *International Man-
    agement Review*, vol. 5, no. 1, 2009, p. 10, quoting Tidd, Bessant, and Pavitt,
    *Managing Innovation: Integrating Technological, Market and Organizational
    Change* (West Sussex, England: John Wiley & Sons, 1997).

5. "Mark Zuckerberg, Moving Fast and Breaking Things," video interview and
    transcript by Henry Blodgett on *Business Insider*, October 14, 2010, http://www
    .businessinsider.com/mark-zuckerberg-2010-10.

6. Ibid.

7. The story of how Best Buy developed its customer-centric approach to
    experimentation—and its subsequent difficulty maintaining its frontline
    focus—is discussed in detail in chapter 8.

8. For example, see Robert G. Cooper and Elko Kleinschmidt, "Screening New
    Products for Potential Winners," *Long Range Planning*, vol. 26, issue 6, December
    1993, pp. 74–81 or Robert G. Cooper, "New Products: The Factors That Drive
    Success," *International Marketing Review*, vol. 11, issue 1, 1994, pp. 60–76.

9. For example, Google software engineer and product manager Orkut
    Buyukkokten is credited with developing orkut as part of his 20 percent time
    allotment (see http://askville.amazon.com/origin-orkut-created/AnswerViewer
    .do?requestId=13006381).

10. For a discussion of the pernicious effects of financial tools when managing
    innovation, see Clayton M. Christensen, Stephen P. Kaufman, and Willy C.
    Shih, "Innovation Killers: How Financial Tools Destroy Your Capacity to Do
    New Things," *Harvard Business Review*, January 2008, reprint R0801F, p. 7.

11. The exact history of the scientific method is debated—tracing its origins to
    multiple philosophers and scientists over more than a thousand years—but it is
    generally accepted that it is a deductive method for determining truth or fact
    from falsehoods or assumptions. In most accounts of the methodology, the
    process must begin by asking a question, conducting observations, posing a
    hypothesis, testing the hypothesis through experimentation or further obser-
    vation, and then reporting results so they can be verified by others.

12. A/B testing was discussed at Amazon in chapter 1 regarding development of
    the "recommended for you" feature. In A/B testing consumers receive different
    versions of a product or Web page (version A or version B) so those conducting
    the experiment can measure how specific changes between version A and
    version B change user behavior.

13. Recorded audio and PowerPoint presentation, "Stories of Invention," http://
    onproductmanagement.net/2009/06/10/scottcook/.

14. Scott Cook, interview with the authors, May 13, 2011.

15. Ibid.

16. Ibid.

17. Ibid.

18. Ibid.

19. Ibid.
20. Ibid.
21. Ibid.
22. Ibid.
23. Ibid.
24. Ibid.
25. Ibid.
26. Ibid.
27. This account was shared in an interview with the authors. For secondary source material that includes some of these details, see also www.antonellapavese.com/2006/04/24/scott-cook-founder-of-intuit-talks-about-innovation-at-chi-2006/ under "3. Savor surprises . . . as learning."
28. Scott Cook, interview with the authors, May 13, 2011.

[Chapter 6: Breaking Down the Hierarchy]

1. Dr. Richard Zimmerman and Eileen Oswald, interview with the authors, January 29, 2010.
2. The estimated number of sepsis cases ranges from 700,000 to 800,000 per year, with mortality rates averaging 28 percent and some studies estimating 30 percent to 50 percent mortality. For summaries of sepsis statistics, see, for example, http://www.oaccm.com/pdfs/Sepsis%20Economic.pdf or http://www.nigms.nih.gov/Education/factsheet_sepsis.htm.
3. Dr. Richard Zimmerman and Eileen Oswald, interview with the authors, January 29, 2010.
4. Ibid.
5. Ibid.
6. Ibid.
7. Ibid.
8. Ibid.
9. Cisco Systems, Inc., "Cisco Announces Streamlined Operating Model," press release, May 5, 2011.
10. Two frequently cited examples are W. L. Gore & Associates, Inc., and Semco SA.
11. Shoshana Zuboff, "Reply Letter," *Harvard Business Review*, vol. 69, issue 2, p. 165.
12. As Noel and Warren G. Bennis discuss in their book *Judgment,* the language that a leader uses to "name and frame" a judgment call can carry great significance for both how people emotionally respond to the call and the speed and clarity with which they take action. See Noel M. Tichy and Warren G. Bennis, *Judgment: How Winning Leaders Make Great Calls* (New York: Portfolio, 1997).
13. For more discussion of the Teachable Point of View and the importance of values, please see chapter 3.
14. While the rule of thumb is that older companies have more pronounced difficulty eliminating bureaucracy, our experience working in Silicon Valley has taught us that even start-ups are prone to institutionalize unnecessary work. Absent a routine process for identifying and eliminating low-value work, trivial tasks and inefficient work processes survive in organizations as a result of inertia.
15. J. C. Spender and Bruce Strong, "Who Has Innovative Ideas? Employees," *Wall Street Journal,* August 23, 2010, p. R5.
16. Work-Out was deployed by General Electric's former CEO, Jack Welch, as a means of eliminating bureaucracy and building the self-confidence of employees at all levels. By requiring managers to act upon employees' ideas, Welch wanted to demonstrate both that employee opinions mattered and that the company abhorred bureaucracy. Noel assisted in designing Work-Out and acted as a Work-Out facilitator for several GE businesses.

17. Leonard Schlesinger, whose work on the Service-Profit Chain is referenced in earlier chapters, holds the copyright to RAMMP (1990).

18. Pepsi Bottling Group was an independent company that merged with PepsiCo in 2009. On August 4, 2009, the date of the announcement, PepsiCo committed to invest $7.8 billion for the acquisition of Pepsi Bottling Group's stock. Eric Foss, PBG's CEO at the time of the merger, committed to stay with the company for two years. He resigned on December 9, 2011, and is currently CEO of ARAMARK.

19. Eric Foss, interview with the authors, April 7, 2009.

20. Ibid.

21. For further background on Zara, see John M. Gallaugher, *Information Systems: A Manager's Guide to Harnessing Technology* (Irving, NY: Flat World Knowledge, 2010), "Zara: Fast Fashion from Savvy Systems," Chapter 3, or Zeynep Ton, Elena Corsi, and Vincent Dessain, "Zara: Managing Stores for Fast Fashion," Harvard Business School Case Study 9-610-042, revised January 19, 2010. Both sources were relied upon for facts and figures that appear in this chapter.

22. As an example of Zara's speed to market, *The Economist* reported in 2005 that when Madonna gave a series of concerts in Spain, teenage fans who attended her last show were able to wear knockoff versions of Madonna's outfits from her first concert in the country.

23. While it may seem that Zara's system relies on significant IT investments, researchers have indicated that Zara actually spends less than one-fourth the industry average. It has smartly invested in systems to capture, analyze, and build on the intelligence of its people. See, for example, Donald Sull and Stefano Turconi, "Fast Fashion Lessons," *Business Strategy Review 19*, no. 2 (Summer 2008).

24. This online job advertisement was for an open position in Mission Viejo, California, and is consistent with the language used for other managerial openings in the United States found on the Web site of Zara's parent company, Inditex. Numerous other examples can be found on the Web site: https://www.joinfashioninditex.com/joinfashion.

25. The term "crowdsourcing" was coined by Jeff Howe in *Wired* magazine in 2006, so while IBM didn't call what it did "crowdsourcing," it has become a prime example.

26. Paul Hemp and Thomas A. Stewart, "Leading Change When Business Is Good," *Harvard Business Review,* reprint R0412, pp. 1–13, December 2004.

27. Osvald M. Bjelland and Robert Chapman Wood, "An Inside View of IBM's 'Innovation Jam,'" *MIT Sloan Management Review* 50, no. 1 (Fall 2008).

28. Joe McKendrick, "Top CIOs Say Social Networks Now Drive Innovation," *FASTforward Blog*, January 14, 2010, http://www.fastforwardblog.com/2010/01/14/top-cios-say-social-networks-now-drive-innovation/.

29. Allen Adamson, "Companies Should Encourage Social Networking Among Employees," *Forbes,* June 2, 2009.

30. There are many structural reasons why police departments are slow to change, including factors such as the expectation of lifetime careers in one department because career opportunities and pensions are based on seniority, which does not typically transfer across departments for the rank and file.

31. All quotes from Dean Esserman are from telephone or in-person interviews we conducted with him between September and December 2009. Esserman served as chief of the Providence Police Department from January 2003 through June 2011. He is currently the chief of police for New Haven, Connecticut.

32. David S. Broder, "A Reformer in Rhode Island," *Washington Post,* June 8, 2006.

33. All quotes and information from Dean Isabella are from discussion with him on December 15, 2009, and July 13, 2010.

34. Involvement included the Ownerville Neighborhood Association, Ownerville Business Association, LISK, Watershed Council, Ownerville Housing Corporation and the PPD.

35. A transcript of Esserman's testimony can be found here: http://www.judiciary
.senate.gov/pdf/3-3-10%20Esserman%20Testimony.pdf.

[Chapter 7: Investing in Frontline Capability]

1. On-site interviews were conducted with Zappos personnel, including Tony Hsieh,
Christa Foley, Donavon Roberson, and representatives of the Customer Loyalty
Team and the human-resources and training departments on November 9, 2009.
Follow-up interviews were conducted by phone between March and June 2010.
2. Tony Hsieh, *Delivering Happiness* (New York: Business Plus, 2010), p. 144.
3. Zappos operates a subscription Web service at http://www.zapposinsights.com
that provides access to management tools, techniques, and advice. Our on-site
research was supplemented by many of the short stories and interviews that
appear on this service. For example, this quote comes from a Web article titled
"Recruiting for Zappos.com, Christa-Recruiting Manager."
4. Rob Siefker, interview with the authors, November 9, 2009.
5. Ibid.
6. While considerable research remains to be done on which specific attitudinal traits
or dispositions may lead to more empowered or capable employees, the academic
literature indicates that those with high self-esteem, proactive personalities, and
preferences for stimulating work are more likely to feel empowered.
7. While this may seem like a large number, consider that it is not unusual for
organizations with large frontline staffs to have 30 percent to 50 percent of their
expenses result from payroll or other human-resource–related activities.
8. For confidentiality reasons, we do not reveal the identity of this company.
9. In addition to changes in training and hiring, the company altered its pay
structure for part-time personnel and amended its dress code and personal leave
policies to address specific concerns raised by female employees. Data regarding
the reduction in turnover was collected via phone interview in July 2009.
10. Fred Hassan, "The Frontline Advantage," *Harvard Business Review,* May 2011,
p. 107.
11. We found the following chapter particularly helpful: Gretchen M. Spreitzer,
Mark Kizilos, and Stephen Nason. (1997). "A Dimensional Analysis of the
Relationship Between Psychological Empowerment and Effectiveness, Satisfaction, and Strain," *Journal of Management,* 23(5): 679–704.
12. We recall one incident at a company that mandated that frontline supervisors
build relationships with their employees. One frontline worker described a
supervisor who asked questions and, without responding, took copious notes
as she spoke. Rather than feeling that the relationship was strengthened, the
employee said she felt the experience had been similar to seeing a psychologist
for a compulsory mental health fitness evaluation.

[Chapter 8: A Never-Ending Process]

1. Miguel Bustillo, "Best Buy Chairman to Resign After Probe," *Wall Street
Journal,* May 15, 2012.
2. Jim Fink, "Best Buy CEO Brian Dunn Resigns: Sex and Consumer Electronics
Don't Mix," *Stocks to Watch,* April 12, 2012.
3. "Best Buy's Board Investigating Dunn's Conduct with Female Staffer,"
Minneapolis Star Tribune, April 12, 2012, http://www.startribune.com/business
/147091815.html.
4. Dell ultimately opened 140 kiosks, mostly in malls, which the company closed
in January 2008, citing an "evolution in its retail strategy" as it focused instead
on channel partners such as Best Buy for distribution.
5. Chuong Nguyen, "Majority of Americans Now Own Smartphones," March 2,

2012, http://www.gottabemobile.com/2012/03/02/majority-of-americans-now -own-smartphones/Aaron Smith, Pew Internet Web site, March 1, 2012, http:// pewinternet.org/Reports/2012/Smartphone-Update-2012/Findings.aspx.

6. This observation came during a conversation we had in early 2011. The theme was reiterated on May 22, 2012, by Best Buy's interim CEO, Mike Mikan, during an investor conference call when he cited the need for Best Buy to improve worker training to deepen customer relationships and the use of data and technology to better enhance customer interaction, predict customer purchase behavior, and improve inventory management.

7. Larry Downes, "Why Best Buy Is Going Out of Business . . . Gradually," *Forbes. com*, January 2, 2012, http://www.forbes.com/sites/larrydowns/2012/01/02/ why best buy is going out of business gradually/.

8. Justin Lahart, "Heard: Best Buy Is Best Avoided," "Heard on the Street," *Wall Street Journal*, April 14, 2012.

[Chapter 9: Corporate Citizenship on the Front Line]

1. Ricardo Salinas, www.ricardosalinas.com.mx.

2. Nuevo Juan del Grijalva was intended as a pilot project to be successfully replicated at scale elsewhere in the world and in Mexico. Current plans call for twenty-five similar hamlets to be constructed over the next few years. In March 2010, a formal ground breaking was held for Santiago el Pinar, the second sustainable rural city in Chiapas, providing evidence of the proven viability of one of the first fully functional sustainably planned communities targeted at base-of-the-pyramid families to have been built anywhere in the world.

3. Dhanin Chearavanont, interview with the authors, February 17, 2011.

4. Alison Overholt, "The Housewife Who Got Up Off the Couch," *Fast Company*, September 1, 2004.

Handbook for Judgment on the Front Line

[Section One: Introduction]

1. Fred Hassan, "The Frontline Advantage," *Harvard Business Review*, May 2011, p. 107.

[Section Three: Developing a Frontline Teachabale Point of View]

1. If you're not familiar with Wawa, you probably don't live in the U.S. Northeast. Each store operates three business lines: (1) convenience products, which include two hundred million cups of coffee and one hundred million bottles of private-label dairy, juices, and teas; (2) food service, with the average Wawa selling as much food as a typical McDonald's franchise and selling more than fifty million built-to-order hoagies annually in its stores; and (3) high-volume gasoline, in which Wawa rang up nearly 2 percent of the United States' total gasoline sales in only five states.

2. As Barbara Ennis shared with us, "Wawa's two-hundred-year history is one of continuous change. Relentless innovation, reinvention, and 'swimming upstream' are hallmarks of Wawa's success."

3. Howard Stoeckel, "Wisdom from the Flock," *Bird's Eye View: The Journal of Wawa CEO Howard Stoeckel,* March 8, 2011, http://www.wawa.com/Blog/ category/Culture.aspx?page=2.

4. Unless otherwise noted, quotes from Howard Stoeckel and Barbara Ennis are from interviews with the authors conducted on January 11, 2011. Additionally, the authors met with store personnel, HR executives, and various Wawa senior executives.

5. This dilemma was solved by a Wawa associate, Matthew Hunt, in Woodbridge, Virginia. When a truck driver lost his wallet while en route to Richmond, he was turned down by gas stations despite offering to have his dispatcher provide the credit-card number by phone. When he asked Matthew, noting that he didn't have enough gas to make it back, he was told that Wawa had the same policy. Hunt then proceeded to dig into his own pockets and lend the man enough money to gas up. The employee not only paid Matthew back but also phoned the Wawa call center to acknowledge the kind gesture and say, "From now on, I will go out of my way to stop at Wawa stores."

6. Frances X. Frei and Amy C. Edmondson, "Yum! Brands, Inc: A Corporate Do-Over," Harvard Business School, Case 9-606-041, January 9, 2006, p. 9.

7. Yum! Brands, 2010–2009 Annual Report, "A Famous Recognition Culture Where Everyone Counts," p. 10.

8. David Novak, interview with the authors, May 24, 2011.

9. Howard Stoeckel, interview with the authors, January 11, 2011.

[Section Four: Teaching People to Think for Themselves]

1. Carmine Gallo, "How Ritz-Carlton Maintains Its Mystique," *BusinessWeek,* February 13, 2007.

[Section Five: Innovation and Experimentation at the Front Line]

1. Eddy Junarsin, "Managing Discontinuous Innovation," *International Management Review,* vol. 5, no. 1, 2009, p. 10 quoting Tidd, Bessant, and Pavitt, *Managing Innovation: Integrating Technological, Market and Organizational Change* (West Sussex, England: John Wiley & Sons, 1997).

2. George Olcott and Nick Oliver, "Capturing Value from Front Line Innovation: Oracle's Innovation Network," case study, University of Cambridge, Judge Business School, June 2006. See http://www-innovation.jbs.cam.ac.uk/pub lications/reports_oracle.html for further information.

3. For example, see Ronny Kohavi, Thomas Crook, and Roger Longbotham, "Online Experimentation at Microsoft," http://exp-platform.com/expMicrosoft.aspx.

[Section Six: Breaking Down the Hierarchy]

1. J. C. Spender and Bruce Strong, "Who Has Innovative Ideas? Employees," *Wall Street Journal,* August 23, 2010, p. R5.

2. Work-Out was deployed by General Electric's former CEO, Jack Welch, as a means for eliminating bureaucracy and building the self-confidence of employees at all levels. By requiring managers to act upon their ideas, Welch wanted to demonstrate both that employee opinions mattered and that the company abhorred bureaucracy. Noel assisted in designing Work-Out and acted as a Work-Out facilitator for several GE businesses.

3. Leonard Schlesinger holds the copyright to RAMMP (1990).

4. The term "crowdsourcing" was coined by Jeff Howe in *Wired* magazine in 2006, so while IBM didn't call what it did "crowdsourcing," it has become a prime example.

5. Joe McKendrick, "Top CIOs Say Social Networks Now Drive Innovation," *FASTforward Blog,* January 14, 2010, http://www.fastforwardblog.com/2010/01/ 14/top-cios-say-social-networks-now-drive-innovation/.

[Section Eight: Citizenship on the Line]

1. Dhanin Chearavanont, interview with the authors, February 17, 2011.

Index